T. K. (Thomas Kelly) Cheyne

Founders of Old Testament criticism

Biographical, Descriptive, and Critical

T. K. (Thomas Kelly) Cheyne

Founders of Old Testament criticism
Biographical, Descriptive, and Critical

ISBN/EAN: 9783743305359

Manufactured in Europe, USA, Canada, Australia, Japa

Cover: Foto ©ninafisch / pixelio.de

Manufactured and distributed by brebook publishing software (www.brebook.com)

T. K. (Thomas Kelly) Cheyne

Founders of Old Testament criticism

PREFACE

THE present volume contains a series of pictures of eminent Old Testament critics from the beginning of the critical movement to the present day, with an attempt in each case to estimate the services of the subject of the picture. It is hoped that it may be not only interesting but instructive, and may tend to remove some current mistakes and misconceptions. Let me mention a few of these. Criticism, it is said by some, is a recent invention; it is arrogant to pretend that it has reached any final or even approximate results. Criticism, say others, is of purely German origin; it is foolish to import what has no roots in our own mental history. Criticism, says yet another school of writers, is purely rationalistic; it has no interest in, and can be of no considerable service to, positive theological truth. Criticism, say a few other respected but isolated observers, is narrow in its methods; it goes on grinding for ever at the same mill, and needs an almost complete reconstruction. In particular, according to these censors, it dreads archæology, and it is time for sober Englishmen to strike out a new method, which will have the additional advantage of being theologically safe.

All these statements are, I believe, based on unfortunate misconceptions, which are best removed by throwing as much light as possible on the history of criticism. To do this adequately would of course be a work of immense labour, nor have I leisure to attempt it. But I venture to hope that the present series of studies may be a small contribution towards the future history, and that the personal elements in the studies may give them a certain value even after the history has been accomplished. For it is not unimportant to notice how the intellectual phases and material surroundings of a writer have affected his criticism. We may see thus how natural and inevitable his course was, and how pardonable were his errors; we may also gather from his life both warnings and encouragements. I have taken special pains to make this clear in the cases of Ewald, who for a time almost seemed to have been annexed by liberal English theology, and of De Wette. And the whole series is concluded by a survey of the present state of Old Testament criticism, without which indeed the volume would have lacked much of any practical helpfulness which it may possess.

Let me explain. The last three chapters, though more predominantly critical than the preceding ones, are by no means an excrescence. The survey of criticism which they contain is not mechanically attached to the sketches of critics, but grows naturally out of a personal study of one of the most blameless and devoted of living scholars. It is an attempt to supply a want which is constantly being brought before me. Introductory works are happily multiplying among us, but on the whole they scarcely give an adequate idea of the actual position of Old Testament problems (especially outside the Hexateuch), and yet, if we all cautiously limit ourselves by the requirements of beginners, our students will be in danger of contracting a somewhat insular and provincial spirit.

The series of studies, which I have thus endeavoured to round off, is far from being as complete as I could have wished. Historically indeed it is continuous, but from an international point of view some plausible complaints may be urged against it. There is but one Dutch critic who is sketched, viz. Kuenen; but one French-writing critic, viz. Reuss; nor are any of the actually living and working German critics (except Schrader, who has now quitted the field of the "higher criticism") either described or criticized. The reasons for these omissions are however not far to seek. Some limitation of the range of the volume was necessary. Prof. S. I. Curtiss had already treated of the earlier precursors of criticism (including Simon and Astruc), and an able young French scholar, M. Alexandre Westphal, had given an equally accurate and interesting sketch of Hexateuch criticism.[1] With

[1] *Les sources du Pentateuque.* Tom. I. Le problème littéraire. Paris, 1888.

regard to German and Dutch critics, I must confess to a feeling of profound sadness at the losses of the last few years; the unexpected deaths of Riehm, Kuenen, and Lagarde seemed to check my pen in its progress. It is true, a similar excuse cannot be offered to French critical workers. But I hope that scholars like Bruston, Piepenring, and Westphal (who work under conditions in some respects analogous to our own) will accept the assurance of my warm interest in their researches, and my expectation of happy results from them for international Biblical criticism.[1]

Friendliest greetings also to all British, American, and Australian fellow-workers! Whether we will it or no, we must all be in some sense English, and it is one of our most characteristic features that we look to the practical results of scientific research. We cannot be mere historical or literary critics; we feel that we must contribute, each in his degree, to the construction of an improved Christian apologetic for our own age. Happily, this is not now an exclusively English characteristic; the same consciousness of Christian duty is visible in representative German critics, such as Hermann Schultz, author of *Old Testament Theology*. Let us see to it that, while our German kinsfolk are learning to be more practical in their theology, we on our side become not less apt

---

[1] For a list of continental as well as British and American critical writers, see part 6 of Appendix to Briggs's *The Bible, the Church, and the Reason* (T. & T. Clark, 1892).

pupils in the spirit and in the methods of critical inquiry. For sound Biblical criticism is neither German nor English, neither Lutheran, nor Anglican, nor Presbyterian, but international and interconfessional. It has a great history behind it, and a still greater one may, let us hope, be before it.

Oxford,
  Nov. 30, 1892.

₊*₊ During my absence in Egypt the correction of the proofs has been kindly undertaken by Mr. G. Buchanan Gray, B.A., Lecturer in Hebrew and the Old Testament in Mansfield College, Oxford.

CONTENTS

CHAP.		PAGE
I.	THE PRECURSORS IN ENGLAND: WARBURTON, LOWTH, GEDDES	1
II.	THE OPENING OF METHODICAL CRITICISM IN GERMANY. EICHHORN AND ILGEN ...	13
III.	DE WETTE, GESENIUS	31
IV.	EWALD (1): THE DEVELOPMENT PERIOD ...	66
V.	EWALD (2): HIS WEAKNESS AND HIS STRENGTH AS A CRITIC AND AS A MAN	99
VI.	HITZIG, [HENGSTENBERG,] VATKE, BLEEK ...	119
VII.	HUPFELD, DELITZSCH ...	149
VIII.	RIEHM, REUSS, LAGARDE, KUENEN ...	172
IX.	THE OPENING OF METHODICAL CRITICISM IN ENGLAND. COLENSO, KALISCH, S. DAVIDSON, ROWLAND WILLIAMS, PEROWNE, A. B. DAVIDSON (1862), RUSSELL MARTINEAU	195
X.	THE MODERN PERIOD. ROBERTSON SMITH, A. B. DAVIDSON, BRIGGS, TOY, [SCHRADER,] SAYCE, KIRKPATRICK, RYLE, FRANCIS BROWN, MOORE, WHITEHOUSE, G. A. SMITH, DUFF, FRIPP, ADDIS, MONTEFIORE, BEVAN ...	212
XI.	DRIVER (1)	248
XII.	DRIVER (2) ...	293
XIII.	DRIVER (3)	334

FOUNDERS

OF

OLD TESTAMENT CRITICISM.

CHAPTER I.

THE PRECURSORS IN ENGLAND—WARBURTON, LOWTH, GEDDES.

A WELL-KNOWN and honoured representative of progressive German orthodoxy (J. A. Dorner) has set a fine example of historical candour by admitting the obligations of his country to a much-disliked form of English heterodoxy. He says that English Deism, which found so many apt disciples in Germany, "by clearing away dead matter, prepared the way for a reconstruction of theology from the very depths of the heart's beliefs, and also subjected man's nature to stricter observation."[1] This, however, as it appears to me, is a very inadequate description of facts. It was not merely a new constructive stage of

---

[1] *History of Protestant Theology*, E. T., ii. 77. For the influence of Deism on Germany, see Tholuck (*Vermischte Schriften*, Bd. ii.) and Lechler (*Gesch. des englischen Deismus*).

German theoretic theology, and a keener psychological investigation, for which Deism helped to prepare the way, but also a great movement, which has in our own day become in a strict sense international, concerned with the literary and historical criticism of the Scriptures. Beyond all doubt, the Biblical discussions which abound in the works of the Deists and their opponents contributed in no slight degree to the development of that semi-apologetic criticism of the Old Testament, of which J. D. Michaelis, and in some degree even Eichhorn, were leading representatives. Transitory as the Deism of Toland and Collins was, it achieved the distinction, not only of calling forth Bishop Butler's *Analogy*, but of influencing or stimulating a number of eminent German scholars of various theological colours, among whom I must not omit to mention the earliest great New Testament critic, J. G. Semler (1725—1791). It is indeed singular that Deism should have passed away in England without having produced a great critical movement among ourselves. If Deuteronomy be, as M. Westphal rightly claims that it is, "Ariadne's thread in the labyrinth of Pentateuch criticism," it is strange that an English theological writer, who saw (for the first time) that this Book was a product of the seventh century,[1] should not have been prompted

---

[1] Parvish, *Inquiry into the Jewish and Christian Revelations* (Lond. 1739), p. 324, referred to by Kleinert (*Das Deuteronomium*, &c., 1872, p. 2). De Wette's epoch-making dissertation on the origin of Deuteronomy was not published till 1805.

by his good genius to follow up his advantage. But in point of fact there are but three isolated English scholars who appear to have shown any talent or inclination for a criticism of the Old Testament which is not merely concerned with various readings of the text—viz. **Bishop Warburton, Bishop Lowth,** and **Dr. Alexander Geddes**; and of these the only one who can properly be called a founder of criticism is the third.

I have first to speak of William Warburton and Robert Lowth. The former was a born pamphleteer and controversialist, and had neither the learning nor the seriousness requisite for the founder of a critical school; he limited himself to throwing out hints on Job and on the Song of Songs in his correspondence with Lowth, which his friend rejected with disdain, but which so far as Job is concerned he himself manfully defended in his *Divine Legation of Moses*. The latter (Lowth) was, for his time, a considerable scholar, but in theology he clung (like Kennicott) to the traditional orthodoxy. Hence he felt constrained to insist on the allegorical character of the Song of Songs, and to maintain the extreme antiquity of the Book of Job. And yet even this circumspect bishop fully admits that the prophets spoke primarily to the men of their own time (see *e.g.* his exposition of Isa. vii. 14),[1] and this admission contains the promise of

---

[1] Cheyne, *Prophecies of Isaiah*, ii. 277. In England the influence of Lowth was chiefly felt in textual criticism (see Blayney's *Jeremiah* (1784), and Newcome's *Ezekiel* (1788). The

the cautiously bold criticism of Eichhorn and Ewald. Both the *Isaiah* (1778) and the Lectures *De sacrâ poesi Hebræorum* (1753) were translated into German, and, enriched with Koppe's notes on the one and with those of Michaelis on the other, were among the revolutionary influences of that unsettled age in Germany.

The third member of our trio is, from any point of view, an interesting phenomenon. Alexander Geddes was born of Roman Catholic parents in Banffshire in 1737, and studied at the Scottish College at Paris, his chief teacher of Hebrew being Ladvocat, Professor at the Sorbonne. For some years Geddes led a simple and studious life as priest of a Roman Catholic congregation near Aberdeen, and from Aberdeen University he received the honorary distinction of a LL.D. degree. Difficulties having arisen from his liberal opinions, he came to London, where he became a notable figure in society, owing to his union of deep learning with wit and liberal opinions. Crabbe Robinson of course met him; he speaks of Geddes's striking appearance, which reminded him of Herder.[1] But again his liberal views, expressed with uncompromising frankness, brought Geddes into suspicion of heterodoxy, and without the help of his munificent patron, Lord Petre, he would scarcely have maintained his position. He himself,

---

study of the literary aspects of the Old Testament made no progress; Lowth was a *vox clamantis in deserto*, so far as England was concerned.

[1] *Diary*, i. 113.

however, never swerved from his allegiance to his ancestral faith, and promoted the cause of moderate and reasonable orthodoxy by a courteous letter to Dr. Priestley, in which he argued that the divinity of Jesus Christ was in some sense held by the ante-Nicene fathers. His great life-work, moreover, was one from which all Christian Churches might have profited—viz. the preparation of a new translation of the Bible with explanatory notes, and so much critical help as appeared necessary for educated and thoughtful readers. In 1786 he published a Prospectus of this work; in 1787 a letter to the Bishop of London (Lowth) on the same subject, and in 1788 (in folio) proposals for printing this new version by subscription. He had much support from influential clergymen (notably Lowth and Kennicott), and in 1792 the first volume appeared, with a dedication to Lord Petre.[1] In the preface, however, he committed himself to critical views of the origin of the Pentateuch, and both Roman Catholics and Protestants opened their batteries upon him. He was, in fact, before his time, and knowing what he did of the temper of the Anglican bishops and the universities,[2] he should perhaps have seen the wisdom of reserving his critical views for a separate work. Vol. ii., continuing the work as far as Chronicles, appeared, under the patronage of

---

[1] The title is as follows: *The Holy Bible, or the Books accounted sacred by Jews and Christians, faithfully translated from corrected Texts of the Originals, with Various Readings, Explanatory Notes, and Critical Remarks.*

[2] See his letter to Eichhorn (Appendix to *Memoir*).

the Duchess of Gloucester, in 1797, but found no more friendly reception. The undaunted scholar, however, brought out a new work in 1800, entitled *Critical Remarks on the Hebrew Scriptures, corresponding with a new Translation of the Bible*, but paid the penalty. He was suspended from his ecclesiastical functions—a lighter penalty, at any rate, than a poor Bavarian priest (Isenbiehl) had paid in 1778 for offering a critical interpretation of Isa. vii. 14. He died in 1802, leaving a nearly-finished translation of the Book of Psalms,[1] and found a competent biographer in John Mason Good, the highly-cultured translator of the Song of Songs.

The plan of Geddes's translation is admirable: as to its execution it would be ungenerous to make much of shortcomings which were inevitable a century ago. Even in the matter of style, one may venture to think that Geddes's ideal of a popular and comprehensible English was a better one than that of the learned Bishop Lowth. To say the least, he deserves to be had in honour as an early worker at the still unsolved problem of Bible-translation. But it is as a pioneer, and to some extent founder of criticism, that he chiefly interests us here. He was recognized by Eichhorn as "almost the only person" whose opinion on his own works he could listen to with respect,[2]

---

[1] This was published in 1807.

[2] "Tu enim fere unicus es, quem, si liceret, judicem mihi expeterem; quandoquidem tu in litteris biblicis habitas, in eodem stadio magnâ cum laude decurris, omnesque difficultates et molestias, quæ talem cursum impediunt, ipsâ experientiâ edoct-

and his *Critical Remarks* were partly translated into German, partly expanded by J. S. Vater in his *Commentary on the Pentateuch* (1802-5), and so gave rise to what is commonly called the Geddes-Vater hypothesis. The following passages will probably interest the reader, as containing Geddes's chief critical conclusions. They are taken from the preface to vol. i. of his Bible (pp. xviii—xix).

"It has been well observed by Michaelis that all external testimony is here of little avail: it is from intrinsic evidence only that we must derive our proofs. Now, from intrinsic evidence, three things to me seem indubitable. 1stly, The Pentateuch, in its present form, was not written by Moses. 2dly, It was written in the land of Chanaan, and most probably at Jerusalem. 3dly, It could not be written before the reign of David, nor after that of Hezekiah. The long pacific reign of Solomon (the Augustan age of Judæa) is the period to which I would refer it: yet, I confess, there are some marks of a posterior date, or at least of posterior interpolation.

"But although I am inclined to believe that the Pentateuch was reduced into its present form in the reign of Solomon, I am fully persuaded that it was compiled from ancient documents, some of which were coeval with Moses, and some even anterior to Moses. Whether all these were written records, or many of

---

us, nosti, ut adeo nemo facile ad judicium tam æquius quam rectius ferendum cogitari possit."—Letter to Geddes (*Memoir*, p. 543).

them only oral traditions, it would be rash to determine. . . . Moses, who had been *taught all the wisdom of the Egyptians*, most probably was the first Hebrew writer, or the first who applied writing to historical composition. From his journals a great part of the Pentateuch seems to have been compiled. Whether he were also the original author of the Hebrew cosmogony, and of the history prior to his own days, I would neither confidently assert, nor positively deny. He certainly *may* have been the original author or compiler; and may have drawn the whole or a part of his cosmogony and general history, both before and after the deluge, from the archives of Egypt: and those original materials, collected first by Moses, may have been worked up into their present form by the compiler of the Pentateuch, in the reign of Solomon. But it is also possible, and I think more probable, that the latter was the first collector; and collected from such documents as he could find, either among his own people, or among the neighbouring nations.

"Some modern writers, indeed, allowing Moses to be the author of the Pentateuch, maintain that he composed the book of Genesis from two different written documents; which they have attempted to distinguish by respective characteristics. Although I really look upon this as the work of *fancy*, and will elsewhere endeavour to prove it to be so, I am not so self-sufficient as to imagine that I may not be in the wrong, or that they may not be in the right. The reader who wishes to see the arguments on which they ground their assertion, may consult Astruc or Eichhorn."

Now, although this rejection of the "Document-hypothesis" of Eichhorn (the details of which Geddes proceeds to give) is not in itself a **proof of** sagacity, yet Westphal seems to me too warm in his invective against the "Geddes-Vater theory," or **the** "Fragment-hypothesis," as an ill-judged return to the crude ideas of Spinoza. The more correct view is certainly that given by Mr. Addis, whose words I have the more pleasure in quoting, because of the justice which he has done on an earlier page to Geddes, not only as a scholar but as **a man**.

"The 'Fragment-theory' was in some respects an advance upon Astruc and Eichhorn. It extended the investigation from Genesis and the beginning of Exodus to **the** whole Pentateuch, and ceased to assume that the only documents in the Pentateuch were documents used **by** Moses. **It argued, with** justice, that the Pentateuch is composed of sections, some of **which had** no original connection with each other, and that even **the** documents which use the word Elohim or Yahweh may be, and are, of various origin. It failed to see that the supposed 'fragments' might, **on closer** inspection, form themselves into two or three documents."[1]

Nor can it be said that Vater was wholly blind to

---

[1] *The Documents of the Hexateuch*, vol. i. Introd. p. xxvii.

the evidence which led Astruc and Eichhorn to form the Document-theory. Vater expressly says that though the fragments of which the Pentateuch is composed had originally no connection, yet it is not impossible that some fragments of the same book may come from the same author, and he is willing to group his fragments in two great families— the Elohistic and the Jehovistic. Ilgen too, whom Westphal praises at the expense of Vater, maintains (as we shall see) that the contents of the three documents of Genesis are derived from as many as seventeen different sources. Two more short quotations from Vater's inspirer Geddes may be added, to illustrate his criticism of the contents of Genesis.

"I will not pretend to say that [its history] is entirely unmixed with the leaven of the heroic ages. Let the father of Hebrew be tried by the same rules of criticism as Greek history."

"Why might not the Hebrews have their mythology as well as other nations? and why might not their mythologists contrive or improve a system of cosmogony as well as those of Chaldæa, or Egypt, or Greece, or Italy, or Persia, or Hindostan?"

So then, in realistic as well as literary criticism Geddes is a convinced adherent of the principles of Eichhorn, from whom however, being a man of great intellectual independence, he does not scruple to differ upon occasion (*e.g.* on the meaning of Gen. iii.). That he has a claim to be reckoned among the founders of criticism, may be seen, not only from his influence on Vater, but by comparing him with our one eminent English *pioneer* of criticism, Thomas Hobbes.[1] It is painful to think that the seed which Geddes sowed fell, so far as England was concerned, on barren ground. What is the cause of this? Geddes, as we have seen, was no Deist, and, though a Roman Catholic, was socially and intellectually on a level with the best English Protestants. Any one who would seek to answer this question would find—to apply some words of Mark Pattison—"that he had undertaken a perplexing but not altogether profitless inquiry."[2]

At any rate, whether we can explain it or not, there are no more Englishmen to mention among the

---

[1] Hobbes was the first modern writer who denied the Mosaic origin of the Pentateuch as a whole on critical grounds. The view expressed by Siegfried, that he borrowed from Spinoza, is not in itself unplausible, since the theologico-political system of the *Leviathan* has points of affinity with that of Spinoza's *Tractatus theologico-politicus*, but is opposed to chronology, the former work having been published in 1651, nineteen years before Spinoza's great work appeared. That the English philosopher borrowed from Ibn Ezra (as seems to be suggested in Bacon's *Genesis of Genesis*, Introd. p. xxiv) is of course not absolutely impossible, but considering Hobbes's singular originality, is hardly probable. That Spinoza borrowed from Hobbes is also possible, but most improbable, the indebtedness of the great Jewish thinker being rather to Jewish than to Western writers (putting aside Descartes). [The passages in Hobbes are—*Leviathan*, part 3, ch. xxxiii.; and in Spinoza, *Tract. theol.-polit.*, ch. viii., "De origine Pentateuchi"; see also ch. vii., "De interpretatione Scripturæ," and comp. Siegfried, *Spinoza als Kritiker und Ausleger des Alten Testaments* (Berl. 1867).]

[2] *Essays and Reviews* (ed. 1869, p. 398).

founders or precursors of Old Testament criticism until we come to our own time. Indeed, I have only given these sketches of Warburton, Lowth, and Geddes because they were natives of Great Britain. Were I to linger over the continental pioneers of criticism—Baruch Spinoza, the lonely Jewish thinker of Amsterdam; Richard Simon, the learned Oratorian of Paris; Jean Leclerc, the French-Swiss Hebraist adopted by the Amsterdam Remonstrants; and especially Jean Astruc, professor of medicine in various French colleges,—I should exceed the limits of this work, and enter into competition with an excellent American writer who has given us a monograph on the early critics of the Pentateuch, Dr. S. I. Curtiss of Chicago.[1]

[1] See his "Sketches of Pentateuch Criticism," *Bibliotheca Sacra*, Jan. and Oct. 1884, and comp. the parallel portions of Westphal's able work referred to in my preface. On Richard Simon see also Bernus, *R. Simon et son histoire critique* (Lausanne, 1869), and a résumé in the *Revue des deux mondes*.

CHAPTER II.

THE OPENING OF METHODICAL CRITICISM IN GERMANY—EICHHORN AND ILGEN.

MY own series of portraits of Old Testament critics begins with **J. G. Eichhorn**, whom, for reasons which I will give presently, I venture to call the founder of modern Old Testament criticism. I wish to show that he was not merely a "dry rationalist," as Mr. Addis represents, but a man of many-sided culture, and not without Church-feeling, a friend of science, and also a servant of religion, sensitive to the best influences of his time, though not in advance of his age. Eichhorn was born Oct. 16, 1752, and was the son of a pastor in a small principality now absorbed in the kingdom of Wurtemberg. At Easter 1770 he went to Göttingen, where the wise liberality of our George II., stimulated by his minister Münchhausen, had founded (in 1734) the famous Georgia Augusta university. There it was only natural that he should be profoundly affected by the *genius loci*. The spirit of classical literature and of historical research, equally with that of a moderate orthodox theology, could not fail to pass into his sensitive mind. These were all subjects which Münchhausen as a statesman desired to foster, and they were cultivated with pre-eminent success in the old Göttingen university. In theology Eichhorn had among his teachers J. D. Michaelis, the Biblical scholar, and Walch, the not-yet-forgotten Church historian; classical philology he studied under Heyne, who admitted him into his *Seminar*, and obtained for him in 1774 his first appointment as rector of the gymnasium at Ohrdruff, in the duchy of Gotha. How Eichhorn came to be smitten with the love of the East, it is not so easy to say. But the titles of his earliest works (from 1774 onwards) sufficiently prove that Mohammedan history, and Arabic and Syriac literature, were the favourite subjects of the young graduate, and this accounts for the fact that in 1775 he was appointed professor of Oriental languages in the university of Jena, where in the preceding year he had already taken his doctor's degree. Hence it was not merely as a theologian (this he could not help being, for theology was then in the atmosphere) but as an Orientalist that he approached the study of the Old Testament. I would ask the reader to take special notice of this fact, because Eichhorn set the tone to his successors, by whom the Hebrew Scriptures were constantly treated, not merely as the vehicle of a revelation, but as in form Oriental books, to be interpreted in accordance with the habits of mind of Semitic peoples. (It is from Eichhorn and his more celebrated friend Herder that the custom of referring to the "Orientalism" of the Scriptures is mainly derived.) I must not pause here to defend or explain this "Orientalizing" of books which the traditional orthodoxy had been accustomed to regard as in all senses unique. The best defence and explanation is to refer, not to the first tentative and faulty efforts of Eichhorn and Herder, but to works of our own time (belonging to different schools), which may be "known and read of all men." It would be possible, no doubt, to gather from Eichhorn explanations of miraculous narratives, and of difficult passages of prophecy, which strike even critics who are no apologists as immature and arbitrary. But this only shows that he is a beginner in the arduous work of entering into the ideas and circumstances of the Biblical writers, and that he sometimes forgets that, on his own theory, there is a divine element in the Bible which no other literature contains in anything like the same degree. And if Eichhorn was sometimes unjust to Biblical narratives and prophecies, not only in his books, but in his academical lectures, yet this was the error of a good and Christian man, who was in his own way an apologist,[1] and whose reverent spirit could not but

---

[1] Comp. Bertheau, art. "Eichhorn," in Herzog-Plitt, *Realencyclopädie*, Bd. iv.; Westphal, *Les sources*, &c., i. 120. How great was the need of critical apologists may be gathered from the appendix to the Wolfenbüttel Fragments published after Lessing's death in 1787, in which, while admitting the Mosaic redaction of the Pentateuch, Reimarus inveighs passionately against the author or compiler. That Eichhorn was equal to the task of defending Biblical religion against its foes, cannot indeed be maintained (see Bleek, *Introduction* (by Venables), § 8). His

neutralize any evil influence from his intellectual mistake. An early biographer in fact assures us that "faith in that which is holy even in the miracles of the Bible was never shattered by Eichhorn in any youthful mind."[1]

Eichhorn, as we have seen, went to Jena in 1775. It was an event of great importance, both for his theological and for his general culture. Seldom has there been a theologian of such a width of interests as Eichhorn, and we can hardly help ascribing this to the varied intellectual stimulus which Jena at that time supplied. In that very same year another young man of promise entered the little duchy of Saxe Weimar: it was Goethe. And in the autumn of the following year, a slightly older man, destined to great things, followed his friend Goethe: it was Herder, who had accepted the office of Court Preacher and General Superintendent at Weimar. That Eichhorn took a keen interest in the literary movement of the time, is certain from his later works on the history of literature. It was his hope to contribute to the winning back of the educated classes to religion, and he may well have thought that in order to do this he must drink full draughts of general culture. In this enterprise he found a natural ally in Herder, who was a theologian among the *littérateurs*, as

---

pupil Ewald was at any rate better equipped, both critically and religiously; for he too was proud to be an "apologist."

[1] H. Döring, in Ersch and Gruber's *Allgemeine Encyclopädie*, (I.) xxxi. (1838).

Eichhorn was a *littérateur* among the theologians. The friends had their first meeting in the summer of 1780. They saw each other often, and began a regular correspondence. In 1780 appeared one of Herder's most charming books (the contents of which have now happily become commonplace [1])—the *Letters on the Study of Theology;* in 1782-83 his still more important work, *The Spirit of Hebrew Poetry*. To both of these Eichhorn was able to give his hearty approval and admiration, and between the two appeared the first part of his own great work, the *Introduction to the Old Testament* (completed in 1783). It was a happy time of mutual intercourse and indebtedness. I think it worth while to state this, because M. Westphal has considerably exaggerated the dependence of Eichhorn on Herder. It is true that Eichhorn in his letters is never weary of confessing that he lives upon Herder's ideas, but it seems to me that it was chiefly a general fertilizing influence which the Weimar divine exercised upon the Jena professor. Such ideas as Eichhorn took from Herder were subjected by him to the testing

[1] Herder's attitude towards the question of Bible inspiration, for instance, is that which all our best critical scholars now take up. "I take vastly more pleasure in winning a lively apprehension of the divine in these writings," he says (Letter xii.), "than in racking my brains as to the exact manner in which it existed in the soul of the writers, or upon their tongue, or in their pen. We do not understand in what a number of human effects our soul displays itself, and shall we decide how manifoldly or how simply God works upon it? We cannot get to the bottom of a single word of God in nature."

C

of a cooler mind, and re-issued with the stamp of his own characteristic conceptions. On reading Eichhorn's third volume, Herder confesses in the frankest manner that his friend has anticipated him in a number of thoughts, as he himself had a few years before anticipated Eichhorn. On the score of learning and critical power, M. Westphal would not deny that the superiority lies with Eichhorn, and Herder himself generously admires the "treasures of knowlege, criticism, and taste" in his friend's work. What indeed would Herder have effected without such a helper as Eichhorn? He could but give general ideas, and stir up an enthusiastic admiration for the "spirit of Hebrew poetry." But how few books were there that he could recommend for the study of details! In the first edition of the *Letters on Theology* (1789), he has to admit that "we have not as yet a proper critical introduction to the Old Testament." In the second (1785) he appends to this the footnote, "We have it now in Eichhorn's valuable Introduction."

But had Eichhorn no like-minded theological colleagues in Jena? He had Griesbach, the famous New Testament text-critic, who could no doubt have cautioned him against attempting too much, and against neglecting accuracy in small things. Somewhat later he had Doederlein, who was a bright, progressive scholar, remembered now chiefly by his *Isaiah* (1775), but in his own day noted as a reformer of the Biblical and other proofs of dogmatic theology. But Herder was all the more valuable to Eichhorn because he was not a professor; width of range, literary insight, and Church-feeling, were Herderian characteristics which Eichhorn needed to carry out his mission. Afterwards it was concentration and the minute study of details that were needed; and then a crowd of illustrious workers appeared—the true "founders of criticism." But all these stand on the shoulders of Herder and Eichhorn, and even if but little of their historical construction should be left standing, Old Testament scholars will still be bound to respect them as pioneers. Well does the aged Goethe, in the notes to the *Westöstlicher Divan*, congratulate himself on having known the time when Herder and Eichhorn together opened up to himself and his contemporaries a new source of pure delight in the Biblical literature! Would that he could have gone further, and expressed obligations of another and a still higher character. For Herder at any rate was a prophet.[1]

In 1788 Eichhorn's residence at Jena came to a close. He was invited back to Göttingen as an ordinary professor in the faculty of philosophy. He found his old professors, Michaelis and Heyne, still alive. With the former he had only three more years of intercourse, and this intercourse does not appear to have been altogether friendly. The great classical scholar Heyne, however (who died in 1812), must have welcomed him with open arms. For in

[1] Haym, *Herder nach seinem Leben und seinen Werken*, ii. (1885), pp. 185, 186.

1789 came an official letter to Herder in Heyne's hand, in which the great poet and theologian was invited to Göttingen as professor of history and chief university preacher. One of the principal arguments urged by Heyne was this—that the theological atmosphere in the university had completely changed, and that even those who had once been hostile to Herder (this was the *second* time that he had a chance of going to Göttingen) now regarded him as a pillar of the Church.[1] How would Eichhorn have rejoiced, if his friend could have joined him in the unromantic and quarrelsome northern university! But it was not to be—Herder, as his friends said, was "too good to be a professor," and was persuaded to remain at Weimar. Eichhorn, at any rate, was not discouraged. He lectured, we are told, twenty-four hours, or more, in the week,[2] and not only on the Semitic languages, but on the whole of the Bible,[3] and even on political history. Another *Fach*, moreover—that of the history of literature—was committed entirely to him. That he lectured thus widely, one cannot, in the interests of accurate study, help regretting. One thinks of Renan's dream of devoting one lifetime to Semitic philology, another to history, and so forth; here is a scholar of such versatility and power, that he can do two or three men's work in one lifetime. How much of this work of Eichhorn's really influenced the

---

[1] Haym.   [2] Bertheau.
[3] His *Introduction to the N. T.*, which appeared in 1804—1814, may especially be mentioned.

progress of science, is of course another question. He taught many things, and produced many works; but did he attain many important results? It may be doubted. On the other hand, he must have stimulated many younger men, and by his books and innumerable articles he opened many discussions, both on the Old and on the New Testament, which lasted for a long time afterwards. He had the privilege of dying in the midst of his work, full of honours, June 27, 1827. His son, K. F. Eichhorn, was the celebrated jurist and Prussian Minister of Worship, a friend and admirer of Schleiermacher, though rather on his practical than on his more strictly theological side.

Let me then pass over all Eichhorn's minor works (with just a brief reference to his services as a reviewer of contemporary literature, from which I have elsewhere derived profit myself),[1] and confine my attention to his *Introduction to the Old Testament*. The success of this work was phenomenal; it went through four editions in the author's lifetime, besides two pirated editions, and exercised as much influence upon opinion in that day as Wellhausen's *Prolegomena* has done in our own time. A long list of books might be given in proof of the latter statement, instead of which I will simply quote the calm assurance of J. P. Gabler, "the father of Biblical theology" (who in 1791-93 republished Eichhorn's early

---

[1] Cheyne, *Job and Solomon*, p. 260.

work, *Die Urgeschichte*,[1] with an introduction), that the analysis of Genesis into two documents "can in our day be regarded as settled and pre-supposed, without fear of any important opposition."[2] This remark of course only applies to Germany. In England the book only seems to have had one warm friend (besides Dr. Geddes)—the Regius Professor of Hebrew at Cambridge, H. Lloyd, who tried in vain to obtain church and university patronage for a translation.

The style of Eichhorn's *Introduction* has been called rhetorical. Certainly it contrasts with the conventional style of seventeenth-century theology. But this was one chief element in its success; it was written for Herder and for Goethe, as well as for Michaelis and the *Zunfttheologen*. As the author himself observes, a new writer is bound to make concessions to the fashionable literary tone, and, as one may add, this work was not only by a new writer, but was the first of its kind, for neither Carpzov nor even Michaelis can be said to enter at all into competition with Eichhorn. Let us listen to his own words—

"My greatest trouble I had to bestow on a hitherto

---

[1] A critical examination of the narratives in the early part of Genesis, which first appeared anonymously in Eichhorn's *Repertorium* (for Biblical and Oriental literature) in 1779. Gabler was about the same age as Eichhorn, and was one of his earliest disciples at Jena, where he afterwards became a professor. Cf. Krummacher's sketch of him in his *Autobiography* (Edinb. 1867), p. 68.

[2] Quoted by Dr. Briggs, *Presbyterian Review*, iv. 91.

unworked field—on the investigation of the inner nature of the several writings of the Old Testament with the help of the Higher Criticism (not a new name to any humanist)."[1] By "higher criticism" he means the analysis of a book into its earlier and its later elements. He comes forward as a defender of the "genuineness" of the books of the Old Testament, but in order to prove this "genuineness," he claims the right to assume that "most of the writings of the Hebrews have passed through several hands." This, he remarks, has been the fate of all ancient books, and he adds that—

"Even the manner in which many of the writings of the Old Testament came into existence makes it necessary that there should be in them an alternation of old and new passages and sections. Very few of them came from the hand of their authors in their present form."[2]

It is true that Eichhorn had been preceded, at least as a critic of Genesis, by Astruc. One might naturally infer from the similarity of their results that Eichhorn was indebted to his predecessor. In this case, the credit due to Eichhorn would still be great, for without him, it might be contended, Astruc's results would have been as completely lost to science as those of Ilgen were afterwards. But it has been proved by Boehmer and Westphal that Astruc's work was only known to Eichhorn at second hand. When therefore

---

[1] Preface to second edition. [2] *Einleitung*, i. 92.

the latter makes the positive assertion that he has arrived at his results independently of Astruc, we have no reason for doubting his veracity; and when he lays claim to being the first to observe the duplicate narrative of the flood in Genesis, we both may and must accept his statement (the article by Michaelis, which was one of Eichhorn's chief sources of information respecting Astruc, misrepresents that critic's view of Gen. vii.).

And now as to Eichhorn's conclusions, more especially with regard to the Pentateuch.[1] The early history, he thinks, is made up chiefly of two documents, Jehovistic and Elohistic, the former of which ends shortly before the death of Joseph (Gen. l. 14), the latter with the first public appearance of Moses (Ex. iii. 25). These documents, according to him, were combined as they now stand at the end of the Mosaic age, or soon afterwards, though often in fragmentary form, and with not unfrequent glosses.[2] The lives of Abraham and of Isaac are almost entirely taken from the Jehovistic, those of Jacob and of Joseph from the Elohistic source. The four later "books of Moses" grew out of separate writings of Moses and of some of his contemporaries. Among the many features of this part of the *Einleitung* which deserve

---

[1] *Einleitung*, iii. (Mosaische Schriften). I have used the fourth edition (1823).

[2] Eichhorn also admits certain separate documents, viz. ii. 4—iv. 24; xiv.; xxxiii. 18—xxxiv. 31; xxxvi.; xlix. 1—27. He thinks too that chap. x. may have been borrowed by the Jehovist from the Phœnicians.

notice are the thoughtful characterization of the documents (in which the Jehovist is rightly distinguished from the Elohist by a diversity of ideas as well as of language), and the distinction between the priests' code of the middle books, and the people's law-book in Deuteronomy. Nothing, we are assured, hangs on the name of the compiler.[1] As to Eichhorn's analysis, it is surely a proof of his sagacity (as well as of the cogency of the evidence) that he has assigned to the Elohist almost all those passages of Genesis which are now unanimously assigned by analysts to the document commonly designated PC or P. These are better grounds for a favourable verdict upon Eichhorn's critical character than those apologetic tendencies which conciliated the regard of the late learned but uncritical Dr. Edersheim.[2] It is a defect and not a merit of Eichhorn that he still thinks the cause of true religion (or at any rate of the Bible) to be to some extent bound up with the Mosaic origin of the Pentateuch. One may excuse him (having regard to the recent Deistic controversy), but one cannot help regretting that even he was touched by the polemical spirit. His other critical results need not be catalogued here. Suffice it to say that, compared with later critics, he is strikingly conserv-

---

[1] In the edition of 1790 Eichhorn says that Moses may have written, or compiled, the books of the Pentateuch. This statement was afterwards modified.

[2] *Prophecy and History*, &c. (1885), pp. 194—196. Appendix I. gives Eichhorn's distribution of Genesis in three parallel columns.

ative, though even he has a clear perception of the Maccabæan date of Dan. vii.—xii. The religious contents of the several books do not, however, receive their due from this early critic, who was a child of the *Aufklärung*, though, partly through the influence of Herder, he strove to overcome its prejudices. In this respect, as we shall see later, he contrasts strikingly with his great disciple, Ewald.

From Eichhorn it is natural to pass to **Karl David Ilgen** (1763—1834), who was Eichhorn's successor at Jena, and most effectually supplemented his critical work on Genesis. In Ilgen the school-master dwarfed the scholar; he is now remembered chiefly as Rector of the scholastic foundation of Schulpforte (for which he did fully as much as Arnold did for Rugby), and as the teacher of the great classical scholar, Gottfried Hermann. A striking sketch of his appearance and character is given by Otto Jahn in his memorial sketch of Hermann, for every word of which there is authority in the short but interesting Latin biography of Ilgen by F. K. Kraft. That such a man should be an eminent Biblical critic, would be surprising in our day, but in the infancy of criticism, when all problems were new, and at any rate appeared simple, it was nothing extraordinary. Ilgen's classical scholarship was extensive, and due more to his own exertions than to his teachers; he was not disposed to fall in with routine, and when duty or inclination called him to Biblical research, it was only to be expected that there should be some fair fruits of his studies. It was in 1789 (while Rector of the gymnasium at Naumburg) that he made his first contribution to Old Testament criticism, entitled *Jobi antiquissimi carminis Hebraici natura atque virtutes.* I will not claim much merit for this early work, which, as Ewald remarks (*Das Buch Ijob*, 1854, " Vorrede," p. xx), nowhere touches solid ground, and actually propounds the hypothesis that the Book of Job is a pre-Mosaic, non-Israelitish work. The hypothesis has long since become antiquated, but seemed not improbable to many scholars of that period,[1] so that we need not wonder that its author was appointed to the professorship vacated by Eichhorn in 1788, and, as it would seem, not at once filled up.[2] While at Jena (1794—1802) Ilgen threw himself into the varied intellectual interests of the place—those were the palmy days when Fichte and Schelling, Wilhelm von Humboldt, and the Schlegels adorned its university. He lectured, we are told, both on the Hebrew Scriptures and on the history of philosophy,[3] and was strengthened in the resolution to practise Biblical criticism "with the same subtlety with which one is wont to practise Greek and Latin literature." In 1795 he brought out a *Commentatio*

---

[1] Cheyne, *Job and Solomon*, p. 97.

[2] I follow the very positive statement of Kraft (*Vita Ilgenii*, 1837, p. 49).

[3] The famous rationalist Paulus, too, thought it a theologian's duty to follow the progress of philosophy (letter to Geddes in Good's *Memoir of Geddes*, p. 540), though he never became very philosophical.

de notione tituli Filii Dei (referred to by De Wette in his early work on Deuteronomy), and in 1799 a critical edition of Tobit (the only special treatise on that book mentioned by De Wette in his *Introduction*). Between these less important works falls one of which I give the title in full,—

Die Urkunden des Jerusalem'schen Tempelarchivs in ihrer Urgestalt, als Beytrag zur Berichtigung der Geschichte der Religion und Politik aus dem Hebräischen mit kritischen und erklärenden Anmerkungen, auch mancherley dazu gehörigen Abhandlungen, von Karl David Ilgen, Prof. der Philosophie und der oriental. Literatur in Jena. Erster Theil. Halle, 1798.

The merits of this remarkable work were to some extent recognized by Ewald (at a time, as Ewald remarks, when his deserts were very generally overlooked) in the first volume of his *History* (ed. 1), but it is only of late years that his right place as a "founder of criticism" has been assigned to him. Although I have not been able myself to see the book on which his fame rests,[1] I venture to endorse the praise which it has lately received from others. It has evidently some rare merits, and its equally striking defects may easily be pardoned in consideration of its very early date. The thesis which it supports is briefly this. The Book of Genesis, as it stands, is composed of seventeen documents, which originally had a separate existence. They proceed,

---

[1] Ilgen's book is, in fact, rarer than Astruc's *Conjectures*.

however, from (probably, or at any rate possibly) not more than three independent writers, whom Ilgen calls respectively *Sopher Eliel harîshôn, Sopher Eliel hashshênî,* and *Sopher Elijah harîshôn* (*i.e.* the first and second Elohist, and the first Yahwist), and whose dates he reserves for future consideration. To recognize and reconstitute these records is no doubt difficult, but this is simply owing to the mutilation which they could not help suffering at the hands of the redactor. Those who are acquainted with recent criticism will at once be struck by the modern air of Ilgen's theory, and will perhaps be surprised that its merits were so long overlooked. The reason is that the more cautious analysts who followed Ilgen and De Wette were startled by Ilgen's large concession to the adherents of the Fragment-hypothesis. They also took offence at his frequent and apparently arbitrary alterations of the divine names, his partiality for the readings of the LXX. and the Samaritan Pentateuch, and his breaking up of the text into minute fragments. More than fifty years afterwards, when the fair-minded Hupfeld read the book, he was repelled (as he informs us) by these characteristics, and it was only after he had himself rediscovered the "second Elohist" that he perceived how many points of contact his own analysis had with Ilgen's, and how many delicate observations his predecessor had made on the linguistic usage of the documents.[1] In our

---

[1] *Die Quellen der Genesis* (1853), "Vorrede," pp. viii—x.

own day there are many critics of Genesis who trace the hand of a second Yahwist (the Yahwists were, in fact, perhaps a school of writers); and this too has been anticipated by Ilgen, who, as we have seen, designates one of the writers in Genesis, "the first Sopher Elijah."[1] No wonder that contemporary scholars are loud in their admiration of this neglected critic, whose achievements in Genesis, had he been able to continue his analysis of the Pentateuch, might have been followed up by others equally brilliant. But in 1802 Ilgen left Jena for Schulpforte, and so his work remained a *torso*; Part II. never appeared.

[1] See especially Westphal, *Les sources*, &c., tom. i., who gives on pp. 140-41 a conspectus of Ilgen's analysis, and Cornill, *Einleitung*, pp. 19-20. Both refer to Ilgen's admirable treatment of the composite story of Joseph, in which this early critic anticipates the best points of Wellhausen's analysis.

CHAPTER III.

DE WETTE—GESENIUS.

To the same little German duchy, to which we are in some sense indebted both for Eichhorn and for Ilgen, we owe the subject of our next sketch—**W. M. L. De Wette.** This great theologian, whose life is so full of suggestiveness to thoughtful readers, was born at Ulla, near Weimar, Jan. 12, 1780. He was the eldest son of the pastor of the place, and was educated at the Weimar gymnasium. During his school-time he came into contact with Herder, whose pleasantness as an examiner and sweet seriousness as a preacher were printed deep in the lad's memory. In 1799 he went to the university of Jena, where for a time Gabler and Paulus converted him to their own cold and superficial rationalism, from the depressing effects of which he was rescued, as he tells us himself, through philosophy. His deliverer was, however, not Schelling (whom he heard with admiration but without conviction), but J. F. Fries, a too little known philosopher, brought up, like Schleiermacher, among the Moravian Brethren, and full of strong religious instincts, who sought to unite the criticism of Kant with the faith-philosophy of Jacobi. In 1805 De Wette took his doctor's degree and became *privat-docent*, offering for his dissertation a treatise on Deuteronomy,[1] in which this among other critical points is argued with much force—that on internal grounds Deuteronomy must be of later origin than the rest of the Pentateuch, and that the kernel of it was written in the reign of Josiah. Some of the critical views expressed or suggested in this work agreed with those of Vater in a famous dissertation appended to his commentary on the Pentateuch, but the generous interest displayed by this scholar in his young rival induced the latter to go on with the preparation of a larger work. This appeared in two duodecimo volumes in 1806-7 under the title of *Contributions to Old Testament Introduction* (I will call it henceforth the *Beiträge*), with a sensible but cautious preface to vol. i. by Griesbach. The opinions which it expressed were, it is true, modified in many respects in the author's later works, and not without cause. In vol. i. De Wette certainly deals too "rigorously and vigorously" (as Matthew Arnold would say) with the Books of Chronicles; in vol. ii. he under-estimates the historical element in the narratives of the Pentateuch. His views on the composition of the Pentateuch are also of a highly provisional character; he hovers between the Fragment- and the Document-hypothesis, and though he

---

[1] This tractate is reprinted in De Wette's *Opuscula* (Berlin, 1833).

is evidently not hopeless of reconciling them, he cannot formulate a distinct theory of his own. Still the work is full of promise, and the youthful author deserves high credit for the large element of truth in all his theories. As Wellhausen remarks, he was the first who clearly felt the inconsistency between the supposed starting-point of Israelitish history and that history itself. And if in his present stage he is too severe both on Chronicles and on the Pentateuch, his predecessor Eichhorn was undeniably too lenient, and the particular critical hypothesis (known as the Supplement-theory) for which De Wette prepared the way, formed a necessary stage in the progress of Pentateuch-criticism. Against these merits must we set the demerit of undevoutness? Let that harshest of contemporary critics, Lagarde, answer. "I remember," he says, "how De Wette's *Beiträge*, against which Hengstenberg warned [every one], worked upon me. [I found in the author] a truthfulness and honesty beyond reproach, with but few results except that great one produced sooner or later upon all candid minds by him who walks before God."[1]

Let us pause a moment here. If it be true (with qualifications) that every earnest thinker passes through three stages—a stage of seeking, a stage of finding, and a stage of applying the truth found to practical life—in which of these stages is De Wette? I think that he has already entered on the second.

[1] *Mittheilungen*, iv. (1891), p. 58.

He has not indeed reached mature and definite critical views, but he is in advance of older workers in the same field, while theologically he has begun to scale the height, from which he hopes to look down on the lower hills of rationalism and orthodoxy. It may be true (see Griesbach's preface to *Beiträge*, vol. i.) that he is at present impeded in his studies by poverty. But his first publication will soon alter this: the completed *Beiträge* will be his passport to a professorship. In fact, the university of Heidelberg borrowed rather largely at this time from Jena. Three eminent members, past or present, of the teaching body of Jena were appointed to chairs at Heidelberg—Fries the philosopher in 1805, De Wette in 1807, and Paulus in 1811. The two friends, Fries and De Wette, were thus reunited, much to the advantage of the latter. A beautiful relation sprung up between them of which we have a fine monument in the dedication of De Wette's first book on Christian Ethics. De Wette had also at this time a growing consciousness that a Biblical critic should work, not merely for criticism's sake, but for the good of the Church. He saw therefore that he must not altogether neglect either historic or theoretic theology. The fruits of this expanded view of duty were not however at once apparent outside his lecture-room. His next work was an attempt to make the results of linguistic Bible-study accessible to the Church at large. It was a new translation of the Old Testament, undertaken by De Wette and J. C. W. Augusti together. This work appeared in 1809, and was completed by a similar version of the New Testament in 1814 (by De Wette alone).[1] All honour to De Wette for the combination of frankness and considerateness which this noble work displays!

In 1810 a great event occurred, which had important consequences for De Wette—the foundation of the university of Berlin. Schleiermacher was the first theological professor appointed, and through his influence De Wette and the speculative theologian Marheineke were called to Berlin from Heidelberg; Neander (put forward by Marheineke) came from the same university later (1813). Here De Wette passed eight years full of delightful academical and literary work.[2] With a character deepened by the trials through which Germany had been called to pass, and a mind susceptible to all progressive ideas, he took his place among some of the noblest of scholars, and contributed to the success of that great creation of Stein and Humboldt—the Berlin university. It is during this period of his life that the third stage in De Wette's development becomes fully revealed. No one can any longer mistake the positiveness of his theology, and the practical character of his aims. Not that criticism is abandoned—far from it; but it

[1] In the second edition of this version of the Bible (1831) the books originally rendered by Augusti were retranslated by De Wette. The third edition appeared in 1838.

[2] A valuable record of this period exists in Lücke's memorial sketch of De Wette, *Theol. Studien und Kritiken*, 1850, Heft 3, p. 497, &c.

becomes more distinctly subordinate to the higher end of promoting the religious life of the Church. In 1813 De Wette published the first part of his *Christian Dogmatics*, dealing with the Biblical division [1] (part ii. on Protestant theology, appeared in 1816); in 1815 a smaller supplementary treatise, *On Religion and Theology;* in 1819, his justly admired *Christian Ethics* (part iii., 1823), with the charming dedication to which I referred above. The last of these works does not concern us here, but the two former, in so far as they deal with the question of "Biblical myths," cannot be passed over.[2] Several of those who were students at that time have recorded the powerful impression which they produced. "De Wette," says one, "in his little work on *Religion and Theology*, a work breathing a youthful inspiration, placed before us a new theological structure corresponding to our wishes," *i.e.* a system which provided a *via media* between a repellent rationalism and a not very attractive orthodoxy. "Indeed," this writer adds, "we now believed that we had won back, in an ennobled form, that which had been torn from us, and only at a later period discovered the delusion (? illusion) by which we had been misled."[3] Such

---

[1] The full title of Part I. is, *Biblische Dogmatik des A. und N. T.; oder kritische Darstellung der Religionslehre des Hebräismus, des Judenthums, und des Urchristenthums.*

[2] For a sketch of the theory of religion contained in them, see Pfleiderer, *Development of Theology*, pp. 99—102.

[3] Krummacher, *Autobiography* (1869), p. 59; comp. Lücke, *Theol. Stud. u. Krit.*, 1850, p. 502, who however only gave up

is the honest verdict of a practical theologian, who had neither time nor ability to rectify the defects in De Wette's system, and who, finding it faulty, pronounced it an illusion, but would not deny the pleased surprise with which he had at first greeted it. Into the causes of De Wette's partial failure, this is not the place to enter. Suffice it to say that in some of his root-ideas he appears to have been before his time. Archbishop Benson has lately admitted the possibility that the Divine Spirit may have made use of " myths," and the influence of Ritschl and Lipsius proves that an unmetaphysical but not irrational theology is becoming more and more attractive in the land of Luther. As to the value of De Wette's third work, the *Biblical Dogmatics*, no doubt happily can exist. It not only forms, historically, a much-needed antithesis to the "naturalism" of Gramberg and his school, but, though somewhat painfully thin, presents many permanent results of criticism in a lucid form. The second edition is graced by a charming and memorable dedication to Schleiermacher.

I remarked just now that criticism was not wholly abandoned by De Wette at this period. Two remarkable works are the proof of this—his *Commentary on the Psalms* (1811) and his *Historico-Critical Introduction to the Canonical and Apocryphal Books of the Old Testament* (1817).[1] The former work, disappointing

---

De Wette's theology because Schleiermacher's suited him better, not because it was too radical.

[1] Six editions of the *Introduction* appeared in the author's

as it is when judged by our present critical and linguistic standard, marks a turning-point in the exegesis of the Psalms. "He was the first," as Delitzsch observes, "to clear away the rubbish under which exposition had been buried, and to introduce into it taste, after the example of Herder, and grammatical accuracy, under the influence of Gesenius." He does not however do justice to the religious origin and theological ideas of the Psalms, which he treats as merely so many national hymns. In his views of the dates of the Psalms, he represents a necessary reaction against the extravagant or at least premature positiveness of Rudinger and Venema. He declines altogether to dogmatize on the occasions when the Psalms were composed, but speaks with no uncertain sound of the historical worthlessness of the so-called tradition. On this point his subsequent course is already foreshadowed in his *Beiträge*, where he frankly declares (i. 158) that "David is as much a collective name as Moses, Solomon, Isaiah." He also gives valuable hints on the marks of originality and imitation in the Psalms, but when he does venture on a positive opinion as to dates, he is not always equally critical; for instance, he thinks that Ps. xlv. is a post-Exilic work, and that it is "most appropriately referred to a non-Jewish king."[1] This is in part certainly

---

lifetime. The seventh (1852) was edited by Stähelin; for the eighth (1869), the work was revised and partly recast by Prof. Schrader, then of Zurich. I may also mention De Wette's handbook to Hebrew Archæology (1814).

[1] De Wette rejects the Messianic interpretation as "incon-

correct, in part a **plausible** opinion. But the same De Wette actually thinks it possible that Ps. cxxxii. may be the work of Solomon, which Hitzig severely but not unjustly describes as a "critical curiosity." Long afterwards, De Wette sought to make good one of the chief defects of his book by a short tractate *On the Practical (erbaulich) Explanation of the Psalms* (1836). The booklet is, naturally enough, in some respects meagre; how indeed could a practical explanation of this monument of the Jewish Church be produced for the educated class without a much **deeper** insight into Biblical theology than even in 1836 the author possessed? But on the subject of inspiration it contains hints which well deserve to be pondered by English students (see especially p. 12).

One of De Wette's most striking faculties—that of condensation and lucid exposition—is specially noticeable in his second critical work of this period. What a pronounced opponent thought of the *Introduction to the Old Testament*, may be seen from these words of Heil on the posthumous *Introduction* of Bleek.[1]

"As our final judgment, we can only state that Bleek's independent conclusions have long since been published by himself in separate dissertations, while the remainder does but reproduce the well-known results of rationalistic criticism, which are put to-

---

sistent with the Hebrew Christology." He is favourably inclined towards a conjecture of his friend Augusti, that the author of Ps. xlv. is Mordecai.

[1] Quoted by the editors of Bleek's *Einleitung*, p. 21.

gether and developed in a much more acute, clever, thorough, tasteful, and complete manner in the *Introduction* of De Wette."

I will not here question this "final judgment" on Bleek, but merely call attention to the earnest study of De Wette which the words of the old apologist imply, and the respect with which this study has inspired him. Other voices, less friendly in tone, have also been heard; the charge of instability has been freely brought against De Wette, on the ground of the variations of view in the successive editions of both his *Introductions*. Is the accusation justified? It is an interesting question, because, should criticism some day be more largely represented in England, the same charge will doubtless be confidently brought against eminent English theologians. And one may reply that it is only justified, if it can be shown that De Wette never reached firm, definite, and consistent critical principles. Change of opinion on problems which from the nature of the evidence cannot with complete certainty be decided, can be no fault, and if due to honest, hard work is a subject for praise rather than blame. Constant development is the note of a great and not of a small character; and he is a poor critic who does not criticize himself with even more keenness than he criticizes tradition. In his willingness to reconsider disputable points De Wette sets an example not unworthy of imitation. As one who knew him says, "he was free from all magisterial obstinacy and vanity, and it cost him nothing to give up even favourite opinions, when the truth was placed before him, and to accept without hesitation even from his junior that which he recognized to be better and more correct."[1] Into the details of De Wette's changes as an Old Testament critic, I cannot here enter. Suffice it to say that in the early editions of his *Introduction* his attitude was predominantly negative. However strongly he felt the difficulties of the traditional views, he could not readily accept the constructive criticism of bolder scholars. Whether he ever attained to a sufficiently positive standpoint of his own, whether in fact he ever gained a large and consistent critical theory, is a delicate question, upon which I may venture to offer an opinion at the close of this sketch.

We have seen that De Wette began his career as a somewhat too pronounced negative critic, and that even when he had reconquered more than his old devoutness, he did not lay aside the sword of criticism. "Only the perfect in its kind is good," he said; "therefore let us venture into unknown fields, trusting to the Guardian of the Church to overrule all things for the best."[2] He had found a subjective reconciliation of reason and faith, and by his philosophy of religion and his symbolic view of Biblical narratives he sought to provide a similar reconciliation for others. This

---

[1] Lücke, "Zur Erinnerung an De Wette," *Theol. Stud. u. Krit.*, 1850, p. 507.
[2] A paraphrase of the last two sentences of the *Beiträge* (Bd. ii.).

however was a thing hitherto unknown among theological paradoxes. Devout philosophy was rare; but devout criticism like De Wette's was unique. His philosophic theology and his symbolizing criticism were alike uncanny to certain devout but narrow-minded "pietists" at Berlin. And when to these two dangerous peculiarities was added a political liberalism, not less intense indeed than that of Schleiermacher, but less under the control of prudence, it will be clear that De Wette's path was not likely to be strewn with roses, for the pietists and the ultra-conservative politicians were allies. De Wette's chief comfort was in the new friendships which opened themselves to him at Berlin. Younger men found an attraction in his freedom from donnishness and youthful readiness to hear others, and preferred, if not his theories themselves, yet his lucid and intelligible way of expressing them, to the dark Heraclitean manner of his colleague Schleiermacher. It was one of these juniors (Lücke) who brought De Wette into closer contact with the latter, by inducing him to attend the church where Schleiermacher ministered;[1] as soon as De Wette discovered the deep religious basis of that great teacher, he gave himself up without reserve to one who was only too glad of his friendship.

[1] For specimens of his sermons, see *Selected Sermons of Schleiermacher*, by Mary F. Wilson (Hodder and Stoughton). Of course, the brief biographical sketch prefixed is only meant to excite an appetite for fuller knowledge. Lagarde's contempt for the piety of Schleiermacher (*Mittheilungen*, iv. 5, 8, &c.) is surely not justified by the facts of his life and writings.

Different as the two men were, they had one thing in common—a complexity of character which brought them for a time into some obloquy. In De Wette the keen literary and historical critic existed side by side with the devout religious thinker; in Schleiermacher the analyst and dialectician made terms with the Christian and the constructive thinker.[1] The tree of friendship grew, and no storms of time could overthrow it. They had indeed one serious dissension; Schleiermacher favoured the appointment of Hegel in 1816; De Wette (who wished to bring Fries from Jena) belonged to a minority of professors who opposed it. But this was soon forgotten, and when in 1817 the position of De Wette seemed to be becoming precarious, Schleiermacher (himself not free from suspicion) prefixed to one of his books[2] a dedication to De Wette which for generosity and for courageous speaking of the truth is unsurpassable in theological literature.

Two years later, the storm which had long been gathering discharged itself upon De Wette under circumstances which no one could have anticipated. In 1817 the prolific dramatist Kotzebue had been appointed a Russian State-councillor, with a salary of 15,000 roubles, and been "sent to reside in Germany, to report upon literature and public opinion." Natur-

---

[1] See a remarkable description of the latter reconciled antithesis in Bluntschli, *Denkwürdigkeiten* (Bd. i.).

[2] It is the *Critical Essay on the Writings of Luke*, translated by (Bishop) Connop Thirlwall.

ally enough, he incurred the displeasure of the Liberals, and especially of the young Liberal students, who were then counted by hundreds in Germany. One of these, named Sand, conceiving Kotzebue to be dangerous to freedom, murdered him, March 28, 1819. The event produced a sensation throughout Germany, and the cry arose among the reactionary party, "The professors and the students are Kotzebue's murderers." Among the most obnoxious Liberal professors were Arndt, Welcker, Schleiermacher, and De Wette.[1] It is almost incredible, considering the known activity of the secret police, that one of these professors actually wrote a letter to Sand's mother, expressing not only condolence but appreciation of the patriotic spirit in which the blameworthy act had been performed. "Only according to his faith is each man judged. Committed as this deed has been by a pure-minded, pious youth, it is a beautiful sign of the time," and, though not concealing his own abhorrence of assassination, De Wette referred in the postscript to Jean Paul's idealistic judgment on Charlotte Corday.[2] No one knew how this letter fell into the hands of the police, but it was suspected that Baron von Kottwitz, the leader of the Berlin pietists, was foremost in urging the Prussian King (Frederick William III.) to take strong measures against the writer. Strange paradox! A scoffer, who described Christianity brought to old Prussia as "a poisonous flower planted in the midst

---

[1] See *Life and Adventures of Arndt* (1879), p. 376.
[2] Frank, art. "de Wette," in Herzog-Plitt, *Encycl.*, Bd. xvii.

of the dry and dead cross,"[1] becomes in death the *protégé* of devout ascetics, and the hireling of a foreign power dictates the expulsion of one of Germany's best patriots. A large part of the university keenly felt the irony of the circumstances. The faculty of theology, led by Schleiermacher, did all in its power to save one of its ablest members, and when De Wette's fate was irrevocably decided, the students presented him with a silver cup, bearing as an inscription the closing words of the great Reformation hymn—

> Nehmen sie den Leib,
> Gut, Ehr', Kind und Weib:
> Lass fahren dahin,
> Sie haben 's kein Gewinn;
> Das Reich muss uns doch bleiben.

So De Wette sadly but proudly left his home, regretted by all who knew him, especially by Schleiermacher. From the Latin biography of Ilgen I learn that the chair which he thus vacated was offered to, but not accepted by, that acute critic of Genesis.

De Wette retired to his native Weimar, nor can one help admiring the moral courage with which he bore his misfortune. To say, with an American biography, that he permanently suffered under a sense of injustice, shows a want of psychological insight. His enemies did but act according to their nature; how then should he accuse them of injustice? That he felt the consequences of their act, need not be denied. But at first he did not even feel them as much as one

[1] Quoted in art. "Grundtvig," Herzog-Plitt, v. 462.

might expect. It seemed to him as if God had called him to another important sphere of work, from which as a theologian he could not but derive profit—that of preaching the Gospel. And while waiting for a summons from the congregation he took up his pen to show that his old doubts had but issued in a firmer Christian character. In 1822 he published a "story with a purpose," called *Theodore, or the Consecration of the Doubter*, which, good in itself, had the additional merit of calling forth Tholuck's equally autobiographical story, *The True Consecration of the Doubter*.[1] And as a fresh proof of his attachment to the principles of the Reformation, De Wette prepared a critical edition of the letters and other papers of Luther, which however only appeared in 1825—1828 (5 vols.). Once during this waiting period he had the pleasure of meeting his old friends Schleiermacher and Lücke at Nordhausen. Lücke has described to us the scene. Friends were coming together in Schleiermacher's room for breakfast. The host sat by himself correcting the proofs of the notes (most remarkable notes) to the new edition of his *Reden über die Religion*. The others listened to De Wette, as he fervently declaimed on the beauty of the preacher's office, and his own

[1] The full title is, *Die Lehre von der Sünde und dem Versöhner, oder die wahre Weihe des Zweiflers* (1823). Both stories had their mission to fulfil for that period. They reflected the different experiences of their respective writers, and therefore appealed to somewhat different audiences. De Wette was the deeper thinker, but Tholuck had passed a more violent spiritual crisis, and consequently had a more Pauline fervour.

joyful hope of studying theology under a new aspect as a minister of the Word.

This hope was soon to be dashed to the ground, at least in the form in which De Wette had cherished it. He was elected shortly afterwards to the principal pastorate in Brunswick, but the reactionary government of our George IV., professedly on moral grounds, refused its sanction. Once more De Wette became a martyr of liberalism, but this time a free Swiss canton intervened in his favour. In spite of strong opposition both within and without the university, he was elected by the town council of Basel (who obtained the most authoritative opinions on the purity of his faith) to a professorship of theology. So, like many a scholar in the olden time, De Wette, for the sake of his life's work, passed into honourable exile. He became a true citizen of the noble little city of Basel, and an unwearied promoter of all its best interests, especially academical and ecclesiastical. Through him, the theological instruction was reorganized on the German model, and after many years a religious service with sermon was set up for the university. If Basel was but a narrow sphere of action compared with Berlin, De Wette's influence there was doubtless all the more intensely felt. And the democratic constitution of Switzerland gave so much theological and anti-theological liberty, that an accomplished and circumspect theologian like De Wette was perhaps more urgently wanted at Basel than at the headquarters of thought.

And what is the effect of this involuntary migration on De Wette? Does he cease henceforth to rank among the "founders of criticism," and pass over, if not to the apologists, yet to the party whose motto is, "Quieta non movere"? Does he become henceforth virtually "orthodox"? It is a common opinion, but it is one which needs some rectification. It is certainly true that De Wette took alarm at many expressions of the newer rationalism; true, that he attached more and more weight to many of the church-formulæ; true especially, that he took every opportunity of practical co-operation with the orthodox, and even with the "pietists," for whose heart-Christianity and good works he entertained a sincere respect. But it is also true, as one of his Swiss-German colleagues has said, that he only advocated old-Lutheran orthodoxy "conditionally and from the stand-point of his philosophical mode of thinking";[1] true, that while disapproving of Strauss the theologian, he assimilated much from Strauss the critic (who indeed had previously assimilated somewhat from him); true, that while rejecting Vatke's reconstruction of Israelitish history as a whole, he admitted that there was an element of truth in many of his views. Again, though it is true that De Wette (unlike Delitzsch) was opposed to the emancipation of the Jews, and would have had both mixed marriages and changes of religion made civil offences,

---

[1] Hagenbach, *German Rationalism*, E. T., p. 358.

it is also true that in his most conservative pamphlet these striking words occur: "I have laboured with all my might for spiritual freedom, and to this freedom my last breath shall be devoted." It must never be forgotten that as a critic De Wette remained fundamentally true to himself, and that even in those old, free days at Jena he expressed strong attachment to the Augsburg Confession. I must confess however that De Wette's later concessions to ecclesiastical conservatism appear to me to come perilously near to a compromise of liberal principles.

Among De Wette's literary works of this period are those lucid text-books, the *Introduction to the New Testament* (1826), and the *Compendious Exegetical Handbook to the New Testament* (1836—1848); also five volumes of sermons (1825—1849), a second didactic story (*Heinrich Melchthal*, 1829), and several treatises on Christian ethics, and on dogmatic and practical theology (besides new editions of older works). From one of his dogmatic works (published in 1846) it is clear that his attachment to the philosophy of Fries grew much weaker in his later years, but that he had no longer the energy to produce a reasoned justification for his "æsthetic" interpretation of dogmas. Altogether, one is led to regret that he gave so much time to subjects for which he had not nearly as much ability as Schleiermacher. Criticism was his strong point, and he would have done well to concentrate himself more upon this. For I must, however unwillingly, admit that De

Wette as a critic never quite realized the promise of his early years. Extensive and useful as his critical work is, we cannot say that it is worthy of "the epoch-making opener of the historical criticism of the Pentateuch" (Wellhausen); in definite literary and historical results it is comparatively poor. And this remark applies to all De Wette's critical writings, alike on the Old Testament and on the New.[1] In both departments of study he begins with scepticism and negativism, and as a rule fails to attain to positive conclusions, much less to an assured historical synthesis. And the reason is that he has a theory of criticism which, though not unsound, is incomplete. He has but a scanty insight into the movement of ideas, and does not take sufficient pains to ascertain the historic background of literary phenomena. Lacking this insight, he could arrive at different critical conclusions, not merely on minor but on fundamental points, at different periods, though it is also possible that in his later years he was unconsciously biassed by his practical conservatism as a churchman. From the same deficiency he was unable to do full justice to specimens of historical synthesis like Ewald's *History of the People of Israel* and Vatke's *Biblical Theology*. It is obviously not enough to say of the former that it throws fresh light on many points in the historical books, and elaborate and respectful as De Wette's

---

[1] Cf. Bleek's judgment on De Wette as a New Testament critic, *Introd. to the New Testament*, E. T., i. 29, with that of Baur, *Gesch. der christl. Kirche*, v. 418, 419.

review of the latter may be,[1] it leads up to a rejection of that able book on the simple ground that it is revolutionary—"its criticism has overthrown nearly all bounds," are the closing words. From this later utterance we turn with a sigh to De Wette's own early experiments in revolutionary criticism— the two little volumes of *Beiträge*.

Would the result of De Wette's work have been less disappointing, had he remained at such a centre of intellectual life as Berlin? It is not impossible. There perhaps he might have had courage to anticipate the conclusions of Vatke from the point of view (introduced by himself in the *Beiträge*) of a realistic and historical criticism of the contents of the Hexateuch. Perhaps too he might have so far overcome his antipathy to Hegel as to absorb something from that philosopher's luminous philosophy of history. Certain it is, that there was much to depress De Wette in his circumstances at Basel. Baron Bunsen, attending the Mission Festival in 1840, brings back a very melancholy report of his state of mind. I will only quote his opening words—

"Professor De Wette was present, closely attending to all that passed: his appearance is shrunk and withered, with deep furrows of reflection and of sorrow in his countenance, and the expression of high and spiritual seriousness. He has married a widow-lady of Basel, but stands alone in the place."[2]

---

[1] *Theolog. Studien und Kritiken*, 1837, Heft 3.
[2] *Memoirs of Bunsen*, i. 576.

The rest of Bunsen's report seems derived from some pitying but misunderstanding friend of De Wette. The great teacher may have been annoyed by foolish misconceptions of his character, and by the prevalence of "pietism" among his own students, but he was not without true friends, such as his colleague Hagenbach (to whose defence of De Wette I have referred), and his gifted pupil Schenkel. And against Bunsen's gloomy sketch we can set this brighter picture by a much closer friend, Friedrich Lücke, in which the reader should especially note De Wette's magnanimous return for Ewald's rudeness (see p. 91).

"I saw my friend," he says, "for the last time in the autumn of 1845 in Basel, still enjoying the cheerful youthfulness of a *vegeta senectus*. He had just finished his *Representation of the Nature of Christian Faith*, and was then preparing for a journey to Italy, with fresh and lively feelings. I was permitted once more to see in union all the beautiful traits of his amiable and lovely disposition. I especially recollect in what terms of recognition and kindness he spoke of Ewald, with whose Commentary on Job he had just been busied; in his noble love of truth and in his modesty he was at no time led astray by the many sharp experiences which he had of being misapprehended, and of the hostility of others. At noon and in the afternoon he mingled, fresh and lively, in a larger circle of friends, in good humour at every stroke of pleasantry, full of joy in the beautiful nature and in all the intellectual life of conversation. So stands he now before my soul in earthly serenity and at the same time in heavenly brightness, along with Schleiermacher. I thank God that He has given me the blessing of having intimately known such men in life." [1]

In 1848 De Wette brought out the last volume of his *Exegetical Handbook to the New Testament*, and so, as Baur has said, worthily " closed his day's work as one of the most faithful labourers in the field of theology." He passed from earth, June 16, 1849, with high and holy words on his lips. What, let us ask, is the great lesson of his life—what was his guiding star in all his wanderings? His old pupil Schenkel has told us. It was this—that " in none of the relations of life, least of all in theology and the Church, can truth exist without freedom, or freedom without truth." De Wette himself was, in the words of Neander, a "genuine Nathaniel-soul,"—" in him was no guile"; and in the midst of comparative failure, he succeeded in this—in presenting probably the best model of a keen but devout critic in his generation.

I have next to introduce the two great philological critics, whose names are still household words among us, Gesenius and Ewald. The former is the older, and indeed represents a phase of religious thought which Ewald from the first almost entirely passed

[1] Condensed from the late B. B. Edwards' translation from Lücke in *Bibliotheca Sacra*, 1850, p. 794.

beyond. His range of study too was narrower, though within that range he attained more undisputed success. It may be added that the idiosyncrasies of the two scholars were as different as their scientific careers, and that they are worth studying, not only as critics, but as men. Wilhelm Gesenius was born at Nordhausen in the Harz district, Feb. 3, 1785. He received his first academical training at the now extinct university of Helmstedt (in the duchy of Brunswick), and it was from the distinguished Helmstedt rationalist, Heinrich Henke, that he imbibed his theology. This was the more unfortunate, because Gesenius's nature was a less devout one than his teacher's, and the young student instinctively fastened on the colder and more negative side of rationalistic thought. Henke himself appears to have been an excellent specimen of the rationalism of that day. There was a manly seriousness in his character, and the devoutness with which he traced a divine inspiration in the philosophy and poetry of Greece finds an echo in the breast of our own best orthodox thinkers. But Henke had little or no sense of the growth of ideas, and of the way in which thought is conditioned by the circumstances of an age, and he applied his own standard of common-sense rationalism to all Christian periods indifferently. He might indeed have learned better things from Lessing, who was still at Wolfenbüttel when Henke began his career at Helmstedt, but he was evidently not as open as Eichhorn to non-professional influences, and

Lessing was a lay-theologian. Such was the teacher who left an indelible mark on the future leader in Hebrew philology. He also made one other important convert among the students of Gesenius's generation. This was Wegscheider, afterwards a colleague of Gesenius at Halle, whose *Institutiones Theologiæ Christianæ Dogmaticæ* had still a waning popularity forty years ago.[1]

From Helmstedt (which lost its university in 1810) Gesenius passed to Göttingen, where Eichhorn and Tychsen were his masters in Biblical and Oriental literature; Ewald, as we shall find, had the same instructors later. There too (like so many other great scholars), he began his public career as a *privatdocent* and *repetent;* by a singular fortune, he had Neander as his first pupil in Hebrew. In 1809 he exchanged academical for scholastic work, but in the following year was transferred to the honourable position of a theological professor at Halle. And at this great seat of theological study he was content to remain. Twice only do we hear of the possibility of his moving elsewhere. The first occasion was in 1827, when the chair of his master Eichhorn became vacant at Göttingen; the second in 1832, when, according to Gesenius's statement to Vatke, Oxford would have gladly given him a position with an income of as many pounds sterling as Halle gave thalers.[2] It may surprise some to hear of Oxford

---

[1] The eighth edition was published at Leipzig in 1844.
[2] Benecke, *Wilhelm Vatke*, p. 83.

offering a home to a German rationalist on the eve of the Tractarian movement, nor can I throw any light on the circumstances referred to. It is true that in the summer of 1820 Gesenius had paid a visit to Oxford (and to Paris) for learned purposes; but what permanent office at the university was likely to be offered at that time to a foreigner? And perhaps it is not less strange that the cause of Gesenius's momentary wish to go to Oxford was a sense of insecurity at Halle. Such however was the case. Two orthodox theologians—Otto von Gerlach (called the Wesley of Berlin) and Ernst Wilhelm Hengstenberg—had in a too famous Church paper (the *Evangelische Kreuzzeitung*) published attacks upon Wegscheider and Gesenius which aimed at nothing less than a dismissal of these "dangerous" rationalists from their office. The attacks, as Bunsen remarked to Niebuhr at the time,[1] "were written without a wrong motive, but were ill contrived and little to the purpose." "An intellectual struggle," he added, "must be fought out intellectually; or practically, when one has to contend against men like Wegscheider, one course only remains—to appoint other individuals of sounder metal to lecture by the side of them, and fairly talk them down." This was exactly the course taken by Altenstein, the Prussian minister of worship;[2] a more severe policy would

[1] *Memoirs of Baron Bunsen*, i. 362.
[2] See Tholuck's sketch of Altenstein, Herzog-Plitt's *Real-encyclop.*, Bd. i.

have been impossible without destroying that scientific freedom which is a fundamental principle of German universities. So Gesenius—the "Clericus redivivus," as Hengstenberg called him—remained, and continued to attract large audiences, while Wegscheider (was it worth while to persecute him?) lectured to nearly empty benches.[1] Once only was his activity interrupted; it was in 1813-14. He had had to close his lectures on Isaiah at the eleventh verse of the fourteenth chapter. On the reopening of the university, Gesenius mounted to his chair, and read aloud the famous ode of triumph which contains the words, "How art thou fallen from heaven, O Lucifer, son of the morning!" He died at the early age of fifty-seven, Oct. 23, 1842.[2] Like Ewald, he visited England twice, in 1820 and in 1835.

Before considering the published works of Gesenius let us ask what made this scholar such a power in his university even during the onward rush of neo-orthodoxy. That he was disrespectful to orthodox explanations of Old Testament problems, and that he indulged in mirth-provoking sallies in his lectures on Church history, is certain. On the other hand, he never sought to inculcate rationalistic doctrines, or to

---

[1] It should be remembered that Tholuck, a man of fascinating personality, and not narrow-minded like Hengstenberg, had been working at Halle since 1827, also that since the war of liberation a sense of the inadequacy of mere rationalism had become more and more prevalent.

[2] On the circumstances attending his death, cf. Benecke, *Wilhelm Vatke*, pp. 391—395.

foist them upon the Biblical writers,[1] and it appears that what the best students of that generation craved was, not a mere revived orthodoxy, but a theology which could adjust itself to a more rational and critical view of the Bible. Gesenius was at any rate accurate in his facts, acute in his criticism, and objective though superficial in his exegesis. The peals of laughter with which his rationalistic sallies were greeted were therefore no proof that Gesenius was injuring the faith of his students, or hurting their religious feelings. Exceptions of course there may have been. Harless appears to have been one of those who were painfully shocked by Gesenius; Krummacher was another; and the American student Hodge (afterwards such a pillar of Calvinistic orthodoxy in America) was a third. In fact, the theological and philosophical superficiality of the lively little man (as he is described to us by an admiring and yet critical student[2]) was only too obvious. What he gave, was in its kind almost perfect—at least for that period; and if he omitted much, there were other professors to be heard, other authors to be read. The description which the student gives of Gesenius, both in his lecture-room and among the members of his *Seminar*, proves conclusively that he was one of the

---

[1] "Die Wissenschaft hatte ich erblickt in einer entschieden rationellen Behandlungsart, aber nicht rationalistische Lebensfragen als Ausgangs- und Zielpunkte aller wissenschaftlichen Untersuchung," says the student about to be referred to.

[2] See *Gesenius: Zur Erinnerung für seine Freunde* (Berlin, 1842; p. 45).

most gifted teachers which Hebrew and Oriental studies have ever had, and that neither Halle nor Germany could have afforded to lose him. That lightness of tone which had the appearance of frivolity in a Church history lecture was precisely what made the dry details of linguistic science interesting; that incapacity for broad philosophical views was but the reverse side of a philological accuracy akin to that exactitude and love of detail which we remark in all successful students of natural science. Gesenius no doubt inherited this from his ancestors. Though not himself a physician like Astruc, he came of a medical family, his father and his great-uncle having both been physicians of some repute, and authors of medical works.[1] And if Gesenius was not too devout, yet he had that absorption in science which has a grandeur not unlike that of religion, and which excites in the devout man an involuntary regretful sympathy.

If this view of Gesenius is correct, we cannot but reckon it as a great loss to Biblical criticism that no direct record remains of his fascinating lectures, which covered the whole range of Old Testament subjects. Had he written nothing, indeed, he would still have been one of the founders of criticism by his university teaching, for in not a few lectures he had over 400 hearers. His works are without those flashes of wit and those instructive analogies which gave so much

---

[1] See Hirsch, *Biographisches Lexikon der Aerzte.*

Anschaulichkeit to his oral discourse.[1] We are thankful for them, but we regret that more time was not given him to mature and to condense the contents of his lectures, and to continue in the path, on which we are assured that he had entered, of progress from mere empiricism to the study of the ideas which underlie phenomena. His first printed work was an essay on the Maltese language, in which he for the first time recognized a corruption of Arabic. In the same year he published vol. i. of his Hebrew-German *Handwörterbuch;* vol. ii. appeared in 1812. This work was translated into English by a pioneer of Hebrew studies in America, Josiah W. Gibbs, in 1824 (from the edition of 1815). The *Lexicon Manuale*, representing much riper study, was published in 1833; a translation of this was published by Edward Robinson of Andover (Mass.). A second edition of the former work appeared in 1834, and of the latter in 1847 (translated by S. P. Tregelles). The printing of the *Thesaurus philologicus criticus* (3 vols. 4to) began in 1826, but was interrupted by the death of the author, whose learned friend Emil Rödiger completed it (1853—1858). Gesenius's hardly less important work as a grammarian began in 1813, when his *Hebräische Grammatik* first appeared (pp. 202). Fourteen editions appeared in his own lifetime, and since his death it has been seven times re-edited by Rödiger, and four times by Prof. Kautzsch of

---

[1] See *Gesenius*, &c., p. 32.

Halle.[1] The *Grammatik* must be distinguished from the *Ausführliches grammatisch-kritisches Lehrgebäude der hebr. Sprache*, which appeared in 1817.

On these important and never-to-be-forgotten works much might be said in another context. They formed in part the basis of the best exegesis of the last generation,[2] and no subsequent Hebrew grammars or dictionaries can fail to be indebted to them, as has been sufficiently shown, from a lexicographical point of view, in the preface to the new Anglo-American Hebrew *Lexicon* (part i., Oxford, 1892). And though Professor Kautzsch in 1878 found himself obliged to put the *Hebr. Grammatik* into a new form, no disrespect to the *Altmeister* was intended thereby. Gesenius's own grammatical work was rooted in the past, and improved as it proceeded. The first edition (1813) is separated by no deep chasm from those which preceded it, while the last owes something to Ewald, whose treatment of Gesenius was, I regret to have to confess, far less worthy than Gesenius's treatment of him. As I hope to show later, the two scholars really supplemented each other; and we at any rate can afford to forget both the undevoutness

---

[1] The *Ausführliches grammat.-kritisches Lehrgebäude der hebr. Sprache*, a separate work, appeared in 1817.

[2] De Wette says, in 1831, in the preface to his Old Testament (ed. 2), "My explanation of the Old Testament agrees for the most part with that of Gesenius, so far as this is known from his *Lexicon* and from other sources; indeed, from the first I am happy to have been in the greatest possible agreement with this excellent friend."

of the one and the uncouthness and irritability of the other.

Another valuable work of Gesenius is his *History of the Hebrew Language* (1815). The work can now only be read with caution, but it will be some time before a trained scholar has the boldness to resume this subject. In one point certainly Gesenius was but ill equipped for his task. This great Orientalist was not deeply versed in later Hebrew, though as he went on he bestowed much pains on utilizing the lexicographical works of the Rabbis. His great contribution to exegesis, the *Commentary on Isaiah* (1820-21, 2 vols.), furnishes many proofs of this. In fact, in all respects this work is a mine of accurate philological and historical information up to its date. Its Biblical theology, it is true, cannot receive high praise. And yet Gesenius's view of prophecy, imperfect as it is in many respects, is superior to the merely æsthetic view often expressed by the older rationalists; he seems to have learned something from De Wette, whom he so earnestly advised young Wilhelm Vatke to read, mark, and inwardly digest.[1] The prophet, according to Gesenius, is not merely a "poet of nature," but a "herald and watchman of the theocracy and the theocratic faith." He repudiates equally the opinion that the "men of God" acted by calculation and with artfully arranged plans, and that

---

[1] Benecke, *Wilhelm Vatke*, p. 27. De Wette, on his side, owns obligations to Gesenius in his translation of Isaiah and in his criticism of Daniel.

the oracles respecting the future are merely veiled historical exhibitions of the present or even of the past. He fails indeed to do justice to the prophetic ideas, and to trace the connexion of the prophets with the progress of the religion of Israel, but this is at any rate better than misrepresenting those ideas and that great progressive movement. Both in criticism of the text and in the higher criticism, the characteristic of Gesenius's *Isaiah* is moderation and circumspection—the very qualities which the keen-eyed student referred to above remarked in his lectures on critical "introduction." For these qualities one may justly praise Gesenius, having regard to the period when he lived. In the previous age there had been an epidemic of arbitrary emendation in the department of textual criticism, and a tendency (at any rate among some "higher critics" of the Pentateuch and Isaiah) to break up the text into a number of separate pieces, which threatened to open the door to unbounded caprice. With a view to sound and safe progress, and in order to bridge over the gulf between extreme parties, it was desirable that some eminent philologist should come forward as an advocate of moderate caution, and, while not denying the more obvious results of the last thirty years' work, should devote himself chiefly to a critical study of the linguistic side of the Old Testament, as handed down to us. No thoroughly trained critic can, in my judgment, now stand where Gesenius stood then, with regard either to the correction of the text or to the "higher criticism." The Massoretic text is not as defensible as Gesenius, with his limited critical insight and too empirical grammatical views, supposed, and, without in the least professing to defend the "fragmentists" in Pentateuch criticism, there can hardly be a doubt that there was a large element of truth in Koppe's disintegrating criticism of Isaiah.[1] It is very singular that a less exact scholar than Gesenius should have taken up a position which, from our present point of view, is more defensible than that of the Halle philologist. Eichhorn, who opposed the "fragmentists" in Pentateuch-criticism, fully (indeed, too fully) admitted the justification for Koppe's disintegration of Isaiah. But then, Eichhorn left his work not half done; he ought to have produced a thorough commentary on Isaiah, showing that a considerable amount of disintegration was not uncalled for on exegetical and historical grounds. Now, it is true that Eichhorn did translate and comment on the Hebrew prophets, but he aimed more than was right at popularity. He had his reward, for he won the ear of Goethe, but he did not win that of deeper Hebrew scholars like Gesenius. Though the disciple of Eichhorn, Gesenius within his own range was far in advance of his old master.

Another attempt had yet to be made to cover the

[1] Gesenius did not, happily, altogether deny the composite origin of Isa. xl.—lxvi., but his concessions were altogether too slight. I have written more at length on this in the *Jewish Quart. Rev.* for July 1891.

same wide range of study which Eichhorn touched—an attempt which, if it did not succeed, yet deserves our admiration and respect. The goal was too distant even for one of the most gifted scholars of that or any age; "quem si non tenuit, magnis tamen excidit ausis." To this great but faulty scholar, who is now in danger in England of a depreciation as excessive as the former worship of him, I now ask the reader to turn his attention.

CHAPTER IV.

EWALD (I).—THE DEVELOPMENT PERIOD.[1]

IT will, I hope, not be thought paradoxical if I associate the names of Butler and Ewald. Different as they are in many respects, I venture to trace a real historical connexion between them. To Queen Caroline's insight was due the promotion of Bishop Butler, and the influence of the same wise queen was not without weight in the foundation of the university of Göttingen. Of that renowned *Hochschule*, Ewald is one of the most typical representatives. History and philology were from the first the most favoured subjects in this emphatically statesmanlike institution, and history and philology constitute the field on which Heinrich Ewald has won imperishable fame. Butler, both as an ethical philosopher and a theologian, would have been at home in Göttingen, where, both in theology and in philosophy, observation and facts have always had the precedence over *à priori* speculation, and where theoretic theology in particular

---

[1] The two chapters on Ewald are mainly composed of two public academical lectures delivered by the author at Oxford, June 1886, and printed in the *Expositor*.

has ever had a moderate and so to speak Butlerian tinge. Ewald on his side would in some respects have been at home in England, at any rate in the more liberal England of to-day. He had always a tenderness for this country; and even if we can partly justify our predecessors for the suspiciousness of their attitude towards him, we may nevertheless hold that, with all their defects, no books can be more important for advanced Bible-students than those of Ewald. He may indeed be as useful to us in our present stage as he was in his earlier period to Germany; and if his influence is waning there, let us not be backward to accord him a friendly reception here. The Germans, it appears, would fain annex Richard Bentley; let us retaliate by annexing or assimilating all that is best in the great, the faulty, but the never-to-be-forgotten Heinrich Ewald.

I am not one of those who think it the duty of a biographer to idolize his hero, and shall have, alas! to admit that Ewald failed in a serious degree to attain his high ideal. But he has been to many, thank God! a source of truest inspiration, and the tragedy of his career diminishes in no respect their reverence for his memory. Suffer me to show you this childlike great man in his strength and in his weakness.

He was born at Göttingen Nov. 16, 1803, and there most of his life was passed. A touch of provincialism was therefore native to Ewald, and this was not counteracted by that variety of culture which many German students gain by a change of university. Ewald himself, it is true, saw no reason to desire a change. He was destined to set an example of concentration, and this object could nowhere be better secured than in Göttingen. Did he want recreation? There was that ample library, then not less famous than the university itself. He had no time for that social intercourse of fellow-students which it is so sweet to most to look back upon, his laborious day being divided between his own studies and private tuition. He was never caught up, like even Michaelis,[1] into the contemporary æsthetic movement, nor did he ever, like Herder, pass under the spell of philosophy. He had indeed, as his works prove, a sense of poetic art, and even more a deep love of ideas, but art and ideas were to him but the historical manifestations of national life. By one of those strange impulses which so often occur in the history of genius, he chose the East for his field of study while still at the gymnasium. If he studied the classics, it was clearly not as the humanities, but as a necessary part of his historical apparatus; for he well knew that no language or literature can be adequately studied by itself. His

[1] See J. D. Michaelis, *Poetischer Entwurf der Gedanken des Prediger-Buch Salomons* (Göttingen, 1751). In the preface he speaks of amusing himself with poetical composition. Ewald very rarely refers to German literature. Herder he only mentions as a writer on the Old Testament. Once he speaks of the good fortune of Eichhorn in working during the blossoming time of the national intellect, and once he highly eulogizes Klopstock in a characteristic note, omitted in the English translation of the *History* (see the German edition, iii. 306, note 1).

Latin is not that of Bishop Lowth, but as a compensation even his early works show a deep knowledge of Arabic literature. Eichhorn and Tychsen, both distinguished Orientalists, were his academical teachers; for both of them he cherished feelings of piety, though he would not own that they had materially influenced his opinions. And yet, though I can easily imagine that Ewald's mind was very early mature, I think he *was* influenced, especially by Eichhorn, to whom his own principles and career present several points of resemblance. Eichhorn, so generously eulogized of late by Dr. Edersheim,[1] was at least as many-sided though not as profound as Ewald. He loved the Bible as being a literature, as well as the record of a revelation; I say the Bible, because, like Ewald, Eichhorn was not merely an *Old* Testament scholar. He was also, in the best sense of the word, like Ewald an *advanced* Biblical critic. And it must be added that, though like Ewald and every other great critic he stood aloof from theological quarrels, he yet retained an unflagging interest in the progress of religious thought. Like Ewald again, he was not merely a Hebraist but a Semitic philologist, and propagated that sound doctrine of the so-called Tenses, which is due especially to that patriarch of Semitic learning, Albert Schultens. He was, like Ewald in his best days, a popular and indefatigable lecturer, but not content with this, he acknowledged

---

[1] See above, p. 25.

a responsibility to the world of scholars in general. For many years,[1] following the example of J. D. Michaelis, he published an *Allgemeine Bibliothek für biblische Litteratur* (all his own work), and a *Repertorium für morgenländische Litteratur*, which reminds us of the *Biblische Jahrbücher* and the *Zeitschrift für die Kunde des Morgenlandes*, the latter mainly founded by Ewald, the former entirely written by him, only that Eichhorn's style is far more lucid than Ewald's, and his tolerance as charming as Ewald's intolerance is painful. Lastly, the influence of Eichhorn on contemporary thought was at least equal in extent, if not in intensity, to that of his great disciple.

Do not think this a digression. Part of the greatness of Ewald's life is its consistency. Such as he was at the opening of his career, such in all essentials he remained to its close. He found much to learn, but very little to unlearn. He tells us himself[2] that he never had to pass through circuitous paths of gloom, nor through grievous inward struggles; that from the first he perceived that the fearful-seeming New is really nothing but the Old, better understood and farther developed. This consistency is not to be accounted for solely by tenacity of character; it implies also that he fell in with wise and congenial teachers. He was consistent, because he lost no time through being badly taught, and because he found a

---

[1] I might have added that from Heyne's death to his own Eichhorn edited the well-known *Göttingische gelehrte Anzeigen.*
[2] *Die poetischen Bücher des A. T.*, iv. (1837), p. 249.

work ready to his hand. He carried on the work of his teacher, Eichhorn, supplementing Eichhorn's deficiencies and correcting his faults, just as Eichhorn carried on that of Herder on the one hand, and Michaelis on the other. The portraits of Herder and Eichhorn, indeed, hung on the walls of Ewald's study as if to remind him of the aim and spirit of their common enterprise. That aim was nothing less than the recovery of the true meaning of the Bible, and the spirit in which it was pursued by these three great men was not less practical than scientific. Herder and Ewald especially had a full consciousness of the religious interests staked on the success of their work, and when Ewald speaks, in the *History of Christ*, of the "wondrous charm of a task which germinates out of a Divine appointment and necessity,"[1] it is difficult to think that the words did not flow from the experience of his youthful days. The Church-historian, Hase, has described Ewald, in language suggested perhaps by a famous saying of Hegel, as a prophet with backward gaze.[2] Ewald's style and manner are often in character with this function, and many a striking passage in his prefaces suggests an inner experience analogous to that of a prophetic call. "Truly," he says in his *Johannine Writings*, "if God did not give us in youth a surplus of boldest enterprise and cheerfullest faith, and thrust us, whether we would or no, into the midst of His truths and ever-

---

[1] *Geschichte Christus*, p. 183.
[2] *Kirchengeschichte*, p. 582.

lasting powers, O how should we find the force and the confidence amid tedious temptations and struggles always to be true to that which we have once for all recognized as the True in itself, and also in His goodness and His grace, as our undeniable duty."[1]

Ewald, then, felt himself called to do a prophet's work for the history and literature of the prophet-people Israel, and called, first of all, to a more special preparation, to which the outer events of his life were to be made subservient. And the very first change which came was advantageous to the future expositor and historian. As a youthful graduate of nineteen, he became in 1823 a teacher in the gymnasium at Wolfenbüttel (in the duchy of Brunswick, thirty-seven miles from Hanover), with free access to that fine library of which Lessing had once been the keeper. There he occupied his leisure by studying and making extracts from Arabic MSS., feeling doubtless already the great importance of Arabic, both for the language and for the literature of the Hebrew race. On this subject let me quote to you the words of Ewald in 1831, "Linguæ arabicæ, semiticarum principis, cognitio diligentior ceterarum stirpis hujus linguarum, hebrææ potissimum, studio non utilissimum tantum est sed necessarium prorsus. . . . Tutoque contendas, qui cultissimam stirpis hujus linguam bene perspexerit hunc demum circa omnes semiticas haud cæcutire incipere";[2] and for the other part of my statement

[1] *Die Johanneïschen Schriften*, ii. "Vorrede," S. v.
[2] *Grammatica critica linguæ Arabicæ*, Pref. p. iii.

those of one of Ewald's greatest pupils: "I have no doubt that the original gifts and ideas of the primitive Hebrews can most readily be understood by comparing Arabian antiquity." [1]

This is not the time to explain the sense in which these two statements are to be understood. Ewald himself used Arabic more for the purposes of philology than for those of what may be called comparative ethnic-psychology. And no doubt philological purposes are the most important from the point of view of exegesis and of theology. Ewald would therefore have hailed the recent institution of an Oriental School or Tripos in our two old English universities. Himself by taste, though not, I admit, equally by endowments, at once philologist and theologian, he would have insisted on the importance not only of Hebrew to the theologian, but of the other Semitic languages to the Hebraist. He was himself by no means a biassed advocate of the claims of Arabic, though circumstances early drew his special attention to it, and the richness and variety of its literature, combined with the exquisite refinement of its style, made it perhaps his favourite among the Semitic languages. His own position on the relationship between the Semitic languages is best seen from his *Abhandlung über die geschichtliche Folge der semitischen Sprachen* (1871), with which compare his remarks in § 7 of his Arabic Grammar.

---

[1] Wellhausen, *Skizzen und Vorarbeiten*, Heft I.

Ewald was now a schoolmaster. But he had no intention of remaining in this profession. He wished to think his own thoughts away from Eichhorn, and to make researches in a fresh library, preparatory to another book. To *another* book, you will say? Yes; for his first book, though published at Brunswick, was the fruit of his student leisure at Göttingen; he must have begun to print almost as soon as he had arrived at Wolfenbüttel. It was called *Die Composition der Genesis kritisch untersucht*, and bears the date 1823. Ewald's acuteness and ingenuity are already abundantly displayed in this volume; he seeks to show that there is a unity in the Book of Genesis and a well-ordered plan which of itself forbids the literary analysis of Genesis, whether into documents or into fragments. "Critics," he says, "will no longer see different narrators where the greatest harmony displays itself, nor divide into separate fragments that which thousandfold bands both join and interlace with such exactness." It was certainly dangerous for so young an author to publish his results; for how few are able to retract what they have once said in print! Happily at this early period Ewald had still the power of self-criticism, and upon further reflection retracted the negative inference referred to. His words are, "I gladly take the opportunity of declaring that the book referred to has now, so far as this single point is concerned, only historical significance." This was in a review of Stähelin's *Kritische Untersuchungen*, published in the *Theol.*

Studien und Kritiken in 1831, the same year, it is not irrelevant to remark, in which he published his critical Arabic grammar. A deeper study of the phenomena of Genesis had shown him the complexity of the critical problem, and the inadmissibility of a simple and, from a purely Western point of view, a natural solution, and a wider acquaintance with the Arabic historians had revealed a process of composition which made him repent his precipitate rejection of both the hitherto current critical hypotheses. It was in fact an epoch-making article—this review of Stähelin's now forgotten work. Some one had at last expressed what many others were privately meditating. A supplement-hypothesis had to be joined to the old document-hypothesis. Ewald himself sought to make this evident in the first volume of his *History*, but his eccentric terminology and his too positive and dogmatic tone deprived him of the influence to which his great ability entitled him.

Ewald, then, had to withdraw from one of the principal positions of his early book. Yet we may be glad that he wrote it. It helps us to refute the charge that he dealt merely in fancy-criticism. It shows that even in youth, when the fancy is generally at its strongest, he was fully aware of the dangers which beset critical analysis, and if at the age of nineteen he could not fully realize the nature of the problem of Genesis, much less solve it, yet he made one positive contribution of value to the critical controversy—he made it impossible henceforth to assert that the Book of Genesis, as it now stands, is without a plan.[1] It is pleasing to be able to say that, though the youthful Ewald freely criticized not only Vater but Eichhorn, the latter did not withhold his commendation, and in the following year (1824) procured Ewald's recall to Göttingen as *repetent* or Tutorial Fellow in the Theological Faculty.

This, however, as might be expected, was only a transition; in 1827 he was promoted to a professorship. Just as Eichhorn, when called to Göttingen, had three years and no more to work with Michaelis, so Ewald, in the like circumstances, had but the same space of time allotted him as the colleague of Eichhorn. The veteran's work was done. He had sketched the main outlines of the right method of Biblical criticism, and had himself brought out by it not a few assured results; but an infinite amount of *Detailforschung*, of minute research, had yet to be gone through, before that historical reconstruction for which he longed could safely be attempted. The captious and arbitrary procedure and unrefreshing results of less able and less sympathetic critics than Eichhorn had disgusted very many with the Old Testament, and we hear Tholuck saying in his inaugural lecture at Halle in 1821, that "for the last twenty or thirty years the opinion has been generally prevalent, that the study of the Old Testament for theologians, as well as the devotional reading of it

---

[1] Comp. Westphal, *Les sources*, &c., i. 182.

for the laity, is either entirely profitless or at least promises but little advantage."[1]

The prejudice lingered on in Germany, and exercised a pernicious influence on the historical and theological views of such eminent personages as Schleiermacher, Hegel, and Baur, the Gnostics of modern times, as Ewald severely styles them. See how much hangs on the completeness of a theological professoriate! If Halle and Tübingen had had Old Testament professors like Eichhorn, or if those three great men had finished their theological studies (for Hegel, as you know, began as a *theolog*) at Göttingen, upon how much sounder a basis in one important respect would their systems rest! Would the youthful successor of Eichhorn be the man to destroy this prejudice? He aspired to be this and even more than this; we shall see later on what it was that hindered his complete success. But we shall do well to remember at this point that other chosen instruments were in course of training simultaneously with Ewald. I need only mention Umbreit, Bleek, and Hengstenberg, the former of whom became professor at Heidelberg in 1823, and the two latter professors at Berlin in 1823 and 1828 respectively. To all these men we in England are, in various degrees, directly or indirectly indebted. It would be unseemly for us to depreciate the merits

[1] *Einige apologetische Winke für das Studium des A. T.'s, den Studirenden des jetzigen Decenniums gewidmet*, translated under the title, "Hints on the Importance of the Study of the Old Testament," in *Philological Tracts*, edited by John Brown, D.D., vol. i. (Edinburgh, 1833).

even of an ultra-conservative like Hengstenberg. Sixty years ago the prospects of a renaissance of Old Testament studies in England seemed hopeless, and without the help of Protestant German scholars of different schools the efforts of the friends of progress would have had but little success.

I am now approaching the most important part of Ewald's life, and am anxious to show that the subject of my lecture has a living interest for English students. Ewald's success or failure in Germany meant, though few doubtless knew it at the time, the success or failure of the cause of the Old Testament in England. I appeal to our young students to regard the life and work of Ewald with something of the same gratitude with which they regard that of our own Lightfoot. Of the religious spirit in which Ewald entered on his career I have spoken already. That inner experience which I have referred to as a call, gave a sanctity, if I may say so, to the most abstruse questions of philological research. In 1825 Ewald published a small treatise on Arabic metres, the results of which were incorporated into his Arabic Grammar, and in 1827 made his first incursion into the domain of the Aryan languages by an essay on some of the older Sanskrit metres. The young scholar, you will see, chafes already at restrictions; he will not be outdone by the great English theologians of the seventeenth century; he will be an Orientalist, and not merely a Semitic scholar. Soon you will see that he is not content with being in the bare sense an Orientalist;

he will be a comparative philologist. And yet we cannot doubt that the religious interest animates all his philological work. He has a deep sense of the wonderfulness of "God's greatest gift"[1]—language, and none of the Biblical conceptions does he appreciate more than that of the Logos. He will delight ever afterwards to trace the resemblances and the differences of the Biblical and the other religions, and in his great series of annual Biblical reviews he is careful not to omit illustrative works on Oriental subjects. In all this he did but act in the spirit of his predecessor Eichhorn, who had a true presentiment of the future importance of the comparative study of sacred books. In 1826 this taste of his was strengthened by a literary journey to Berlin, where he had fruitful intercourse with one of the older Sanskrit scholars, F. A. Rosen. One incidental result of his Sanskrit studies was the discovery (as it seemed to him) of the manifold use of Sanskrit for the correct explanation of Hebrew. It is, in fact, in this early period that he allowed himself the widest range. In 1826, the year of his Berlin visit, he began to lecture on Sanskrit, to which he afterwards added Persian, Turkish, Armenian, Coptic: I need not mention specially the various Semitic languages.[2] It is as if he had taken to heart the saying of Bp. Pearson,

---

[1] Max Müller, *Science of Language*, i. 3.

[2] Among the Orientalists who passed through the school of Ewald may be mentioned Schleicher, Osiander, Dillmann, Schrader, and, one of the latest, Stern the Egyptologist.

"Non est theologus nisi qui et Mithradates." He even planned a work on the history and comparative grammar of the Semitic languages.[1] His taste, however, was chiefly for Arabic, though the only text which he published was that of Wakidî on the Conquest of Mesopotamia, in 1827. He once hoped to compose a history of the intellectual movement among the Arabs, closing with the death of Mohammed;[2] a task, it would seem, for which the materials are still too scanty. I should suppose that a vast number of ideas were continually arising in his fertile brain, and slowly taking shape in lectures, articles, and reviews. But none of them, I am sure, was allowed to obscure the master-project on which he said, in 1859, that his mind had been working for far more than thirty years—the project of a history of the growth of true religion in the midst of the people of Israel.

It is remarkable that the first Old Testament book to which Ewald devoted himself in the maturity of his powers, was one "in less direct connexion with lofty interests"—the Song of Songs. By selecting it, he not only evidenced his firm adhesion to the view of the Old Testament as a literature, established by Lowth, Herder, and Eichhorn, but took the first step towards ascertaining that frankly human basis of a sound and healthy popular life on which alone the

---

[1] *Grammatica critica linguæ Arabicæ*, vol. ii. Præf. p. iii.; comp. "Vorrede" to the Hebrew Grammar of 1827.

[2] *Abhandlung über die geschichtliche Folge der Semitischen Sprachen* (1871), p. 61, note.

superstructure of what he loves to call the true religion could possibly be reared. He is proof against the temptation to which a lamented Cambridge Orientalist (E. H. Palmer) succumbed, when he said, "If you would feel that Song of Songs, then join awhile the mystic circle of the Súfís." The extravagant mysticism to which Tholuck had not long before introduced the European world [1] was alien to the thoroughly practical, and in this respect Jewish mind of Ewald. The Song of Songs is to him not the work of a theosophist—that is too high a view; nor yet is it a mere collection of love-poems—that is too low a view; it "is one whole, and constitutes a sort of popular drama, or, more correctly speaking, a cantata," describing the victory of true love, and thus, without the least sign of conscious purpose, promoting the highest ends of morality. This is not one of Ewald's greatest works, but it is one of the most pleasing from the delicacy of its tone, a quality in which Hitzig's work on the Song is lamentably deficient. The author is doubtless too ingenious in restoring what he thinks the proper form of the poem,[2] and yet, though neither in this nor in any other book of Ewald has the last word of criticism been spoken, his very freshly written first edition marks a real step in the explanation of the Song.

[1] *Ssufismus s. theosophia Persarum pantheistica*, 1821. Comp. Vaughan's *Hours with the Mystics*, vol. ii.

[2] Ewald's scheme of the poem is given, with some slight modifications, in Dr. Driver's *Introduction*, pp. 413—416.

All this was most creditable work, but not enough for an aspirant to the chair of Eichhorn. There was an older scholar who had strong claims on the appointment, himself an old pupil of Eichhorn—need I mention Gesenius?[1] The too general and æsthetic treatment of the Old Testament, introduced by Herder, was profoundly repugnant to this somewhat dry commentator, but most accomplished master of the Semitic languages. Herder was for soaring into the infinite; Gesenius was perfectly satisfied with the finite. Ewald had in his nature something of both, reminding us of those lines of Goethe:

> Willst du in's Unendliche schreiten,
> Geh nur in's Endliche nach allen Seiten.

Ewald might well expect that the chair of Eichhorn would be offered, as in point of fact it was in the first instance, to Gesenius, but he would also seek to strengthen his own claims by competing with that scholar on his own ground. Great as were the merits of Gesenius's Hebrew Grammar, or rather grammars, from the point of view of the learner—their clearness and simplicity, in fact, left nothing to be wished—there was still a demand for a grammar more independent in its relation to the older systems, more philosophic in its explanations, more in harmony with the scientific principles of Franz Bopp and his distinguished colleagues. As an English friend and pupil of Ewald said in 1835, "The elements of a

[1] See p. 55.

further development of Hebrew grammar were already ripening in silence; but the honour of effecting the reformation was reserved for Prof. Ewald."[1] The *Kritische Grammatik* (1827) at once drew all eyes upon its author, and it may safely be said that with this book in his hand he won his professorship. Gesenius himself had no mean jealousy of his young rival; he was even in the habit of sending his most promising pupils to Göttingen to complete their studies under Ewald, who, he said, was "ein exquisiter Hebräer, auch ein selten gelehrter Araber."[2] In 1828, hungry for fresh distinction, Ewald actually brought out a second Hebrew grammar, "in vollständiger Kürze bearbeitet," which appeared in 1835 in a second edition, thoroughly revised, as the preface states, and greatly improved. The most important addition consists of a treatise on the accents, based upon a previous essay of Ewald's published in 1832 in his *Abhandlungen zur Oriental. u. Bibl. Litteratur* (part 1; a second part was never issued), in which the relationship of the Hebrew to the simpler Syriac accentuation is pointed out. Throughout his life Ewald continued to improve his grammar, to which in 1844 he gave the title *Ausführliches Lehrbuch der hebräischen Sprache des Alten Testaments*. The earlier editions are however of much historical interest,

[1] Preface to the English translation of Ewald's Hebrew Grammar, by John Nicholson (Lond. 1836), p. xi.
[2] See the sketches of Hitzig and Vatke, and cf. Benecke, *Wilhelm Vatke*, p. 27.

and a few passages from the preface to Ewald's second Hebrew Grammar may be quoted, as illustrative not only of the views of the author, but of his modesty at this point of his career. He is speaking of the new period in the study of Hebrew grammar. "I myself may have only the merit of the first impulse to improvement, if even that may be called a merit, since the idea of an improvement in this science is less owing to me than the claims of our time, and this idea has perhaps only been awakened somewhat sooner and more vividly in me. Even after the firmer form which I have been able to give the Hebrew grammar in this new work, there nevertheless remains, as I partly confidently believe and partly suspect, much for future inquirers, or, perhaps, for myself to add or to define more strictly, not only in the syntax, which follows logical laws and is therefore more easily thoroughly understood by a consistent thinker, but also in the doctrine of the sounds of the language."[1]

It is not, I think, superfluous in England to lay stress on the services of Gesenius and Ewald (but especially of Ewald) to Hebrew grammar. Quite recently an English bishop, addressing the clergy of his diocese, declined to recognize the supposed results of "higher criticism" until it could be shown that the Hebrew language was much better understood in our day than in the time of Ainsworth and Broughton.[2] And it is precisely from the want of a

---

[1] Nicholson's translation (see above), p. xii.
[2] Dr. Ryle, *Guardian*, Oct. 26, 1892.

philological exegesis such as Ewald and others have founded that our popular commentaries on the Old Testament are in many respects so misleading. The late Dr. Pusey at any rate thought differently from Bishop Ellicott. He cordially admitted [1] the "philosophical acuteness" with which "as a youth of nineteen (? twenty-four) he laid the foundation of the scientific treatment of Hebrew grammar," though I cannot see that in his own commentaries he made the most of Ewald's grammatical principles. This is not the place to estimate with precision the services of Ewald as a grammarian. The very interesting preface of Dr. John Nicholson to his translation of the second edition of the *Grammatik*, well describes some of the most valuable characteristics of the book, and the impression which they produced on acute and well-prepared students like himself. Other schools of grammarians have arisen since Ewald's time, and his successors can certainly not afford to imitate him in what König calls the style of assertion. Much that Ewald in his later years considered himself to have settled, has now become very properly a subject of debate. But the stimulus which he has given to the study of Hebrew grammar is immense, and a general indebtedness, visible in most if not all of his successors, is quite consistent with many differences on points of detail. I need not say more on this subject, because my friend, Prof. Driver, has given the best illustration

---

[1] *The Minor Prophets* (Oxf. 1879), p. iii.

of what I have been urging in his beautiful text-book on the Hebrew tenses.

Ewald has sometimes been reproached with being too theological. But his interest in grammar at any rate was purely disinterested. He loved it for its own sake, as the most wonderful product of the human faculties. To Arabic grammar he devoted himself at first with almost as much zeal as to Hebrew grammar; and the pages of his linguistic works [1] testify to his keen interest in the most outlying languages, from which indeed he often drew illustrations for Hebrew. The composition of his Arabic Grammar (vol. i. 1831; vol. ii. 1833) falls between the first and second editions of the second or smaller Hebrew grammars, and must have contributed greatly to the improvement of the latter work. The book is written in very clumsy Latin, but contains much interesting matter for a Hebraist or a comparative philologist, its object being not merely to register phenomena, but to give simple and consistent explanations.

The author never had leisure for a second edition, in which perhaps he would have given more detailed criticism of the Arabic grammarians. Writing the book was a recreation. From Arabic grammar, from the *Mu'allaqât* and the *Qur'ân*, he returned with renewed energies to Hebrew grammar, to the psalmists and the prophets of the Bible.

I speak of this as a return, for you will remember

[1] See especially the two first of his *Sprachwissenschaftlichen Abhandlungen*, 1861-62.

that Ewald is already well known to Biblical scholars. Both on Hebrew grammar and on Hebrew poetry he has published results which have been found worth hearing. A grand ideal beckons him onward, but he has the self-restraint to listen to the warnings of an inner voice, which bids him proceed slowly, *ohne Hast ohne Rast*, trusting that God will grant him time enough to finish his work. In 1826 he began the investigation of the poetical books; in 1835 he resumes this by the publication of a book on the Psalms, which is followed in 1836 by Job, and in 1837 by Proverbs and Ecclesiastes. These volumes form parts 2—4 of a series called *Die poetischen Bücher des Alten Bundes;* the first part, containing introductory matter on Hebrew poetry in general and on the Book of Psalms in particular, did not appear till 1839. He takes, you see, a different line from that recommended by Abraham Kuenen. He thinks it safest to begin his Old Testament researches, not with the prophets, but with the poets, as bringing us nearer to the primitive spiritual forces at work amidst the people of Israel. Thus he hopes to gain a vantage-point for comprehending as well the far loftier speech of the prophets, as the recollections of the spiritual movement (using the word "spiritual" in a wide sense) of Israel's bygone times recorded in the historical books.[1] There

---

[1] See p. vi. of "Vorrede" to *Die poetischen Bücher*. Compare Ewald's view of the right plan for those who would read the Bible for instruction, *Die Lehre der Bibel von Gott*, i. 465-66. Here again note Ewald's consistency from youth to age.

is something to be said for this plan. That peculiar spiritual state which we call inspiration is less distinctly visible in the poetical than in the prophetical books; not less truly, but less distinctly visible; and it is perhaps a good exercise to study this phenomenon first of all as displayed upon the frankly human and popular groundwork of poetical compositions. The only danger is that such a course is liable to prejudice the investigator unduly in favour of an early date for the poetical books; for if these books are very late, they seem to become a mere reflection of prophecy, a sort of substitute for the living oracle. It was, at any rate, very unwise of Ewald to hamper his future course as a critic by venturing thus early on a chronological rearrangement of the Psalms. It is however, in my opinion, much to his credit that he recognizes so fully a large captivity and post-captivity element in the Psalter. In fact, he stands aloof both from the extreme conservative and from the extreme liberal party, and foreshadows that *via media* for which the progressive conservatism of our day so ardently longs. The fault of the book is of course its fragmentariness. But as a supplement to other works, it still has its use. Ewald's view of the connexion of thought in the Psalms is always worth considering, and his emotional sympathy with the psalmists is altogether unique.

But I think that his book on Job is, if not greater, yet more complete and freer from faults. If we look at the translation, how many brilliant examples of grammatical tact occur to us! while the commentary shows equal skill in tracing out the often subtle connexions between the speeches. The introduction is brimful of insight, and stimulates even where it fails to convince, and Ewald's "higher criticism" is here, I think, for once final and authoritative. The study of the wonderful character-drama of Job has, I trust, a great future before it, but only on condition of our starting from the point where Ewald has left it. I cannot stop to speak of his Proverbs and Ecclesiastes—works less fruitful, as it seems to me, in suggestions of permanent value; and of the opening volume of the series I can only give the general verdict of Biblical scholars, that, putting aside the meagre pages on the Psalms, strange to say, the only part accessible in English,[1] it is one of Ewald's most original and satisfactory works.

But now to return to the personal history of the author. We have seen him in his greatness; we are soon to sympathize with him in his trials and infirmities. He has had the discipline of prosperity, but has shown a strong imaginative sympathy with those in the depths of affliction. The *Book of the Trial of the Righteous One* has found in him a congenial interpreter; soon the question of the poem is to come back to him with a personal application, "Dost *thou* serve God for nought?" Looking back on this early

---

[1] Dr. Nicholson's translation of the general introductory portion is buried in the Old Series of the *Journal of Sacred Literature.*

period, Ewald was in the habit of idealizing it, just as the patriarch idealized the "months of old" in that most touching elegiac retrospect, the 29th chapter of Job. Still there is no doubt that Ewald was more firmly rooted in Göttingen, and his relations with scholars both in and out of Göttingen more agreeable at this time than afterwards. A truly noble band of professors, especially historical professors, illustrated the *Georgia Augusta*. There was Lücke the commentator and Church-historian, Gieseler the Church-historian, Dahlmann the historian of Greece, Ritter the historian of philosophy, Gervinus the historian of literature, Otfried Müller the archæologist, Jakob Grimm the Germanist; among others may be added the two friends, Weber the great electrician and Gauss the celebrated mathematician, the latter of whom in 1830 became Ewald's father-in-law. None of these was more distinguished than Heinrich Ewald. Honours crowded upon him; he had large classes, attracted by his enthusiasm and his thoroughness, and exercised a wide and salutary influence on the critical movement.

True, there was already a root of bitterness in his self-concentration. That same spiritual "recluseness" which, in the words of Edward Irving, led "that soul of every excellence, the glorious Milton," into "the greatest of all intolerance,"[1] was the bane of Ewald. He had a noble and unselfish ambition, but he had it

---

[1] *Miscellanies from the Writings of Irving*, p. 153.

too absorbingly. It bade him "separate himself" from his kind and "intermeddle with all wisdom,"[1] forgetting that more than one prophet is wanted to accomplish a Divine purpose, and that he himself, no less than Eichhorn, needed the support of independent fellow-workers. At first there was only a vague danger that a naïve self-confidence might develop into a tormenting intolerance. His expressions of feeling were too childlike to irritate, and as yet he left the world and its rulers to take care of themselves.[2] In 1836 however there are indications of a change; the conclusion of the fourth part of *Die poetischen Bücher* contains, among much very interesting matter, full of rude but striking eloquence, a painful attack on that sweet-natured, conscientious, and gifted scholar, De Wette. Ewald had, it seems, been spending a holiday in Italy, but it was a holiday against his will; his mind preyed upon itself, and even the historical treasures of the Eternal City gave out no balm for his wounded spirit. Ancient art scarcely speaks to him; he writes epigrams in verse,[3] breathing a Luther-like scorn of the Romans and their Church, and of those who, tempted by false promises, have become converts to Rome. Except where his faith darts upwards, as for instance in the last lines, which remind us of Arthur Clough's "Say not the struggle nought

---

[1] Prov. xviii. 1, A. V. I need not criticize the translation.

[2] "Ich schrieb dort mit leichtem um die Welt bekümmertem Sinne" (*Die poet. Bücher des A. B.*, Bd. i. "Vorrede," S. viii.).

[3] "Mussestunden in Italien," *Ibid.* iv. 231—246.

availeth," his pen is dipped in gall, and he seeks a much-needed excuse in some wrong which has been done him at home. I cannot myself understand his obscure allusion to a "speech of tyrannous cruelty," but certain it is that in the following year a grievous wrong did befall him, which threatened for an indefinite period to thrust into idleness—"in thatenlose Musse zu versetzen"—one whose spirit was wholly academical, and who viewed with perfect justice even his authorship as an outgrowth of his professional position. In 1833, as a consequence of the attempted revolution of 1831, King William gave his sanction to a *Staatsgrundgesetz* or Constitutional Statute; in 1837 King Ernest Augustus signalized his accession to the throne by refusing to recognize this as binding. It was an event which deeply stirred academic society, and not to Otfried Müller alone may these words of a scholar-poet be applied :

> Und als der Donner zürnend eingeschlagen,
> Wer hat den Muth mit tapferm Wort erregt,
> Dem Manneswort : "So wir uns selbst nicht fehlen,
> Wie mag uns Furcht vor Drang und Unbill quälen ?"[1]

But what could academical teachers do, knights of the pen and not of the sword ? Seven at any rate found their duty clear ; they addressed a solemn protest to the curators of the university at Hanover. Their names deserve to be chronicled ; Dahlmann was the leader, the others were the two Grimms, Gervinus,

---

[1] From a memorial poem on Karl Otfried Müller, by Dr. Ellissen, Hellenist and Liberal politician.

Weber, Albrecht, and the subject of this sketch. The consequences were serious for themselves, for in December of the same year they were all dismissed from their office. Upon Ewald, not merely a patriot, but essentially a provincial, the blow fell with double force. No exile ever felt **his** banishment more. For the moment he found occupation in the English libraries;[1] but it seemed at first as if **the Guelphic** ban were to exclude him and his friends from academical office anywhere. Fortunately indeed such fears were groundless; the reputation of **the** seven professors was as much enhanced by a protest against arbitrary power as that of our own seven bishops, and Ewald was the first to receive an appointment.

Ewald's call to Tübingen in 1838 opens **a** fresh chapter in his history; it brought him, we must add, face to face with his second great trial. Would the recluse scholar be enriched or impoverished by transplantation? Would he catch something of the characteristic warmth of Wurtemberg religious life, **and** communicate in return that earnestness and questioning reasonableness which he had inherited from his fathers? And looking to his new university relations, would the man who could so well give their due to the different types of teaching in the Bible show equal flexibility in dealing with **a** colleague so unlike

[1] This is **strictly** accurate. Blenheim could not tempt him from the Bodleian. Some of his Oxford acquisitions are to be found in vol. i. of *Beiträge zur ältesten Auslegung des A. T.*, by Ewald and Dukes (Stuttgart, 1844).

himself as Ferdinand C. Baur? It was a difficult position for Ewald. Even Karl Hase, as he has told us in his charming autobiography, found it a work of time to get thoroughly naturalized in Schwabenland. One so awkward as Ewald in social intercourse, and so conscious of his own merits, could not but experience in some respects even greater hindrances than Hase. He was thus thrown back more than ever on himself, and his old infirmities gathered such a head that they made life a burden both to himself and to others. He had even before 1837 begun to express himself with unjustifiable positiveness on the errors of contemporary theologians, not indeed as a rule mentioning their names; but after that date things went from worse to worse. The fundamental differences between himself and Baur seemed to him to demand an ever-renewed protest on his part.[1] I need not say how painful such a feud between colleagues must have been, and I have no doubt that, even more than in the case of Ewald's quarrel with Gesenius, the fault was on Ewald's side. But indeed no one was safe from this self-appointed censor. The English nation came off best; but our own Pusey, who never retaliated on Ewald, had the fortune to be joined with Hengstenberg and Delitzsch in the same unqualified condemnation. To Ewald, as a political martyr, political errors, too, were now equally obnoxious with theological. With unmeasured violence, but without

[1] Contrast the respectful language of Dorner and Ullmann to Baur at this same period.

any of that wit which redeems the violence of great satirists, he chastised by turns most of "the powers that be," and when no notice was taken, it was a proof to him that he was in the right. Alas for a true prophet who mistook his functions, to the injury not only of his own fame, but of the truth which it was his privilege to make known! Alas, that instead of gratefully learning wherever he could, and appreciating high moral purpose, when he could do no more, he at once rejected all but his own results, and imputed intellectual divergences to moral defects! "Woe to that study," says the gentle Spenser's too fiery friend, Gabriel Harvey, "that misspendeth pretious Time, and consumeth itself in needlesse and bootlesse quarrels."[1] For Ewald's "railing accusations" were fully avenged on Ewald himself. Had he but taken his proper place as an honoured member of Truth's household, how much more would he have effected, and how much more easily could we estimate the comparative value of his work![2]

I have omitted as yet to mention one great blow which befell Ewald, too great to be referred to in the middle of a paragraph. It removed from his side the

[1] *Foure Letters, and certaine Sonnets, etc.* (1592), p. 27.
[2] The controversial treatises of Carl Wex and August Knobel may be here mentioned, the one entitled *Herr Prof. Ewald als* **Punier** *gewürdigt* (1843), the other *Exegetisches Vademecum für Herr Prof. Ewald* (1844). Literature of this kind justifies the remark of a French-Swiss scholar, "Les philologues allemands du xixme siècle ont souvent le tempérament aussi batailleur et la critique aussi âpre que les érudits de la Renaissance" (Pref. to Pictet's *Les origines indo-européennes*).

one softening influence which remained to him in his banishment. In 1840 his wife died, a more serious loss to him, as he himself says, than any of which his foes had been the cause. His only comfort was in high ideas, and he became more and more sensitive to any supposed disparagement of them. He had quenched his burning thirst for religious truth at the fountain of the Bible, and it both grieved [1] and angered him when some critic of large gifts misused them, as he thought, to the detriment of the Bible —that is, of Ewald's opinions about the Bible. It is true that the grief in Ewald's mind was too commonly overpowered by the indignation. But, we may ask, have there been no instances of this confusion of truth with opinion, and of intellectual error with moral obliquity among critics of another school and divines of another Church? If I had a right to be intolerant of the intolerant, I would quote those words of the ancient seer:

> O my soul, come not thou into their council;
> Unto their assembly, O my glory, be not thou united.[2]

In Ewald's case, however, this inability to do justice to other workers detracts in only a slight degree from the comfort of the reader, for as a rule he confines controversial allusions to his prefaces. None of his

---

[1] "Ich möchte vergehen vor Schmerz, sehend dass ein so armseliger Zustand von Exegese von Männern fortgesetzt wird, welche vielleicht Besseres leisten könnten" (*Die poet. Bücher*, iv. (1837), p. 253). [2] Gen. xlix. 6.

writings is more bathed in the peace and sanctity of
the spiritual world than the two volumes on the
Prophets, which appeared in the opening years of the
bitter Tübingen period. What can I say that would
be sufficient of this grand work, the treasures of
which are still far from exhausted, and which, as a
specimen of exegesis, has extorted the admiration of
a critic who so much dislikes Ewald's believingness
as Eduard Meyer?[1] Full and free as is my own
appreciation of other "founders of criticism," I cannot help noticing in Ewald's *Die Propheten* a power
of sympathetically reproducing primitive experiences,
Nachempfinden, as the Germans call it, in which his
teacher Eichhorn and most of his contemporaries and
successors are sadly deficient, and which I ascribe
partly to Ewald's possession of a deep spiritual theistic
religion, uncoloured and undistorted by non-Semitic
formulæ, partly to that peculiar personal experience
which I have ventured to call, by analogy, prophetic.
The first edition of the work appeared in 1840 and
1841; the second only in 1867—an instance of
self-restraint and noble dissatisfaction which may
mitigate our disapproval of the author's dogmatism.
"Not as though I had attained," he seems to say,
"either were already perfected." The two editions
deserve to be compared; philologically, I am not
sure that all Ewald's corrections are improvements;
though the study of the higher criticism is in some

[1] *Geschichte des Alterthums*, i. (1884), p. 204.

respects advanced by the new edition. But let all theological students, however strong their prejudices against the critical analysis of ancient texts, read, mark, learn, and inwardly digest that noble introduction which, by what might seem a miracle, deals even-handed justice both to rational criticism and to the realities of faith.

CHAPTER V.

EWALD (2).—HIS WEAKNESS AND HIS STRENGTH, AS A CRITIC AND AS A MAN.

COULD that true prophet who saw **Israel's past so much more clearly than his own life or his own time**, have looked back with purged eyes on this **point of his career,** he might have taken up the words of a poet-prophet who went before him: "Midway the journey of our life, I found myself in a dark forest; for the straight way was lost." Short though sharp was his mental agony, and then, like Dante, he saw the hill close by with its shining summit, for which all his life through he had been making. And as he "took his way on the *desert* strand,"—for who was there that rightly shared his aim?—and was **now at** the point to climb, three cruel forms appeared from the recesses of the wood, seeking to "drive him back to where the sun was mute." That is to say, arbitrary political power, blind theological conservatism, and recklessly destructive criticism, were agreed, as Ewald thought, in fearing and in seeking to oppose the regeneration of Old Testament studies. The story of Ewald's mistakes and half-mistakes is not on the outside indeed as poetic, but quite as tragic, as that of Dante's, and no one will form a right judgment of it unless he recognizes, first, that from Ewald's point of view his apprehensions were justified, and next, that, however we may blame his arrogance towards man, we must admire and reverence his constant sense of dependence on God. The one was the source of his weakness; the other, of his strength. But for his faith and his unworldliness, he could not, even with his great talents, have done as much and seen as clearly as he did. He was his own worst enemy; he would have attained, even as a scholar, more uniformly substantial results, had he worked more in concert with others. But his fidelity to the voice within was absolute, and I have no doubt that when he says that he will joyfully recant his whole system, if "a man of insight and of conscience" can prove it to be necessary, his profession is an honest one. But observe the qualification, "insight and—*conscience*." He is not only a born critic, but a born "apologist"; in one place he candidly says that though "Apologete" is a "Tübingischer Schimpfname," he will accept the description. Ewald cannot tolerate in Biblical matters a perfectly dry criticism. In all his work upon the Old Testament he is partly thinking of the New, which he regards, too completely even for some orthodox critics, as the crown and climax of the Old. He cannot admit the usual division of the field of exegesis between professors of the Old and professors of the New Testament. He must himself have a hand in the development of New Testament studies, not (as has been sometimes said) in opposition to Baur and Strauss, but because to him the New Testament forms the second part of the record of Israel's revelation. This can be proved, I think, by chronology. As long ago as 1828, before Baur had begun to touch the New Testament, Ewald published a Latin commentary on the Apocalypse. This work is at any rate more solid and significant than that of his old master, Eichhorn, and contributed to bring about that sound historical interpretation now so generally current. Writing it was Ewald's recreation amidst the serious linguistic studies which preceded his Hebrew Grammar: "unter hundert Bedrängnissen jener Jahre wie in eiligen Nebenstunden verfasst." But not all the brilliant successes of F. C. Baur as an author and as a teacher could tempt his self-centred colleague to compete with him on the field of the New Testament. In 1850 Ewald did indeed break through the appointed order of his works, and express himself on the three first Gospels; the book appeared in a second edition, which included the Acts of the Apostles, in 1871. But though its first appearance was opportune from the point of view of "apologetic" criticism, the bias of Ewald being distinctly "positive," *i.e.* inclining him to believe that we have firm ground beneath us in the Gospels in a higher degree than Baur could admit, it was neither Baur nor Strauss who forced him, almost, as he says, against his will,[1] to anticipate the time for speaking his mind on the Gospels. It was his concern for those ideal goods which Germany seemed to him to be losing. What Ewald dreaded, was the spirit of the revolution, and the chief reason why he so disliked Baur and Strauss was, that he thought *their* " Tendenz" revolutionary. Not, however, till 1861 did he touch the fourth Gospel, though the rejection of the traditional authorship of this Gospel rifled, as he thought, the "most attractive" product of the whole Biblical literature. Here, however, too, as in all Ewald's works, there is no direct controversial element. No one hates controversy more than this critic. *Nachempfinden* (Ewald's own word) was his motto from the first. It was the spell with which, even as a youth, he conjured the monsters of extreme criticism; and though later on he somewhat changed his mind as to friends and foes, never did he cease to insist upon a direct relation between the expositor and his author, a relation so close and sympathetic as to exclude any great care for the opinions of others. If he feared radicalism more as represented by Baur than by Vatke, it was because he thought that there was a fatal, however undesigned, connexion between the conclusions of Baur and those of his too brilliant friend, David F. Strauss, and the revolutionary excesses of 1848; for Vatke seemed sufficiently guarded against, as well by his heavy style and by the slight

[1] *Die drei ersten Evangelien*, "Vorrede," S. iii.

echo which he found in German universities, as by those general warnings given by our arch-dogmatist, not only in his prefaces, but, as it seems, also in his lectures.[1] Once begun, there was no intermission in his New Testament work. The *Sendschreiben des Apostels Paulus* appeared in 1857; the second volume of the *Johanneïschen Schriften* in 1862; and ten years later we find the books of the New Testament complete in seven volumes, which, in spite of their deficiencies, will never quite lose their interest, from the peculiar character of the author, and from the Hebraistic eye with which, even when writing his first Grammar, he regarded the New Testament writings.

Thus, while fully admitting that Ewald's New Testament work lost something through his antipathy to Baur, I am bound to deny that it was in any sense inspired by that too vehement feeling. So far as his researches on the Synoptic Gospels had any controversial reference, they may be said to have been his answer to the Revolution. It is true they were more than this, and in explaining my allusion, I resume the thread of my narrative. The publication of *Die drei ersten Evangelien* in 1850 was a sign that Ewald was thoroughly settled again in his old university. Much as he feared and hated the revolutionary movement, he had at least to thank what he somewhere calls the shipwreck year for bringing him back to port. Ill at ease, both on public and on private

---

[1] Benecke, *Wilhelm Vatke*, p. 613. In 1835, however, Ewald judged more favourably of Vatke's book. *Ibid.*, pp. 168—175.

grounds, and equally unable to assimilate the Biblical mysticism and the speculative rationalism of Tübingen, he had resigned his post in the great southern theological university. The senate of the Georgia Augusta supported an application which he himself made for his recall, and in September, 1848, Ewald resumed his old position at Göttingen. His reputation as a scholar had certainly not diminished during his absence. I have spoken of his *Die Propheten*. On the completion of this work, he began one of much wider range, the greatest of all the great Göttingen histories; need I mention the *Geschichte des Volkes Israel?* On two grounds this work is fitly described as epoch-making. It is in the highest degree original; every line exhibits a fresh and independent mind, and mature and long-tested research. It is also, if you will allow the expression, in a scarcely less degree, unoriginal. In spite of many ideas which are the sole property of the author, it sums up to a considerable extent the investigations of a century, and closes provisionally that great movement which, beginning as it did with Lowth, ought to have been throughout Anglo-continental. Twenty years hence, when the next great history of Israel will be due, may we venture to hope for a native English Ewald? Great is our need of him. The old Ewald must in England be for the most part the teacher's teacher; peculiarities of style and of exposition, not unpleasing to those who are interested in the author personally, are real hindrances to beginners. The new Ewald will be born into a world which is not so academical as that of Heinrich Ewald. He must be free at all costs from the moral drawbacks of his predecessor, and must have an English as well as a German training. A mere wish will not bring him into existence, but a strong enough wish will be the parent of action. Unless we see our goal, we shall never shake off our guilty torpor. Therefore—

> Flash on us, all in armour, thou Achilles;
> Make our hearts dance to thy resounding steps.[1]

The reader will pardon this abrupt transition. The memory of Lowth, whose books made no epoch in England, but kindled a flame in Germany, pursues me, and doubtless many of the younger generation who are no longer repressed by a needless dread of rationalism. Now to return. I am of course not asking any one to accept Ewald as a master. There was a time when Ewald was in some quarters almost an unquestioned potentate, the Ranke of Hebrew history. I have no wish to revive the belief in his infallibility. Over and over again we shall have to fight with him, but let us mind that we do so in his own spirit and with his own weapons. Does some one ask, What *is* Ewald's spirit? "To be scientific" —he tells us himself—" is to have a burning desire to push on more and more towards the high goal which science has set up, and to come from certainty

[1] Browning, *Paracelsus*.

to certainty."[1] But the goal with Ewald is the knowledge of a self-revealing God ("they go from strength to strength, and appear before God in Zion"); Delitzsch postulates this, Ewald works towards it. And if the question be added, Which *are* Ewald's weapons?—I reply in the words of Niebuhr, "History has two means by which it supplies the deficiencies of its sources—criticism and divination." "Both are arts," continues this great historian, "which may certainly be acquired from masters, and which a man must himself understand before he can judge of their productions."[2] Niebuhr, I know, is superseded as a critic, and Ewald is in course of being superseded. But the man who finally supersedes him will only do so in virtue of a more penetrating criticism and a better regulated though not more intense divination. Lord Acton, in the *Historical Review* (No. 1, p. 25), has lately said, "It is the last and most original of [Ewald's] disciples . . . who has set in motion" in Germany the new Pentateuch controversy, and Julius Wellhausen himself inscribes his now famous work, "To my unforgotten teacher, Heinrich Ewald." Most certainly, this eminent critic cannot be appreciated without a true knowledge of the influences which formed him. In one sense he has no doubt broken with his master. He has identified himself

---

[1] *Beiträge zur Geschichte der ältesten Auslegung*, by Ewald and Dukes, p. xviii.
[2] "Essay on the Study of Antiquities," in Niebuhr's *Life and Letters*, ii. 219.

with that "so-called criticism" (Ewald's phraseology) which has "given up Moses and so much that is excellent besides," and which leads on directly to the contemptuous rejection of the Old Testament, if not also of the New (again, Ewald's phraseology). But in another he carries on his old teacher's work; he stands where so fearless a critic as Ewald would stand, could he begin his career again.

It is a proof of the moral and intellectual force of the *History of the People of Israel* that the most advanced critical hypothesis did not become a power in Germany thirty years earlier. Strauss's *Leben Jesu* coincides (as we shall see) in date of publication with more than one remarkable work which anticipates the theory of Julius Wellhausen. It was a subversive influence of the first order; Vatke's *Biblische Theologie des Alten Testaments* was not. Vatke, it is true, had not the pointed pen of David F. Strauss; still the Carlylian denunciations of Ewald's prefaces would have been a too ineffectual breakwater by themselves. Ewald dies, and Wellhausen sets all Germany in a flame, commits treason, as Lord Acton calls it, against his old master. In another sense, however, Wellhausen is a faithful disciple of Ewald, whose principles he does but apply more consistently, and therefore with different results. It would be well for students of Wellhausen to begin by learning something from Wellhausen's "unforgotten teacher."

It was inevitable that a reaction should set in sooner or later against Ewald as a historian. The range of his researches was too wide; his self-confidence too strong; his deficiency in dialectic power too complete. But never will his great historical work be out of date as a monument of the union of faith and criticism. From this point of view it deserves the attention of all theological students. Ewald's original idea was to bring the narrative down to the time of Christ. It took nine years to complete the publication on this limited scale, the first volume being published in 1843, the fourth in 1852; in 1848 a supplementary volume was given on the *Antiquities of Israel*. This work was an admirable introduction, worthy to be put by the side of the introduction to the Prophets. Our excellent apologists who are defending ultra-conservatism against Julius Wellhausen, would have done well to practise their hand on such a work as this. Other men have been as distinguished as Ewald in the analytic department of criticism; but no one yet has been his equal in the synthesis of critical material—he is an architect of the first order. I know that there are two great faults in that part of the Introduction which relates to the sources. One is common to Ewald with most of his contemporaries—it is the comparative neglect of the archæological side of Pentateuch-research; the other is a peculiarity of his own—it is his somewhat arbitrary treatment of the component parts of the Hexateuch, and his perplexing nomenclature. But I also know that the literary analysis to which Ewald much confined himself has produced some assured and permanent results, and that his analysis is not really so very divergent from that of his fellow-critics;[1] his dogmatism in this particular is less misleading than might be supposed.

I am unwilling to stir the ashes of smouldering controversies. But there is another serious fault, as I know but too well, which still attaches to Ewald in many minds. Undevout he cannot be said to be. Prof. Wilkins has rightly emphasized Ewald's piety as well as his profundity and eloquence.[2] Our critic never treats the Old Testament as if he were a medical student dissecting the dead. He believes that the religion of Israel was the "nascent religion" of humanity in quite another sense from that in which the philosophy of Greece was its "nascent philosophy." He reveres, nay loves, the great personalities of the Old Testament; he even almost makes the anonymous historical writers live before us. But his treatment of the miracles has shocked some religious minds. Even Erskine of Linlathen speaks of Ewald in one of his letters as giving "the history of Israel divested of miracle, and (Israel) as a nation choosing God, not chosen by God."[3] All that is true, however, is that Ewald has no scholastic theory of miracles, and that to him as a historian the fact is not the miracle but the narrative of a miraculous occurrence. Those who wish to know more can now

---

[1] See Merx, *Nachwort* to the introduction of Tuch's *Genesis*, ed. 2 (1871), pp. cxvii, cxviii.
[2] *Phœnicia and Israel*, p. 148.   [3] *Letters*, p. 407.

refer to Ewald's own brief treatment of the subject of miracles in the second part of the third volume of his great work on Biblical Theology. There, however, he speaks predominantly as a theologian; in his *History of the People of Israel* he speaks, and ought to speak, as a historian.

Time forbids me to enter into a detailed examination of Ewald's greatest work. I spoke in my last chapter of his love of high ideas. This is one source of the attractiveness which he possesses for young students; it is not however without its dangers. It tempts him to idealize certain great periods of Israel's history, as for example the age of Moses and the age of David and Solomon. As Pfleiderer puts it, "when any historical figure impresses him, he is immediately carried away by his feelings, and ascribes to his heroes, forgetting the requirements of sober criticism, all the noble moral thoughts and feelings which he, the historian, entertains at the moment."[1] This is why all recent investigators have turned aside from the paths of Ewald. Prof. Oort for instance has pointed out what a *petitio principii* it is to make the volume on the Antiquities of Israel an appendix to the history of the judges and the early kings, as if the customs and institutions, as well as the beliefs of the people, underwent no change in the following centuries.[2] But it is not a member of the Leyden

---

[1] *Development of Theology* (1890), p. 257.
[2] Oort, *De tegenwoordige toestand der israelit. oudsheidskunde* (Redevoering aan het Athenæum illustre te Amsterdam den 31 Maart, 1873).

critical school, it is the coryphæus of the later orthodox theology, Dr. Dorner himself, who complains, perhaps too strongly, that "the internal and religious history of Old Testament development is not brought out by Ewald," and that "the religious matter of the Old Testament, the Messianic idea not excepted, dwindles in his writings into a few general abstract truths, devoid of life and motion," and that "he fails to perceive the progress of the history of revelation, and its internal connexion with that national feeling which prepared for it,"[1] in short, that Ewald has not entirely thrown off the weaknesses of the eighteenth century. Dr. Dorner speaks as it were out of the soul of this generation; it is something to have welcomed the discoveries of Darwin and to have lived in the same capital with Leopold von Ranke.[2]

With his fourth volume (the fifth in the English translation) Ewald arrives at the original goal of his narrative. There is no period in the earlier history of Israel in which so much still remains to be done as that which extends from the Exile to the Birth of Jesus Christ. It is no discredit to Ewald that his volume, full of interest as it is, presents considerable *lacunæ*. How imperfect for instance, in spite of its masterly grouping, is his treatment of Philo! We

---

[1] *History of Protestant Theology*, ii. 437.

[2] "The historical spirit among the rising generation of German clergymen is chiefly due to his fostering care" (Max Müller). May we some day be enabled to use such words of an English Dorner!

must henceforth look to the co-operation of Jewish and Christian scholars for the filling up of these gaps. Ewald was not as friendly as could be wished to Jewish scholars, and much work, not indeed of equal solidity, has been done in this field since Ewald's last revision of his fourth volume.

By his *Geschichte Christus*, Ewald distinctly affirmed the view, which is not indeed the only tenable one, but which is the only possible one to a Christian, that Israel's history culminates in Jesus Christ. He showed in it that he was not inclined to withhold his opinion on the great and burning questions of our time. Great are its faults; great also are its merits. Ewald as a historian reminds us here something of Maurice as a philosopher. It is an expository sermon on a grand scale that he gives us—not a history; a luminous haze blurs the outlines of his picture. Nowhere is this scholar's literary criticism so disputable as in the introduction to the Synoptic Gospels published in the second edition of *Die drei ersten Evangelien*, and presupposed in the *Geschichte Christus*. English readers, however, will perhaps not be severe upon him; indeed, he shares some of his faults (so far as they are faults) with other respected German theologians of different schools, such as Neander and Karl Hase. I say, so far as they are faults; for to me, as to Ewald, a strictly historical biography of the Christian Messiah is a thing which cannot be written. The sources are too incomplete, and Christian and non-Christian alike are driven to complete them by divination. I will not therefore blame Ewald, except for venturing to call his book *Geschichte Christus*.

Here let us take breath awhile. The *History of the People of Israel* was completed in 1859; the dream of the author's youth was fulfilled. Soon after this he took another holiday in England, when I believe he paid a visit to one who in some respects was very like him, and with whom he sympathized, Dr. Rowland Williams, at Broadchalke. It would have been well if Ewald could oftener have allowed himself these distractions. I like not to criticize his personal character. But that serene atmosphere which envelops all his New Testament work did not penetrate his outward life as we could wish. Had he but enjoyed the same deep religious experience as Tholuck, for instance, or Franz Delitzsch, that most humble-minded of great critics; had he, moreover, but shared their satisfied longing after the brotherly fellowship of the Church—how differently would his inward and consequently also his outward history have shaped itself! It is all the sadder, because of the noble words on the past, present, and future of the great rival Western communions contained in the appendix to *Die poetischen Bücher* (vol. iv. 1837). All the sadder, because there were in Ewald, as these passages seem to me to show, the germs of better things. Lucian Müller has remarked that the life of a German philologist is, by the necessity of the case, uneventful. I wish that Ewald's life had been more uneventful. He became in his latter years more irritable than ever, and more unwise in the expression of his opinions. His Hanoverian patriotism too led him astray. He had never forgotten nor forgiven the violent conduct of Prussia towards Hanover in 1801 and 1806, and on the annexation of Hanover in 1866 he refused, on conscientious grounds, to take the oath to the king of Prussia. For a long time no notice was taken of this privileged offender; but after much provocation on Ewald's part, he was placed on the retired list, with the full amount of his salary for pension. There is a curious irony in the concatenation of events by which the very man whom a Guelph deprived, was now again dismissed from office for loyalty to the Guelphs. The truth is, however, that he was treated very leniently, but unfortunately became the tool of his party. He might have done almost as good work as ever; he might perhaps have been alive now, had not his friends ("amici quàm parum amici," as Casaubon says) formed the desperate resolution of sending this most unpractical, because most uncompromising,[1] of men as the Guelphian representative of Hanover to the German Reichstag. Let us draw a veil over the melancholy issue of that ill-advised step, but respect the sense of duty which would not let him "brood over the languages of the dead,"

[1] Heinrich Thiersch, indeed, sees nothing but good in the rigid consistency of Ewald: "Dieses seltenen Mannes, der in dieser Zeit des Verfalles der Charaktere, da die Vertreter der verschiedenen Partheien wetteifern, ihren Grundsätzen untreu zu werden, fest und ungebeugt dastand, unter der Menge der haltlosen ein christlicher Cato."

when, as he thought, "forty millions of Germans were suffering oppression."

The last short chapter in Ewald's life is at hand. But I must not open it without some inadequate lines, which I would gladly make fuller, on the most recent of his works, *Die Lehre der Bibel von Gott*, the first volume of which has been translated into English under the title, *Revelation, its Nature and Record*. The publication began in 1871, and the printing of the last volume was only finished after Ewald's death. It is not often that a man's time is so exactly proportioned to the life-work which he has set himself to do. This book too had to be written, if the depths of truth in the Holy Scriptures were to be fully explored. In 1844 two young Oxford students, one of them named Stanley, called upon Ewald at Dresden. They never forgot the noble enthusiasm with which this dangerous heretic, as he was then regarded in England, grasped the small Greek Testament which he had in his hand, and said, "In this little book is contained all the wisdom of the world."[1] This was the spirit in which Ewald wrote his grandly conceived work on one of the subjects of the future, Biblical Theology. He wrote it at a time of much anxiety, both on public and on private grounds. The war with France stirred him greatly; and much as he disliked the French, he had no confidence in the rulers of his country. Still he worked on, though

---

[1] Stanley, *Jewish Church*, vol. iii. Pref p. 17.

the excitement of the time hindered consecutive thought and the clear expression of his ideas.

But however faulty this work may be, as compared with the great *History of Israel*, it has special claims on the notice of all who are interested in theology. First, because its design is a practical one. Strange as it may seem, Ewald writes here for the great public. He thinks, poor dreamer, that the men of this world will attend to a system based on the historical study of the Bible. Like Maurice, he is persuaded that even in the Old Testament truths are contained which the world cannot afford to neglect. He does touch, however clumsily and ineffectually, on some of the great subjects of the day. He does not bury himself in his study, like too many German divines, but seeks to bring himself into relation with the people and its wants. He began in 1863, by co-operating with others, including the great theologian Richard Rothe, in founding the "Protestanten-Verein"; he now, with his old prophet-like confidence, offers that which he has found in the Bible as "a banner because of the truth." And next, because the book suggests to us a new criterion of the relative importance of doctrines. Do they stand in a line of direct continuity with the Old Testament? We may not altogether agree with Ewald's results, or with Ritschl's,[1] but they have both done good service

[1] Albrecht Ritschl, author of *Die christliche Lehre von der Rechtfertigung*, perhaps the most independent and influential of recent German theologians.

in pointing us back to the roots of theology in the Old Testament. Lastly, however weak as a theological system—and remember that Ewald, almost alone among famous theologians, had no special philosophical training[1]—the book is full of suggestive exegetical details, combined with something of the old architectonic skill. The right hand of the veteran scholar has not forgotten its cunning; and on this and other grounds, I think that the translation of the first volume is of primary importance, not only to teachers, but to students.

To the last Ewald remained in outward bearing as he had ever been. No one who has once seen it will forget that tall, erect form, and those eyes which seemed to pierce into eternity. His loss as an academical teacher was not greatly felt. His enthusiasm indeed had not cooled, but it ceased to attract students. He was however to his very last *semester*, as I well remember, an eager and exacting lecturer on Semitic philology, and if in his Old Testament lectures he repeated himself too much, the few who came to them were doubtless repaid by the privilege of hearing Ewald. His death was the fitting close of a great scholar's career. Only four days before it occurred he sent in a paper on a Phœnician inscription, for a meeting of the Göttingen *Gesellschaft der Wissenschaften*. But his mind had

---

[1] He might almost pass for English in his repugnance to modern German philosophy (see e. g. *Die Lehre der Bibel von Gott*, ii. 45, note 1).

other and higher occupations than this. His old child-like faith never left him. "There he sat," says one who visited him, "in his long grey fur-trimmed gown, in the little green upper chamber. On the walls hung, not only copies of two well-known modern paintings, but the Saviour of the World by Carlo Dolci." "His words" (so my author continues) "were full of a bold assurance that took no account of earthly opposition."[1] But the end was near. He passed to the land where faithful servants of Truth do not "strive nor cry," and where all problems are solved, May 4, 1875. We will neither praise nor blame him, but thankfully accept all that is good in his life's work. No one has better expressed the spirit of his life than Karl Hase in one of his exquisite vignettes of eminent theologians,[2]—"Nach Gesenius hat Ewald die Geschichte des alttestamentlichen Volkes aufgerollt, er ein rückschauender Prophet mit der orientalischen Zungengabe, kühn und zu Opfern bewährt für die Freiheit, nur durch seine sittliche Entrüstung gegen jede abweichende Meinung leicht verstört."

[1] *Einsame Wege* (1881), an anonymous work by a leading Lutheran divine, pp. 300, 301.
[2] *Kirchengeschichte*, p. 582.

CHAPTER VI.

HITZIG—[HENGSTENBERG]—VATKE—BLEEK.

THE same year which is marked by the death of Ewald is also memorable for the decease of **Ferdinand Hitzig**, who passed away at Heidelberg, Jan. **22,** 1875. Less known in England, he does not appear to claim so full a notice in these pages as Ewald, but it were shameful ingratitude to pass him by altogether, nor need I, in eulogizing his merits, show myself blind to his defects. He was born at Hauingen in the Baden Oberland, Jan. 23, 1807. Both in his home and in his scholastic and academical training he was subject to rationalistic influences, which were not corrected, as in the case of De Wette, by subsequent acquaintance with deeper philosophical systems. At Heidelberg he heard the lectures of Paulus, but speedily moved to Halle, where Gesenius induced him to devote himself to the Old Testament with a view to an academical position. That he worked hard under such an exacting teacher, can be easily believed, but soon, at Gesenius's instigation, he went away to Göttingen to study under Ewald : we shall presently find Gesenius giving the same unselfish counsel **to** Vatke. The opinion **which young** Hitzig formed of

Ewald may be gathered from the dedication of his Commentary on Isaiah: "To the founder of a new science of the Hebrew language, and thereby of the exegesis of the Old Testament, G. H. A. Ewald, in Göttingen, as a mark of recognition of manifold and great deserts." In 1829 Hitzig, as a young graduate, returned to Heidelberg, and became *privatdocent* of theology. His income however was so small that he was on the point of taking a small cure of souls, when at the last moment he received a call to a professorship in the young university of Zurich. Here for twenty-eight years he lived and worked happily, and of the many German scholars who found a home in Zurich about this time, few so thoroughly appreciated the peculiar character of the Swiss people. Still more gladly however would he have returned to Heidelberg, and on the death of Umbreit in 1861, the opportunity offered itself.

At the time when I made Hitzig's acquaintance, the number of students of theology at Heidelberg was not large. It was otherwise in 1861, when he took the students by storm, and gathered a large class of interested hearers. No one indeed could see or hear Hitzig without feeling that there was a man behind the scholar,[1] and that his researches were controlled by a strong, manly character. I ventured to write thus of him on the news of his death:—[2]

---

[1] Read the letters prefixed (with biographical sketch) to his posthumous *Biblical Theology* (1880).
[2] In the *Academy*, Feb. 6, 1875.

"Great as an Orientalist, greater as a Biblical critic, he was greatest of all as a disinterested, truth-loving character. From first to last he never wavered in his adherence to that dry, but clear-cut, sternly moral Rationalism, which he had received from his university teachers, Paulus and Gesenius. He was not indeed without his faults. He could not be induced to learn from any other but himself. His love of far-fetched etymologies—not all of them, we may hope, intended seriously—makes his works, especially the later ones, unreadable — *ungeniessbar* — to a pure philologist. The application of that method of criticism, which seeks to determine the date of a book from internal characteristics alone, led him to many results, especially in his work on the Psalms, which are not likely to hold their ground. But he knew Hebrew well; he had an exegetical tact far surpassing that of Ewald or any other scholar with whom we are acquainted, and the substance of his works has become the common property of critics. Two of these deserve special recognition—his suggestive and absolutely unrivalled commentary on Isaiah (Heidelberg, 1833), and his contribution to the *Exegetisches Handbuch* on Jeremiah (first edition, Leipzig, 1841), remarkable for its judicious treatment of the complicated question of the text. But his brilliant capacities were already fully displayed in a still earlier work, *Begriff der Kritik am Alten Testamente praktisch erörtert* (Heidelberg, 1831). He also wrote on the Psalms, the Minor Prophets, Ezekiel,

Daniel, Ecclesiastes, the Song of Songs, the Proverbs, and—but last year—Job. His *History of the People of Israel* (Leipzig, 1862) is in the highest degree stimulative, but too Hitzigian, if we may be allowed the term, to produce much effect on criticism. His raids on the New Testament had also too much divination in them to be successful. Nor will students of Cuneiform acquit him of arrogance and unscientific haste in his unfortunate essay on the Language of the Assyrians. But his faults were those of a generation accustomed to a less severe philology than the present. His virtues were his own."

To this I venture to add some supplementary notes. (1.) Hitzig was not less wide in his range of study than Ewald: change of study was his recreation. From his youth he delighted in classical studies, and sometimes (according to Redslob) even lectured in this department. An incomplete Turkish dictionary was found among his papers, and it is known that in his latter years he studied the Slavonic languages. That his imperfect acquaintance with Sanskrit and Zend led him astray in Old Testament research, is well known. On New Testament criticism too he ventured to offer new and ingenious suggestions (see *e.g.* Holtzmann, *Kritik der Epheser und Kolosserbriefe*, pp. 22, 33, 87, 158—160, 165—168, 306). (2.) As to Hitzig's services to Old Testament criticism. As a "higher critic" he errs, like Ewald, by attempting to solve too many obscure points of detail: he forgets the necessary limits of human knowledge. This fault can be traced even in his two earliest critical works. Thus (*a*) in the *Begriff der Kritik* he claims a number of psalms for Jeremiah, partly at least because certain expressions (prosaically interpreted) correspond with facts mentioned in the narrative chapters of the Book of Jeremiah. So too Ps. lxxii. is treated as referring to Ptolemy Philadelphus, not merely on the legitimate ground of a *general* correspondence between the background of the psalm and the story of the early days of the Ptolemy, but on the illegitimate ground that parts of the psalm, when realistically interpreted, agree exactly with the narrative. And (*b*), in the dissertation called *Des Propheten Jonas Orakel über Moab*, he endeavoured to show, not only that that much-disputed passage, Isa. xv. 1—xvi. 12, is not by Isaiah, but that, though almost without any historical allusions, it is certainly the work of Jonah ben-Amittai (2 Kings xiv. 25). There are many other instances of this same dogmatism in both his works on the Psalms. I do not deny that there is now and then much plausibility in his conjectures, and had they been brought forward much more sparingly, and with a due admission of their uncertainty, they would deserve praise rather than blame (assuming of course that on other grounds the period—I do not say, the year—to which Hitzig assigned the particular psalms was probably correct). There are also many startling conjectures in his *History of the People of Israel*, where Hitzig also complicates matters by his strange ideas of comparative philology. So startling indeed are some of them that they would infallibly have ruined the reputation of any other scholar.

Happily there is much more to be said on the other side. On the larger critical questions Hitzig may not be conclusive, but what he says is always rich in stimulus, and even his excess of positiveness, when dealing with those problems of detail in which he delights, can be excused as a reaction against De Wette's scepticism. And probably no one has done so much for that accurate explanation of the text upon which, after all, the "higher criticism" must be largely based. He is, in the first place, under no illusion as to the state of the Hebrew text, and though his emendations require sifting, they are often really brilliant. Certainly he is never so ineffective as an emender as Ewald, from haste and inattention to his own grammatical rules, sometimes unfortunately is. And next, as a grammarian, Hitzig is not inferior to the master to whom in this field he has so fully owned his indebtedness, and though, as an exegete, he is not equally sensitive with Ewald to some psychological phenomena, yet he seizes many delicacies of thought which that too eager commentator overlooks; he may indeed sometimes be even too subtle, but this is one of the *défauts de ses qualités*, and is not likely to mislead many English readers. I will quote what another master of exegesis (Delitzsch) has said of Hitzig; the passage is of much biographical as well as critical interest, and deserves respectful attention.

"In spite of the difference of our religious standpoint and the bitter words which we have often exchanged, I ever respected in Hitzig the extraordinarily gifted master of the art of exegesis, and there existed between us a sympathy which found various modes of manifestation. Hitzig himself gave hearty expression to this feeling, as lately as Jan. 6, 1875, shortly before his decease, in a letter bearing his own tremulous signature."[1] Alas, that the religious difference here referred to should have been so strongly marked! Both scholars indeed were sincere Christians (see, for Hitzig's position, *Geschichte des Volkes Israel*, p. 3), but Hitzig's view even of the higher religion of the Old Testament erred by meagreness as much as that of his friendly rival erred by exaggeration. But let us not censure either scholar. Fidelity was a leading feature in the character of both, and of Hitzig it may be said that he was loyally devoted to the clear but shallow rationalism of his parents. The effect was seen in his narrow view, not only of Hebraism, but of Christianity itself, as is well pointed out by a great Jewish scholar (J. Derenbourg) in a review of Hitzig's *History of the People of Israel*.

"M. Hitzig est quelque peu de l'école de MM. Lassen et Renan. La race sémitique est pour lui une race inférieure, incomplète, dominée par les sens, privée de toute délicatesse morale, bornée du côté de

---

[1] *Hiob* (1876), "Vorwort," p. vi.

l'esprit, une race sans aucune largeur de vue, pour laquelle l'âme n'est que le souffle de ses narines, ou le sang qui coule dans ses veines, une race dont la langue elle-même, par la pauvreté de son fond et de ses formes, reflète l'insuffisance et les imperfections. Le christianisme, pour cette école, est avant tout un fait arien, un produit de l'esprit hellénique légèrement mélangé d'éléments hébraiques, à son détriment selon les uns, pour son profit selon les autres." [1]

It is not surprising that the shallowness of Gesenius and Hitzig, and the vagueness of Ewald, were profoundly obnoxious to those who resorted to the Scriptures simply and solely for supplies of spiritual life.[2] Even had the new exegesis been more free from rationalistic assumptions, it would have required unusual strength of faith to admit in practice (what most admit in words) that divine revelation is progressive, and that the records of it are not free from earthly dross. "It is not every interpreter who is able, like Luther and Calvin, to place his novel views in a light which shall appeal as strongly to the religious experience of the Christian as to the scholarly instincts of the learned. The rise of new difficulties is as essential to the progress of truth as the removal of old puzzles; and it not seldom happens that the defects of current opinions as to the sense of Scripture are most palpable to the man

---

[1] *Revue critique*, 7 mai, 1870.
[2] Some passages here are taken from my *Prophecies of Isaiah*, ii. 280, 281.

whose spiritual interest in Bible truths is weak. . . Thus the natural conservatism of those who study the Bible mainly for purposes of personal edification is often intensified by suspicion of the motives of innovating interpreters; and even so fruitful an idea as the doctrine of a gradual development of spiritual truth throughout the whole course of the Bible history has had to contend, from the days of Calvin down to our own time, with an obstinate suspicion that nothing but rationalism can make a man unwilling to find the maximum of developed spiritual truth in every chapter of Scripture."[1]

Only by such feelings as these can we account for the unvarying opposition of **Hengstenberg** (1802—1869) to the new criticism and exegesis—an opposition, I must add, intensified by his editorship of a Church newspaper,[2] which kept him in a continual atmosphere of party strife. Anxiety for his personal religion, which he had learned in the school of trial, and not of this or the other theologian, converted the youthful Hengstenberg into an ardent champion of revelation (as he conceived it), and a certain heaviness of the intellect (which no English reader of his works can fail to observe) made him regard any attempt, such as Bleek's, at a *via media*, as sophistry or self-delusion. Hengstenberg had no historical gifts, and

[1] Prof. W Robertson Smith, *British and Foreign Evangelical Review*, July 1876, p. 474.
[2] To the attacks upon Gesenius in this paper I have already referred. Neander marked his disapproval of them by ceasing to write for it. Gesenius was not the only sufferer.

never seems to have really assimilated that doctrine of development which, though rejected by Pietists on the one hand and Tridentine Romanists on the other, is so profoundly Christian. He was therefore indisposed to allow the human element in inspiration, denied the limited nature of the Old Testament stage of revelation, and, as Dorner[1] has pointed out, made prophecy nothing but the symbolic covering of the doctrines of Christianity. These, even in the opinion of not unfriendly judges, are grave faults which seriously detract from the value of Hengstenberg's work. It must be remembered, however, that the exegesis which he so earnestly opposed had been equally one-sided, and had still many infirmities to overcome. Even from a scientific point of view, it was desirable that the traditional theories should be once restated in a modern form, that they might be more completely overcome, and that justice might be done to any elements of truth which they might contain.

I need not say much respecting the outward life of this militant theologian, who would himself have been surprised at the company into which he has been thrown. It is fair to mention, however, that at the university he studied Aristotelian philosophy under Brandis, and Arabic still more eagerly under Freytag (who somewhat later had our own Pusey for a disciple). From Bonn he passed to

---

[1] *History of Protestant Theology*, ii. 436-7.

Berlin, to study theology under Neander and the youthful Tholuck. In 1825 he became licentiate of theology and *privatdocent*. The following year, Tholuck went to Halle, and Hengstenberg, partly through his learning, piety, and orthodoxy, partly through having married into an influential and only too zealous orthodox family, became the recognized head of the anti-rationalists of Berlin. In June 21, 1827, he put forth an announcement of his newspaper, the *Evangelische Kirchenzeitung*, and in 1828 the first numbers appeared. The controversial spirit of this famous Church organ gained him many enemies, and Pusey would, I am sure, have disapproved of the unseemly tone of the articles, and of the unworthy means which were adopted to support their attack on the liberties of theological professors. But I do not think it is fair for such or similar reasons to condemn Hengstenberg as bitterly as one of those great scholars whom we have lately lost (Lagarde) has been impelled to do. Hengstenberg was a good and sincerely pious man, though not what Lagarde with his English tastes would call a "gentleman." And the fact that he endeavoured, so far as he could, to modernize orthodoxy, deserves to be mentioned in his favour.

It is this fact which makes it possible to regard Hengstenberg as in a certain sense one of the "founders of criticism," especially for English and American students of the last generation. No one who looks into his various exegetical works can fail to see that

he was not a Church father "born out of due time,"
but rather that he had sat at the feet of Gesenius and
Ewald for grammar, and received some intellectual
stimulus both from the older and from the newer
rationalism. The latter point will be abundantly clear
to any one who will examine the theories on prophecy
expressed in his greater work, the *Christologie des A.
T.*[1] The book is ill translated, but should not be
altogether overlooked by students: it was a brave
attempt (such as Pusey with his Church views could
not have made) to save the citadel of orthodoxy at
the cost of some of the outworks. Of his other
works, I need only mention the *Beiträge zur Einleitung ins A. T.* (3 vols., 1831—1839), of which vol. i.
deals with Zechariah and Daniel, vols. ii. and iii.
with the "authenticity of the Pentateuch," and
the *Commentar über die Psalmen*.[2] It is needless to
say that on questions of the "higher criticism"
Hengstenberg is almost uniformly conservative.
Ecclesiastes indeed, unlike Pusey, he denies to
Solomon,[3] and in explaining the Psalms he admits
the representative character of the speaker so often
as to damage the case for the Davidic authorship to

---

[1] First edition, 2 vols., 1829—1835; second, 4 vols. 1854—1857 (recast). Translated in Clark's Theol. Library.

[2] First edition, 4 vols., 1842—1847; second, 1849—1852. Translated in Clark's Library.

[3] The historical background, says Hengstenberg, can only be the period of the Persian rule; the language is post-Exilic. The position of the book in the Canon confirms this view (*Der Prediger Salomo*, 1859, "Einleitung").

a very serious extent. Among the English-speaking scholars whom he introduced to a modernized conservatism (thus preparing the way for greater changes to come) is Joseph Addison Alexander, professor at Princeton Seminary, N.J., an accomplished linguist though not an original critic, known by two useful commentaries on Isaiah and on the Psalms, both of which (but especially the latter) are to a great extent a reproduction of Hengstenberg.

On April 21, 1828, a young student arrived at Berlin from Göttingen, who was destined for many years to be a thorn in Hengstenberg's side.[1] This was Wilhelm Vatke (born March 14, 1806), the son of the much-respected pastor of Behndorf, a village in the Prussian province of Saxony, not far from Helmstedt (in 1806 still a university town). His father (who was a near friend of the father of Gesenius) was an earnest rationalist in theology and a Kantian in philosophy. It was in the orchards and woods of Behndorf that Vatke drank in that love of trees which, together with the love of music, contributed so much to his happiness throughout life. On his father's death (1814), in the midst of war-troubles, the family moved to Helmstedt, where young Wilhelm received a good education, which was completed in the Latin school of the Waisenhaus at Halle. In 1824 Vatke began his university studies at Halle, and after four *semesters* spent in that

[1] I am much indebted here to the excellent memoir of Vatke by Benecke (1883).

famous seat of philology and theology, and three at Göttingen, he came, with a modest supply of funds, to the still more brilliant though younger university of Berlin. Seldom has a theological student been better prepared for critical studies. At his schools Vatke had enjoyed a thorough classical training, and at his two former universities he had been well grounded in the Semitic languages (Gesenius had passed his pupil on to Ewald), and had been interested in history and historical criticism, while from De Wette, all of whose books (at Gesenius's instigation) young Vatke had devoured, he had adopted the principle that "every truth is better than even the most edifying error, and a faith which is inconsistent with the truth cannot possibly be the right one."

Such was the young student who now came to Berlin to complete his theological studies. He had as yet no definite idea of becoming an Old Testament scholar. Theology was a wide field, and he wished to take a survey of the whole before selecting a field of more special study. Göttingen had never been strong in philosophy, while Berlin at this time counted Schleiermacher, Hegel, and Marheineke among its philosophers and philosophic theologians, besides being well provided with teachers in every other *fach* except that of the Old Testament. Let us note at the outset that Vatke was on the look-out for a deeper philosophy than either Wegscheider or even Fries and De Wette could supply. Also that he took up the study of philosophy in good earnest, and that he combined it with the study of historical theology in Neander's *Seminar*. Such a student of philosophy, if he ever returned to his first love (that of Old Testament research), was likely to throw some fresh light on the progress of religious thought and belief among the Israelites. But young Vatke was in no hurry to return. Hengstenberg, at that time a young, newly-appointed professor, failed entirely to attract him, not so much because he was not speculative (for Neander, whom Vatke liked, was not this), as because he had no historical sense, and barred the way of historical and philosophical inquiry. Vatke was therefore free to follow his own instincts, and told Neander that he should work longer at Arabic and Syriac and at the New Testament; inwardly, however, he had resolved to give his best time to the labour of fathoming the deepest philosophy of the age.

We must bear in mind that Vatke was one of those born scholars who can combine difficult subjects of study without becoming mere *dilettanti*. Thus at this period of his life we find him turning from Hegel to Church history, and then to Rabbinic (in which he had the tuition of Biesenthal). But beyond question his dominant interest (putting aside music) was in Hegel (not in Schleiermacher, be it observed), and it is a noteworthy fact that, directly he had mastered Hegel's system, the Old Testament began to appear to him in a new light. Starting from De Wette's conclusions, he went with intuitive certainty far beyond his teacher, and his clue to the labyrinth of critical problems he derived from Hegel. It was not strange that he should now think of lecturing on Old Testament subjects, especially as, by the exchange of Bleek [1] for Hengstenberg, the theological faculty was now without any representative of the "higher criticism" of the Old Testament. Vatke had no personal dislike to his slightly older rival, but could not abide the dangerous views and domineering spirit of one who so dreaded the light (*ich denke nicht gern an den lichtscheuen jungen Mann*). On public grounds, therefore, which even Neander could thoroughly estimate, it was needful for some one to oppose Hengstenberg on his own ground, and this was what Vatke did after his first *semester* as a lecturer. No doubt (as I have admitted) Vatke also obeyed the inner impulse of a pioneer. No sooner did the young Hegelian return to the Old Testament than the theory of his *Biblische Theologie* began to take shape. "Courageously he made a way for himself through untrodden fields, and his pioneering boldness counted for much in the attraction which he exercised upon the academic youth." [2]

It was in Vatke's second year as a *privatdocent* that Hegel died (Nov. 14, 1831), and only too soon afterwards followed the decease of Schleiermacher (Feb. 12, 1834). Both events were misfortunes for Vatke, though not in the same degree. To the

---

[1] See p. 143.   [2] Benecke, p. 59.

former of these teachers he owed the best part of his intellectual possessions; to the latter, endless food for reflection, but no lasting satisfaction. For Vatke's own sake, one is tempted to wish that his relations to Schleiermacher could have been different. His inner life would, as one thinks, have been somewhat more normal in its devoutness, and, granting this, we might perhaps have received from him a more sympathetic treatise on the history and meaning of the higher Old Testament religion—I do not here merely mean, a more readable book, but one which appeals more to one's religious sympathies. And then, who knows?—perhaps Schleiermacher himself might have been led to take a higher view of the best parts of the Old Testament than with all his devoutness he had been able to do. The wish, I say, is natural, but I am bound to add, that it is not one that could have been realized. It was probably impossible in those days to pick and choose among the treasures of Hegel—to receive stimulus and instruction from his Philosophy of History,[1] and there stop, without committing oneself to Hegelianism as a whole. And so Vatke suffered in some sort (if a non-speculative student may thus express himself) for the general good. The step which he was now about to take in the constructive criticism of the Old Testament could only have been taken by a thorough Hegelian; no other critic of his

---

[1] The fertilizing influence of Hegel on historical inquiry has been well pointed out by Pfleiderer, *Development of Theology*, p. 71.

time would so intuitively have discerned order in the midst of conflicting phenomena. And I hasten to add that if Vatke suffered some loss, it was not in the sphere of his moral character. If in him religion was far too much overlaid by theology, its presence was sufficiently proved by the fruits which it alone could have put forth. What De Wette was to theologians, Vatke has become to a larger circle of students by his exhibition of such truly Christian virtues as meekness under provocation, courtesy to opponents, friendliness to social or intellectual inferiors, contentment, unpretentiousness, inward collectedness, resignation.[1]

In the year 1835 appeared two remarkable books, one of which has passed through edition after edition, whereas the other may still be obtained new in its original edition—two remarkable books, the less successful of which, from a commercial point of view, commands much more general assent among competent students than its fellow. These books are—Strauss's *Leben Jesu* and Vatke's *Die biblische Theologie wissenschaftlich dargestellt*, Band i.[2] Into the relation of the two writers and their respective books

---

[1] See especially the tribute paid to Vatke in his lifetime by Delitzsch's friend and collaborator J. H. R. Biesenthal, author of *Das Trostschreiben des Apostels Paulus an die Hebräer*, 1878 (who, as we have seen, instructed Vatke in Rabbinic), Benecke, p. 620.

[2] The second title-page calls the book *Die Religion des Alten Testamentes nach den kanonischen Büchern entwickelt*, Erster Theil.

it is not necessary to enter here. Suffice it to say that, while the *Leben Jesu* addressed itself to the thousands of ordinary educated readers, the *Biblische Theologie* appealed solely and entirely to professional theologians. This needs, I think, to be emphasized. The author even went to the extreme of refusing all readers but those who understood the Hegelian terminology. He thus lost many of the most qualified judges; a glance at the table of contents was enough to deter Reuss, and of those who read the book we may conjecture that not half did justice to its underlying historical criticism. That this was an error in judgment, Vatke himself afterwards saw. It is true that his insight into the development of the higher religion of Israel was quickened by his Hegelianism, but his conclusions were not philosophical but historical, and could to a large extent have been justified without the help of an abstruse philosophizing. A convenient summary of these results will be found in Pfleiderer's *Development of Theology*, but the student will do well to glance at some of the pages of the book itself. Whether readable or not, the treatise is at any rate admirably arranged, and the central idea, round which all the details group themselves, is one which is no longer the heresy of a few,—viz. that the religion of Israel, like all other movements of thought or belief, is subject (we need not at present ask for qualifications) to the law of development. Many of the details moreover are such as now commend themselves to an increasing number of students. Notice for instance the clear distinction drawn by Vatke between the religion of the Old Testament and nature-worship in all its forms; he points out *e.g.* how even in such a relatively pure religion as Mazdeism the conception of creation differs in some points from that of Hebraism (p. 603). Vatke sees moreover that the true standard of Old Testament religion is that supplied by the prophets (p. 593), and for the first time forms an equitable judgment upon Jewish "particularism" (pp. 614—617). For "higher criticism" too the book furnishes many valuable hints. Wilhelm Vatke in this work and Leopold George[1] (in his *Die älteren Jüdischen Feste*, 1835) independently put forward what is now becoming the prevalent view on the date of the Levitical legislation; Vatke has also again and again extremely acute critical theories on the prophetical writings (*e.g.* on Joel's and on Isa. xxiv.—xxvii.) and on the Hagiographa. Surely to have produced such a book in 1835 entitles a man to a high place among the "founders of criticism."

That the book has many faults, is not less obvious. Though the author admits the religious importance of highly gifted individuals (p. 645), it is doubtful[1] whether he does justice to their intuitional originality, and whether he recognizes at all adequately

---

[1] Von Bohlen too in the same year published his view that Deuteronomy was composed under Josiah, but the rest of the Pentateuch not before the Exile (*Genesis historisch-kritisch erläutert*, 1835).

the germs of New Testament religion contained in the Old Testament. It stands to reason moreover that a number of details have been rendered uncertain by subsequent critical and archæological research. Vatke himself in his later years retracted his speculations on Saturn, and became willing to modify his statement on the symbolism of the temple. It is a still greater fault, from the point of view of the "higher criticism," that the sharp-sighted author gives no prolegomena on the critical analysis of the Hexateuch. Most important questions of analysis were still but half solved, and if Vatke would not contribute to solve them, how could he expect the literary critics to attend to his solution of the less pressing historical problems? And yet from the most competent judges, such as De Wette, Nitzsch, and Ewald,[1] most gratifying words were heard, qualifying and mitigating an almost unavoidable rejection of the main positions of the book, while in our own day one critic vies with another[2] in admiration of a writer who was so much before his age.

However little effect he may have had as an author, as a lecturer Vatke was among the most successful of his time till the fatal year 1849. In 1837 he became extraordinary professor, and in 1841 published his second great work, called *Human Freedom in its Relation to Sin and the Divine Grace.* This is not

[1] Ewald however was not always so equitable. Both in books and in lectures he afterwards violently opposed Vatke.
[2] See especially Wellhausen, *History of Israel.*

the place to discuss this remarkable piece of constructive speculation. One may remark however that Vatke's genius was clearly more synthetic than analytic, and that consequently we need not be surprised at his slowness to publish. Moreover after 1849 various influences contributed to lessen Vatke's productivity. Fear of failing in their examinations through knowing too much kept away students from his lectures; and within his own mind a change was going forward in his relation to Hegel, whom he no longer regarded as a philosophical Messiah. One may ask whether Vatke's critical attitude towards Hegel does not partly explain the change in his opinions on the origin of the Pentateuch. In his posthumous *Introduction to the Old Testament* (1886), published from the manuscript of his academical lectures, these striking sentences occur:—

"In the year 1835 two writers came forward, who sought to prove that the Elohim-document cannot have been written before the Exile, viz. Vatke himself and George. Graf adhered to this view, and Reuss in Strassburg has also asserted that there could be no rest for criticism till it had been proved that this legislation was the later. But it can be shown that those priestly laws proceed from the author of the Elohim-document, and that he is older than the Jehovist and the Deuteronomic writer . . . In order to explain the Elohim-document historically, we must ascribe to its author the large plan of a reform of the entire life (of the nation), which was probably occasioned by Hezekiah's partial reformation."[1]

Elsewhere Vatke expresses his view thus:—

"The priestly writer knew the second Elohist; he therefore wrote after 716, towards the end of the eighth or at the beginning of the seventh century, probably in the last years of Hezekiah, and was perhaps one of those who brought about the reform of the cultus undertaken by that king." "The priestly supplementer of the Elohim-document (the author of Lev. xvii.—xx., xxvi., Num. xxxiii. 52—56) forms the transition from the older form of representation to Deuteronomy. . . . We shall have to place this writer immediately after the Jehovist, perhaps in the middle of the seventh century, so that the work which he closed consisted of the writings of the second Elohist, the Elohim-document, and of the Jehovist. This work was found in 624, and it was the supplementing additions (perhaps made with a view to publication) which produced such a deep impression on Josiah."[2]

This change of opinion shows, first, the comparative isolation in which Vatke lived, rarely quitting his beautiful Berlin domain; secondly, his love of truth, and willingness to correct himself to the best of his

---

[1] Vatke, *Einleitung*, p. 402.

[2] *Ibid.* pp. 388-89. Vatke's view on the date of Deuteronomy (which he places in the last ten years of the kingdom of Judah) is the same in both his books. It is connected with his theory on the law-book found by Hilkiah in the temple (on which see Kuenen, *Hexateuch*, p. 216).

ability. It does not however perhaps do much credit to his critical sagacity, and has been passed over in respectful silence by contemporary critics. It is of course possible that, had Vatke been able to work out his later theories for the press, he might have been led to question their soundness. But he put this off too long; in his last days the requisite mental elasticity was wanting. His last great pleasure was the grateful recognition given to him by the theological faculties of Berlin and Jena, and by many of his old pupils,[1] on the occasion of his jubilee as an academical teacher. As long as he could, he amused himself with his favourite composer Bach, and died peacefully April 19, 1882.

Our next "founder of criticism" was in many respects most unlike Vatke. Friedrich Bleek was an able and truth-loving critic, but like Reuss strongly opposed to an *à priori* construction of history. Born in Holstein, July 4, 1793, he spent his first two years of academic study at Kiel. But more important for his development were his student-years at Berlin (1814—1817), where he came into close contact with De Wette, Neander, and Schleiermacher. By the influence of these friendly teachers he was appointed theological *repetent* (tutorial fellow), and succeeded so well as a teacher that he was nominated by the

---

[1] Among those who attended his lectures even after 1849 was the New Testament critic Heinrich Holtzmann, who in his *Einleitung* (1885, Pref. p. viii) ascribes his interest in criticism entirely to Vatke.

minister Altenstein to an extraordinary professorship. But—who could have believed it?—that same terrible police, which ruined De Wette, interfered to check De Wette's pupil, and it was not till the end of 1823 that the official notice of his appointment was given.[1] At Berlin Bleek remained till the end of 1828, when he moved to the new university of Bonn, thus leaving the field clear at Berlin for the two opposing powers —Hengstenberg and Vatke. There he worked with much acceptance for thirty years. He passed away suddenly in the midst of his devoted labours for the university and the Church, Feb. 27, 1859.

Bleek had a more harmonious development than his master De Wette, and supplies an example of easier imitation. He was one of those divines who (to use his own words), "with all their susceptibility to the teaching of revelation, refuse to identify the Word of God and Holy Scripture, and regard it as their primary object to discern the Word of God *in* Holy Scripture." His essentially evangelical character cannot be denied, but the *via media* which he put forward failed to satisfy, not only Hengstenberg, but even such a sensible English churchman as Canon Venables, to whose only too balanced commendations we may partly ascribe the failure of the English translation of Bleek's *Introduction to the Old Testament*.[2] Certainly few books of German origin were

---

[1] Kamphausen in Herzog-Plitt's *Encycl.*
[2] See preface to English edition (2 vols., 1869). Probably, however, the blame must be shared by Mr Venables the translator.

more fitted to succeed, and no English scholar being ready to provide a substitute, one would have thought that our Church leaders would have recognized the duty of pressing the claims of Bleek, as I ventured to do myself in 1870.[1] But it was not to be. Colenso's brave but ill-regulated criticism was not to be welcomed as the first step towards something better, but to be put down, and the Church has had to suffer the bitter consequences. It is right however to scan some of the features of the book which ought to have done so much for us. Let us notice then, (*a*) that Bleek's *Introduction* is not a mere handbook, but can be read with pleasure. Though it does not go deeply into disputable points, what it gives is full enough and clear enough to be taken in. (*b*) That its critical tone is not negative, but positive; it avoids the faults of the early editions of De Wette's handbook. (*c*) It does not aim at giving a complete and consistent critical history of the Old Testament literature; it does but make contributions to this (see preface of the German editors). The student therefore is not in danger of supposing that his teacher is "biassed." Of course, this attitude was somewhat easier in Bleek's time than it is in ours. (*d*) Though the book is in the main non-theological, the author does not disguise his own theological stand-point. Like all our leading critics, he has a positive theology (though not a theological *system*), to which upon due occasion

[1] Review of Schrader's edition of De Wette's *Introduction*. *Academy* (Aug. 13, 1870).

(see *e. g.* § 193) he refers, and his theology is that genuine historical evangelical theology, which in the Anglican Church appears as yet to have only a few scattered representatives.

May I not venture to say that by producing such a book (based as it is upon the academical teaching of many years) Bleek would have established **his** claim to be one of the "founders of criticism," even if **he** had done nothing more? One may cheerfully grant that many of the conclusions of the book **are** now out of date. In Pentateuch criticism, for instance, he now appears far too conservative. When for instance the venerable K. J. Nitzsch (one of the most earnest opponents of Vatke) reckons among Bleek's merits " the proof of the Mosaic age of fundamental laws of the Pentateuch and of the historicity of the scaffolding of the patriarchal narrative," we hesitate to give full assent, knowing that there was much crudeness in the views of Bleek, and having lost that dread of an "attenuation" (*Verdünnung*) of Abraham and Moses[1] which beset the reviewers of Vatke's *Biblische Theologie.* But in his own day such conservative-liberalism as Bleek's was a wholesome element of thought. **And** plain, not to say self-evident, as his remarks **on** the Book **of Daniel** may **now** seem, we must not forget that by his early dissertation on " the authorship and object of Daniel " Bleek contributed much **to** make them so. Nor have

---

[1] See Nitzsch, in Benecke, *Wilhelm Vatke,* p. 216 ; **cf. p. 551.**

all Old Testament scholars yet reached to the very moderate degree of critical progress indicated in Bleek's important paragraphs on the analysis of Isa. xl.—lxvi. Altogether, one may safely say that Keil's unfavourable judgment on Bleek's *Introduction* is not justified.

It has not yet been mentioned that the work referred to is a posthumous publication. The first edition came out in 1860, under the care of Johannes Bleek and Adolf Kamphausen. In 1878 the book appeared in a much altered form, which seemed to the publisher to be dictated by the altered aspect of critical problems. The editor was Julius Wellhausen, who re-wrote parts of it, and would doubtless have re-written more, but for the fear of seeming to anticipate the opinion of scholars on his own recent articles on the composition of the Hexateuch. This fourth edition is therefore virtually a criticism (and a valuable one it is) on Bleek's *Introduction to the Old Testament*.[1] Nor is this the only posthumous work of Bleek. In 1862 his *Introduction to the New Testament* was published,[2] and in the same year his *Synoptical Explanation of the Three First Gospels*, and his *Lectures on the Apocalypse;* in 1865, his *Lectures on Colossians, Philippians, and Ephesians*,

---

[1] In ed. 5 (1886) much of the editorial element has been withdrawn.

[2] In the third and fourth editions (cared for by Mangold) the views given by Bleek have been considerably modified (see B. Weiss's review, *Theol. Lit.-Ztg.*, Jan. 8, 1876. The English translation (by Urwick) is made from the second German edition.

and his *Lectures on the Epistle to the Hebrews*. And before passing on, I may remark that Bleek is even more important in the exegesis of the New Testament than in that of the Old. His great work on the Epistle to the Hebrews (1828-36-40) is neglected by none of our best scholars, and his second larger work, *Contributions to the Criticism of the Gospels* (1846), is especially important in the annals of the criticism of the Fourth Gospel. The latter book was dedicated to Bleek's old teacher De Wette, upon whom it evidently produced a deep impression.[1] The positive tendency of Bleek on the Johannine question reminds us that he was a devoted pupil of Schleiermacher.

In fact, the relations between De Wette and his younger friends Bleek and Lücke illustrate one of the most pleasing traits in the character of the former, viz. his willingness to receive suggestions from his juniors. He never himself reached such positive views either on the historicity of the Pentateuch or on the authorship of the Fourth Gospel as Bleek, but he let himself be impressed by Bleek's arguments. In 1822 the latter, at that time merely a theological *repetent*, published in Rosenmüller's *Repertorium*[2] (Bd. i.) an article called "Some Aphoristic Contributions to Pentateuch Researches," which, as Westphal remarks, produced a sensation. "Bleek parut, sans hardiësse et sans passion : on l'écouta."[3] De Wette was the foremost

---

[1] See quotations in Watkins, *Bampton Lectures* for 1890, p. 309.   [2] Cf. Bleek's *Introd.* § 74.
[3] *Les sources du Pentateuque*, i. 166.

to admit the weight of Bleek's objections, and retreated (in the third edition of his *Introduction*) from his most advanced positions. Later on (in his fifth edition) the same candid critic accepted from Bleek and Tuch the famous Supplement-hypothesis, towards which he himself in his *Beiträge* had been unconsciously moving—*i.e.* the hypothesis that an Elohistic *Grundschrift* or "fundamental writing" (as Tuch first called it) was "worked over" and supplemented by a second writer commonly called the Yahvist. For Bleek's view on this subject see (besides the *Introd.*) his *De libri Geneseos origine atque indole historicâ observationes quædam contra Bohlenium*[1] (1836). I part from this truly Christian scholar with sympathy, though as a critic I cannot think that he was sufficiently keen. Among his other works I would mention his epoch-making dissertation on the origin and composition of the Sibylline Oracles (Schleiermacher's *Zeitschrift*, 1819-20), and his inquiry into the origin of Zech. ix.—xiv. (*Theol. Stud. u. Kritiken*, 1852, pp. 247—332; see also Bleek's *Introd.*), the results of which should be compared with those of De Wette in his *Introduction*.

[1] Bleek's criticisms of von Bohlen's *Genesis* illustrate the difference between himself and Hitzig. The latter also reviewed von Bohlen (*Theol. Stud. u. Krit.* 1837); he found something to praise, but more to blame, or at least to reject. But whereas Bleek charges von Bohlen with *protervia* and *arrogantia*, Hitzig declares that the censure is unmerited; he can only see the *Keckheit* of a young scholar rejoicing in his strength.

CHAPTER VII.

HUPFELD—DELITZSCH.

It is natural to pass from Friedrich Bleek to **Hermann Hupfeld**, who stands in the same rank as a clear-headed, accurate, dispassionate, and fundamentally devout scholar.[1] Looking at the early history of the latter as described by himself, one can see that it throws much light on his character as a scholar. He was born March 31, 1796, at Marburg. His father was a pastor who held the usual rationalistic views in no extreme form, but at the age of thirteen the lad passed into the house of an uncle, a pastor of "pietistic" views, who carefully superintended his studies, but was compelled to leave him for many hours alone. The consequence was that while on the one hand the inquisitive boy made great progress in his studies, on the other he became too thoughtful and critical for his years, and was without the stimulus

---

[1] A *Lebens- und Charakterbild* of Hupfeld was published by his pupil and friend Eduard Riehm (now himself deceased); Kamphausen's article in Herzog-Plitt contains a good summary of facts, with an appreciative estimate of Hupfeld as a man and a scholar.

supplied to the imagination by history and poetry. From a religious point of view, he gained much from this residence with his uncle; he became heartily attached to Christian truth, and desired nothing better than to become a pastor himself. So, after spending a year and a half at the gymnasium at Hersfeld, young Hupfeld matriculated at the Hessian university of Marburg. There he came under the influence of a decided supernaturalist, A. J. Arnoldi, who, though not famous in research, was an eminent teacher, and grounded him in Arabic and Syriac as well as in Hebrew philology. But it was entirely by his own efforts that, after leaving the university, he reached a view of the Old Testament, independent of modern theological theories, and equally satisfactory to his historical and to his religious sense. The charm of the view which thus opened itself to him was so great, that he felt that only as an academical teacher could he do his best work, and that, " cost what it might," he must obtain admission to this office.

It became necessary therefore to resume his student life, and after a year and a half's quiet study, he went to Halle in 1824, not so much however, as it would seem, for training (for he only remained in Halle a year), as for stimulus. In 1825 he first lectured as *privatdocent* at Marburg, and as an extraordinary professor. In the same year he won his spurs as a grammarian. For more than a hundred years Ethiopic philology had been almost entirely neglected, and it was Hupfeld who, by his *Exercitationes Æthi-*

opicæ (published in 1825), gave the first impulse to a resumption of this study. Soon after, he became full professor, and the following years were the happiest of his life, not only because of his love for Marburg, but because they were the years of wedded happiness. In 1843 Hupfeld had the honour of being called to Halle as successor of Gesenius, and scarcely three months afterwards (Jan. 1844) he lost his "angelic" wife by low fever.

There is little more to tell about Hupfeld's outward history. At Halle, where he had the illustrious Semitist Rödiger for a colleague, he exercised a wide and beneficial influence on theological students. Surely his path ought to have been a smooth one. How Gesenius was treated by Hengstenberg, we have seen; but Hupfeld was very different religiously from his predecessor. It is therefore strange indeed to have to report that in 1865 he was delated to the Prussian government as an irreverent critic of divine revelation—a charge which the entire theological faculty of Halle university, including Tholuck and Julius Müller, repelled on his behalf. Soon afterwards (April 24, 1866) this unweariable worker passed to "where beyond these voices there is peace." Something must however be added on his philological and theological position. I have already compared him to Bleek. It is true, he did not belong like Bleek to a definite theological school. Bleek was and remained a disciple of Schleiermacher; Hupfeld, on the other hand, came from the school of the old-fashioned supernaturalist Arnoldi, and when he ceased to think with his teacher, he does not appear to have put himself under another master. Now Hupfeld's own tendencies were, not philosophical, but philological. A historical view of the Biblical literature, and of the progress of the kingdom of God, gave him basis enough for his own personal theology. In practical Church matters he evinced a profound interest, but in a theological dispute he but once took part (1861); it was to counteract the theosophic theology of Hofmann of Erlangen (the friend of Delitzsch), which no doubt had an exegetical basis.[1] Hupfeld and Bleek moreover had somewhat different fields of work. The former concentrated himself more upon the Old Testament, and was specially attracted by the problems of Old Testament philology and exegesis: he thus became the fitting successor of Gesenius. And though both agreed, as I have said, in certain high moral qualities, yet there was a sharpness in Hupfeld's manner from which Bleek was entirely free, and which is certainly no essential characteristic of a truth-loving man. To Hupfeld's inconsiderate condemnation of Delitzsch, that lovable scholar replied in the gentlest terms, which pricked the conscience of Hupfeld, and awakened echoes of happier days.[2] We must not

---

[1] As Baudissin says, "Die Erlanger 'Heilsgeschichte' ist keine eigentliche Geschichte. Sie besteht darin, dass ein im Himmel von vornherein fertiges Gefüge in seinen einzelnen Gliedern allmählich herniedersteigt in das Irdische" (review of Delitzsch's *Iris*).

[2] Preface to second edition of Delitzsch's *Psalms*.

forget the great sorrow which had befallen the Halle professor in 1844, and also the intense dislike of Hupfeld to mysticism.

By his special linguistic work, our scholar early won a deserved reputation. His Hebrew Grammar (1841) unhappily remained a *torso*, but again and again he returned to grammatical and lexicographical subjects, and once he resumed the study of Ethiopic. His dissertations on certain obscure and misunderstood passages of the history of the text of the Old Testament (*Theol. Stud. u. Krit.* 1830, 1837) were also fruitful in important results. But his two great works are, 1. *The Sources of Genesis, and the Mode of their Combination, investigated anew* (1853), and 2. *The Psalms, translated and expounded* (4 vols. 1855—1861). Of the former it is possible to speak in the highest terms. Ilgen's discovery of the second Elohist had (as we have seen) to be made over again, and it was Hupfeld's good fortune, or rather merit, to make it. He also showed clearly that each of the three documents of Genesis was originally an independent work, upon which, as Mr. Addis remarks,[1] the Supplement-hypothesis came to a natural end. Of the latter I find it more difficult to speak as I could wish. No doubt, upon its appearance it exercised on the whole a healthy influence both upon criticism and upon exegesis. It uttered a not unjustified protest against extravagances of all sorts, in linguistics, in Biblical theology, and in the

---

[1] See his sketch of Hupfeld's work, *The Documents of the Hexateuch*, Introd. pp. xxviii—xxix.

"higher criticism," in which third department it continued the work of De Wette. What it says is always worth reading; Hupfeld's eye was constantly directed on facts, and if he did not see all the facts, nor always explain or combine them aright, this does not render his laborious work superfluous. For my own part, I think that Hupfeld's conclusions are very often erroneous. He is far too unsuspicious in his attitude towards the received text, and is wooden in his exegesis. In his Biblical theology he is not profound or comprehensive enough, though only ignorance can excuse Dr. Binnie's suggestion that he is "incompetent in matters lying within the domain of spiritual religion."[1] And in the "higher criticism" he errs by defect even more than Hitzig errs by excess of daring. Nor does he, so far as I know, redeem his comparative failure as a critic of the Psalter by luminous suggestions on the "higher criticism" of other books (except indeed to some extent on that of Genesis). All that he says, for instance, about the origin of Joel is that the Book has not yet been understood,[2] though in all essentials Vatke already understood it in 1835.[3] Still, Hupfeld's historical position among critics is well assured. Not only did he contribute to the linguistic

---

[1] *The Psalms, their History, Teachings, and Use* (1886), p. 144. Against Dr. Binnie, it is enough to refer to Riehm's decisive statements in his *Lebensbild*. I concur with this writer however in his unfavourable criticism upon Hupfeld's view of the Tora-psalms.

[2] Kamphausen in Herzog-Plitt vi. 383, note.

[3] *Biblische Theologie*, pp. 462-3.

basis of criticism, not **only** did he seek to restrain **some too** eager spirits, not only did he write the *Quellen der Genesis*, but **he** manfully defended the rights of criticism within the Church in a time of theological and political reaction.

There are still perhaps some theologians left who hesitate to recognize the "scientific" (*wissenschaftlich*) character of the work of **Franz Delitzsch**,[1] and I will candidly admit that just as there are many half-theologians, so Delitzsch is but a half-critic.[2] But that is no reason for excluding him from my series of "founders of criticism." Eichhorn too was only a half-critic, and yet he was a "founder"; and no one more than Delitzsch has helped to win for critics their full rights of citizenship in the historic Christian Churches. Nowhere, too, can it be more clearly seen how largely investigation may be influenced by the idiosyncrasy of the investigator than in the life of

---

[1] Much of this chapter appeared in the *Guardian*, April 9, 1890. About the same time (April 5) Prof. Graf. v. Baudissin published in the *Theol. Lit.-Zeitung* a most delicate character-sketch of his **revered** teacher, nominally as a review **of** Delitzsch's *Iris*. It has been translated in the *Expositor*, June 1890. From a Jewish point of view we have a graceful sketch by Prof. Kaufmann, *Jewish Quarterly Review*, 1890, p. 386, &c. **A short but** trustworthy biography has been published by Dr. S. I. Curtiss (T. & T. Clark, 1891). The authoritative memoir by W Faber is still delayed.

[2] As a literary critic of the Old Testament Delitzsch had certainly not reached the limit of his possible concessions; a historical critic he never professed to be. Cf. Curtiss's article, "Delitzsch on the Pentateuch," *Presbyterian Review*, 1882, pp. 553—588.

Delitzsch. And lastly, I should be sadly wanting in gratitude if I did not recognize the bond of sympathy which (since 1871) united the old professor and myself. Delitzsch had an attraction for me, partly because he was so lovable, and partly because he was a psychological puzzle. I noted with interest his strangely blended character and opinions—his insistence on spiritual experience as a condition of successful exegesis, his combination of mystical philosophy and sober, accurate philology, his fondness for relieving a too arid discussion by a flashing subtlety or paradox, his love for the ideas of the Bible, which to him were as much facts as the best attested external events. Nor must I forget to mention his tolerance (without which indeed he could not have been the virtuoso in friendship that he was), his love of the young (to whom he unbosomed himself more completely perhaps than to the old), and his passion for poetry and for flowers. Those who would form an idea of Delitzsch in his lighter moods would do well to read a volume of popular essays by him called *Iris* (1888), of which there exists a good translation.

The story of Delitzsch's outward life is simple. He was born at Leipzig, Feb. 23, 1813. The reign of rationalism in that famous Protestant town was drawing to a close; but it was not at the gymnasium, but at the university, that Delitzsch first came under evangelical religious influences. He says himself, "The person of Jesus Christ remained shrouded in mist for me till my university time began in 1831.

He remained so, as long as I sought truth and satisfaction in philosophy, through the fascination of Fichte." Friendship was already the blessing of his life, and some earnest-minded friends made evangelical religion, in the form which it assumed at that time, a reality to him. Delitzsch ever remembered the day and hour of his great spiritual change—one of those points in which he differed from mere traditional forms of religion. Even in old age he declared that he still loved to remember the days when the soul-struggles which he witnessed rendered scientific arrogance distasteful to him for ever.[1] In 1832 he became a student of theology. This was the year of the publication of Zunz's *Die gottesdienstlichen Vorträge der Juden*, and three years after appeared Vatke's *Biblische Theologie (Die Religion des A. T.)*,—the former a work of immediate importance for his studies, the latter destined to influence him indirectly through Wellhausen. It is important to notice that young Delitzsch came under no great theologian's personal influence. At Berlin there were Schleiermacher, Marheineke (the disciple of Hegel in dogmatic theology), Neander, Hengstenberg. Who was there to match these great luminaries at Leipzig? There was, no doubt, Winer, a devout man and a specialist

---

[1] See "The Deep Gulf between the Old Theology and the New," an address delivered at a pastoral conference, and translated in the *Expositor*, 1889 (1); and comp. the qualifications of Delitzsch's two fervid statements in my letter, *Guardian*, Jan. 9, 1889.

of the best kind (see his Chaldee and Greek Testament Grammars), and there was August Hahn, who not only met rationalism by argument, but penetrated Leipzig by a warm Christian spirit; but neither of them had a faculty for the deepest problems. I think that this seeming misfortune was really a gain for Delitzsch. He was too original to be moulded; himself was his best teacher, or rather, as we shall see, Providence guided him step by step, so that his life was a continuous self-education. Perhaps a more complete historical training in philosophy might not have hurt him. He was attracted by Heinroth, the psychologist, but a turn for mysticism and theosophy, fostered doubtless by his deep Jewish studies, seems to have interfered with his progress. At any rate the result in later years showed a singular absence of sound method in philosophical study. In one point, however, Leipzig had perhaps more to offer Delitzsch than Berlin. Fürst was a greater Hebrew scholar than Biesenthal (afterwards a missionary to the German Jews and Delitzsch's fast friend), and in the young Arabist Fleischer Leipzig possessed the man whom all European scholars were to acknowledge as their leader. What Fürst and Delitzsch were to each other may be learned from the preface to Fürst's *Hebrew Concordance* (1840); what Fleischer was to Delitzsch appears from many philological notes marked *Fl.* in the commentaries of the latter, and from Delitzsch's *Festgabe* on the jubilee of his teacher, *Jüdisch-arabische Poesieen aus vormohammed-*

anischer Zeit; ein Specimen aus *Fleischer's Schule* (1874).

Delitzsch had now a well-defined aim. He had begun to learn Hebrew at the gymnasium. But it was the apparent accident of his meeting two agents of the London Missionary Society for Promoting Christianity among the Jews which made him "draw all his cares and studies this way"—viz. to make the Old Testament better known to Christians, and the New Testament to Jews. Between 1835, when he became Dr. Phil., and 1842, when he became a *privat-docent*, he lived entirely for his studies and for religion. Oriental and religious books began to appear at frequent intervals. In 1836 came out a charmingly written book on the history of post-Biblical Jewish poetry (*Zur Geschichte jüdischer Poesie*); in 1837, M. Ch. Luzzatto's מגדל עז, a Hebrew adaptation of Guarini's *Pastor Fido*, edited from an Italian MS.; in 1838 *Wissenschaft, Kunst, Judenthum; Schilderungen und Kritiken*, and *Jesurun, seu Isagoge in grammaticam et lexicographiam linguæ Hebraicæ*, in which, as a disciple of Fürst, young Delitzsch expressed etymological views which he afterwards found cause to abandon (see the criticism by his son, Friedrich Delitzsch, *Studien über Indogermanisch-Semitische Wurzelverwandtschaft*, 1873, pp. 6, 7). I mention this, not to disparage Delitzsch, but as a proof that genius may shoot wildly at first, and yet afterwards hit the mark. In 1839, the year of the Reformation jubilee, the young doctor's heart was hot within him, and he openly joined the strict Lutheran party, to whose critical organ, edited by Rudelbach and Guerike, he shortly afterwards became a contributor (it was here that he printed those valuable Talmudic illustrations of Greek Testament phraseology which so well deserve to be reprinted). The literary monument of this period bears the speaking title, *Lutherthum und Lügenthum*. Let us say at once that Delitzsch never wavered in his theological allegiance. I do not think he was ever tempted to do so. "By the banner of our Lutheran confession let us stand," he said in 1888; "folding ourselves in it, let us die."

The year 1841 is marked by a singular book, dedicated to "the scattered confessors of the Lord," and entitled *Philemon oder das Buch von der Freundschaft in Christo*. It consists of essays on Christian friendship, signed with initials which have since been interpreted—" c "= Fräulien von Klettenberg; " x "= her younger sister, Marie Magdalena; " p "= Friedrich Carl von Moser, a statesman and author of the last century; and " d "= the editor, Delitzsch himself. Grace of style there is none; but as an expression of the inner life of the authors, especially of the *schöne Seele*, for whom Goethe had so tender a reverence, these fourteen essays have an interest of their own. How Delitzsch obtained the manuscripts is not stated, but I remember his telling me of his friendly relations with Walther von Goethe. In 1844 he published one of the most popular altar manuals of the Lutheran Church, for which special thanks were rendered to

God by one of the speakers at the service of March 7
—*Das Sacrament des wahren Leibes und Blutes Christi*.
This shows how thoroughly he combined the High
Churchman and the scholar. Meantime, in conjunction with Fleischer, he had been cataloguing the
Oriental manuscripts of the city library, at the conclusion of which task he published some *anecdota* on
the mediæval scholasticism among Jews and Moslems
(1841). He now (March 3, 1842) acquired the right
of lecturing by a dissertation on the life and age of
Habakkuk, which was followed in 1843 by an exhaustive philological commentary on the same prophet,
a companion volume to the *Obadiah* of his friend
Caspari (better known to some by his elaborate work
on *Micah*, and by his Arabic Grammar, which the late
Professor W. Wright adopted as the basis of his own).

But why was not Delitzsch a professor? His call
did not come till 1846, when he succeeded Hofmann
at the small university of Rostock; he had married
the year before. But he was not to be long in this
northern home. In 1850 he joined the author of the
Weissagung und Erfüllung and the *Schriftbeweis* at
Erlangen. For sixteen delightful years the friends
worked together.[1] The "Erlangen school" became
almost as famous as that of Tübingen. It seemed as
if the orthodoxy for the new age were about to be
found. Hengstenberg's criticisms and apologetics

[1] The theological correspondence of the friends was published
by Prof. Volck in 1891 (cf. *Expositor*, 1891 (1), pp. 241 &c.
361 &c.).

were alike mechanical; Hofmann and Delitzsch agreed in rejecting them. They sought something better, but it must be confessed that not even Delitzsch (though, as he assures us, he had already "taken up the standpoint of free inquiry") was at all a scientific critic when he went to Erlangen, and his theories of prophecy, not less than those of Hofmann, bear the stamp of immaturity. Hofmann's works I have mentioned; Delitzsch had already entered the field with his *Die biblisch-prophetische Theologie* in 1845, the theosophic element in which, partly derived from Crusius, he must afterwards have greatly modified. Delitzsch's first Erlangen book had indeed nothing to do with prophecy. But it was not unconnected with Hofmann's prophetic theories. Hofmann's view of the Song of Songs was, if I understand right, that it had a typical or *quasi*-prophetic character, arising out of the contemporary historical situation. Delitzsch was dissatisfied with this view, and proposed another which, with more right than Hofmann's, may be called the typical. The work in which it appears, *Das Hohelied untersucht und ausgelegt* (1851), is not now on the list of Delitzsch's publications, but the view is still endorsed in his later book. In 1852 appeared the first edition of his important work on *Genesis*. Important I may already call it, though Delitzsch himself thought but little of the early editions. There are no doubt startling peculiarities in his explanation of Gen. i.—iii., which brought upon him the sarcasms of less devout writers. But by his distinct assertion of the composite authorship of the book, Delitzsch thoroughly proves his own title to speak in the conclave of critics. In 1853 he ventured to touch the problem of the composition of the Gospels (*Untersuchungen über die kanonischen Evangelien*), but his comparison of the structure of the Pentateuch was not helpful. In 1855 he returned to philosophical speculations. The *System of Biblical Psychology* has interested and perplexed not a few English readers. This is not entirely the fault of the translator. There is a touch of Talmudic condensation in much of Delitzsch's writing; in the *Psychology* there was the additional rock of "newly coined words and daring ideas" (author's letter in the translator's preface). Still, wherever light pierces through, striking suggestions are seldom wanting. He attempts too much, of course, but there is more to be learned from Delitzsch when he is wrong than from ten ordinary men when they are right.

The year 1857 saw the publication of two less brilliant but really more important works—the critical appendix to Drechsler's *Isaiah* (edited by Delitzsch and H. A. Hahn) and the commentary on Hebrews. The former is important for the subtle theory mentioned below, the latter for its masterly treatment of a subject specially appropriate to a Hebraist. The suggestion of a work on Hebrews may have come from Hofmann. That eminently original theologian, in commenting on passages of Hebrews in his *Schriftbeweis*, had propounded a theory of the Atonement which gave rise to a trying controversy. Probably on this account Delitzsch wrote his commentary, at the end of which is a dissertation on the "sure Scriptural basis" of the ecclesiastical doctrine of vicarious substitution. In 1859-60 a still greater treasure was given to the Church by one who had more than most a natural affinity to the subject. It was fit that "*aller Heiligen Büchlein*" (the Psalter) should be commented upon by the loving hand of Franz Delitzsch, and one regrets that Hupfeld, a dry though not undevout scholar, should have accused the book of faulty taste and Rabbinic philology. That Delitzsch's later editions are the best both from a literary and from a philological point of view is certain, but the first edition (which I have never seen) cannot be so vastly inferior to the succeeding ones as to deserve such a criticism. One is glad that Hupfeld lived to repent it. In 1861-62 appeared *Handschriftliche Funde, mit Beiträgen von S. P. Tregelles*, containing studies in the textual criticism of the Apocalypse and a notice of the *Codex Reuchlini*, which had been used by Erasmus in 1516, but had been lost for centuries, till it was rediscovered by Delitzsch himself. The Book of Job had its turn in 1864, and Isaiah in 1866. To the latter commentary I was early under obligations which I am delighted once more to express. The subtle, poetic theory by which Delitzsch accounted for the Babylonian horizon of (speaking generally) the second half of Isaiah never seemed to me critical, but philologically I was conscious of a *Gründlichkeit*, a penetratingness, which no other commentator on Isaiah seemed to display. In 1867 a further proof was given of the same quality by the second edition of the *Psalms*, which is conspicuous for the completeness with which all that is most worth referring to in the psalm-literature of the preceding seven years has been utilized, errors corrected, and exegesis made more definite. The preface is dated July 7, 1867. By the October *semester* of the same year he had said farewell to the old Bavarian university; he had been recalled to his native city as the successor of Tuch.

It is sad to think what havoc death has wrought in the faculty of which Delitzsch became such a distinguished member. Luthardt indeed remains—a valiant and skilful champion, not only of Lutheranism, but of Christianity. But Lechler, G. Baur, and above all Kahnis, have all passed away—Kahnis, the brilliant dogmatic theologian, orthodox, but not of an unprogressive type, and sympathizing with Delitzsch in his willingness to meet Old Testament critics half-way. That Delitzsch enjoyed returning to his *Vaterstadt* is clear from the preface to his inaugural lecture, delivered October 1867. Need I say how full of recondite learning the lecture is? The subject is, "Physiology and Music in their Relation to Grammar, especially Hebrew Grammar," which reminds us that in the preface to his earliest book he expresses his intention to write on Jewish music. Delitzsch's first Leipzig book (if my dates are correct) was, however, not philological, but apologetic. The *System der Christlichen Apologetik* (1869) is full of a gentle persuasiveness. And here, perhaps, I may mention the series of descriptive sketches, partly imaginative, of the times of Christ, most of which have been translated—*Jesus and Hillel* and *Artisan Life in the Time of Jesus* (these came out at Erlangen), *A Day at Capernaum*, and *Jose and Benjamin* (these are of the Leipzig period). The descriptions of Palestine are so vivid as to suggest that the author had travelled in the Holy Land. Many valuable essays from his pen might well be collected from *Daheim* and other periodicals. They would illustrate, not less than those in *Iris*, the versatility and wonderful productiveness of this gifted man. Nor can I pass over his earnest interest in the Jews. *Jesus and Hillel* was first published in *Saat auf Hoffnung*—one of the few missionary periodicals which have to some extent a critical interest. Towards the close of his life Delitzsch regarded his work for Israelites as one of his greatest privileges. How he laboured on his Hebrew New Testament, he has told us himself in an interesting pamphlet called *The Hebrew New Testament of the British and Foreign Bible Society* (1883). The first specimen of his work was published as a separate work in 1870. It contained the Epistle to the Romans in Hebrew, with Talmudic illustrations which render the booklet indispensable to New Testament students. The New Testament has now received its definitive revision, through the loving help of G. H. Dalman; it is (as

Kaufmann says) "not an inspired masterpiece, but the matured fruit of learning, working and advancing step by step." Nor did Delitzsch give less attention to the Hebrew text of the Old Testament. Besides publishing those *Complutensian Studies* which will be mentioned presently, he entirely by his own exertions induced the great Massoretic scholar, S. **Baer, to** edit separate portions of the Old Testament in a revised text, to each of which Delitzsch prefixed a learned Latin introduction.

The year 1870 was one of keen anxiety for Delitzsch. He lost a son in the war, and could not repress the mournful words addressed to his students, *Ach, ich bin ein armer Mann geworden.* In 1876 he lost another son, a promising young theologian, known by an able work on Thomas Aquinas. His son Friedrich was spared, and to him are due most of those Assyriological notices which adorn his father's more recent commentaries.

It was in 1871 that I first saw Delitzsch. A work **that I** had published in 1870 on Isaiah at once opened his heart to me. Perhaps he judged the book from a German, not from a contemporary English, point of view. His *Studies on the Origin of the Complutensian Polyglott* began to appear in 1871 (Part II. in 1878, Part III. in 1886); they are a model of minute research in many manuscript collections. His *Proverbs* came out in 1873, *Song of Songs and Ecclesiastes* in 1875, the second edition of *Job* in 1876, the third of *Isaiah* in 1879, the fourth of the *Psalms* in

1883   Nor must I omit Delitzsch's *second* article on Daniel in the second edition of Herzog's *Encyclopædia* (vol. iii. 1878), in which he concedes the Maccabæan date of the book as a whole, and takes much pains to show this to be consistent with devout reverence. Evidently his mind was at this time in a somewhat painful state of transition. In the summer *semester* of 1873 he had spoken confidently of the victories gained by Hengstenberg, Hävernick, and Keil over the "higher critics." But during the long vacation of 1876 he began a more careful study of the newer criticism by a perusal of Kayser's recent work, *Das vorexilische Buch* in connexion with Graf's older book, *Die geschichtlichen Bücher des A. T.* "He had never," says his pupil and friend Dr. Curtiss, "recognized the strength of the critics' positions until he came to study Kayser's little book." His change of view on the subject of Isaiah probably took place shortly afterwards. I cannot easily believe that he accepted the plural authorship of the book when he published the third edition of his commentary (July 1879), in which the unity of authorship is still earnestly maintained. But it is certain that in the winter *semester* of 1879-80, when lecturing on Messianic prophecy, he *assumed* that Isa. xl.—lxvi. was written at the close of the Exile.[1] Henceforth he

---

[1] See *Messianic Prophecies*: Lectures by Franz Delitzsch (ed. Curtiss, 1880); and cf. *Old Testament History of Redemption*, p. 154, &c.; *Messianic Prophecies in Historical Succession*, p. 197, &c.

did not scruple to use the terms "deutero-Isaiah," "Babylonian Isaiah," though it was not till 1889 that he finished recasting his old book (not with perfect success) in accordance with his new views.

Meantime Delitzsch began to take Church theologians into his confidence. In 1879 appeared vol. i. of Wellhausen's *Geschichte Israels*, and it became necessary for such a trusted orthodox leader to state his position. This Delitzsch did in two series of articles called *Pentateuch-kritische Studien* and *Urmosaisches im Pentateuch* in Luthardt's *Zeitschrift*. Students of Delitzsch's *Commentary on Genesis* (1888) ought certainly to look into these articles. They prepared the way for that great fifth edition of his *Genesis* which he justly regarded as a new work. For an estimate of the latter I would refer to the article in the *Theol. Studien und Kritiken* (1889; pp. 381—397) by Delitzsch's old pupil Kautzsch. The book is indeed open to much criticism, as this reviewer has indicated in the most tenderly considerate way. But it is both stimulating and instructive, and is a proof not only of physical but of moral energy. Yes, this veteran required great moral energy so elaborately to revise his old opinions. English reviewers could not easily understand his procedure (see a well-meant article in the *Guardian*): he seemed to them to be untrue to himself, and to be playing with fire. It was a mistake on their part. Delitzsch had never identified himself with traditionalism like Hengstenberg, and the alternative to critical progress was a violent theological crisis. It was natural, too, for a sympathetic teacher to enter into the thoughts of younger minds, Stade and Kautzsch, once members of Delitzsch's class, now convinced adherents of the newest critical school, though differing on many not unimportant points. And there were many more, troubled and perplexed, feeling that neither they nor the Church could put off a reasonable solution of pressing problems. One of Delitzsch's last printed utterances speaks of a compromise which the Church (as an educational institution) can safely make with criticism. Where shall we find this informal, provisional compromise better indicated than in his article on Daniel, his *New Commentary on Genesis,* and his fourth edition of *Isaiah?*[1]

The last-mentioned work, which shows no abatement of thoroughness, is a κειμήλιον to Dr. Driver and myself, because of its gracious dedication. Of Dr. Driver the young-hearted old man always wrote to me in the warmest terms. The Oxford professor's delicate scholarship was of the utmost service in the revision of the Hebrew Testament, and Delitzsch

[1] I have tried to work out this idea in an address on reform in the teaching of the Old Testament delivered to a clerical audience, and published in a revised form in the *Contemporary Review* for August 1889 (see especially pp. 221—224). Professor H. Strack informs me that I might have quoted him as more decidedly in favour of the critical analysis of Isaiah than I have ventured to do. He, like myself, thinks Professor von Orelli's hesitating criticism (see *The Prophecies of Isaiah,* T. & T. Clark, 1888) not even provisionally tenable.

refers with evident pleasure in the new *Isaiah* to Dr. Driver's *Hebrew Tenses* and his handbook on Isaiah. The goodwill which Delitzsch showed to us, he showed to all honest and earnest students (witness his preface to a young Canadian professor's recent work on the text of Jeremiah). That he came at last to approximate so much to my own first book on Isaiah, and to Dr. Driver's work (both of which are relatively conservative), is an abiding satisfaction. Would that I could have seen him again! But that erect form and those flashing eyes now live only in memory. Delitzsch was taken ill in September, but was enabled to carry his last work through the press —*Messianische Weissagungen in geschichtlicher Folge*, the preface of which is dated five days before his death.[1] The Hebrew text of Jeremiah, edited by himself and Baer, and published after his death, has a preface dated Jan. 1890. He died at Leipzig, March 3, 1890. "Jew and Christian alike mourn the loss of a great man: one must go back to old times to find his equal," are the words of a sympathetic Jewish scholar, to which I will add that those who value the love of truth even more than scholarship, will thank God for the bright example of this high quality given by the aged Delitzsch.

[1] Translated by Dr. S. I. Curtiss.

CHAPTER VIII.

RIEHM—REUSS—LAGARDE—KUENEN.

THE group of Old Testament critics to which, by the date of his death, Franz Delitzsch belongs contains other eminent names besides his own. Riehm, Reuss, Lagarde, and Kuenen have all been snatched from us within the last few years. The youngest of these is **Eduard Riehm**, who was born in 1830 and died in 1888. A pupil of Hupfeld in his youth, he had the happiness of returning to Halle as the colleague of his old master in 1862, and upon Hupfeld's death in 1866 Riehm succeeded to the vacant chair. It is worth noticing that, like so many of our own professors of theology, Riehm had had the advantage of practical experience of pastoral work. For good or for evil this seems to have affected his work as a lecturer and a writer. For if there is one quality more striking than another in the writings of Riehm, it is that of sympathy with orthodox believers. He took an early opportunity of displaying this in an address to the *Unionsverein* of Halle on the special religious importance of the Old Testament for the Christian Church (*Gemeinde*),[1] in which he meets the objection that the adoption of the modern critical standpoint disqualifies a man for ministering to the congregation; and shortly afterwards, in the *Theologische Studien und Kritiken* (1865—1869), he published three studies on *Messianic Prophecy*, which are not less effective from a church-theological than from a historico-critical point of view.[2] The same rare quality is conspicuous in his two posthumous works, the *Introduction to the Old Testament* (2 vols. 1889-90) and the *Old Testament Theology* (1889). Sympathy with the orthodox seems to have become a part of Riehm's nature; he could not, even in critical inquiries, divest himself of the preoccupations of a practical clergyman. Now, shall we be glad or sorry for this? For my own part, though I fully appreciate Riehm's feeling, I regret the extent to which he has allowed it to influence him. Painful as it may be to one who would fain spare Church students the least distress of mind, there must be no compromise in "scientific" (*wissenschaftlich*) investigation, since as De Wette said in 1807 "only that which is perfect in its kind is good," and true and pure religion cannot be subverted by any criticism.

[1] *Die besondere Bedeutung des A. T.*, &c. (Vortrag gehalten am 13 Oct. 1863).

[2] These studies, which on their appearance taught me much of which I was ignorant, were republished in a volume in 1875. They are now accessible in the faithful translation of the Rev. L. A. Muirhead (1891), who bases his work on the second German edition (1885).

Riehm's criticism was not, as I think, free from the spirit of compromise; and the consequence is 1. that he fails to reach a consistent view of the development of the religious literature of Israel, and 2. that in his tenderness towards orthodox prejudice he does not sufficiently consider the interests of that spiritual religion which is the "orthodoxy within orthodoxy."

My judgment upon Riehm, both as a "higher critic" and as an interpreter of criticism to the Church, is therefore not entirely favourable. But I utter it, not as a censure, but as a criticism of something which, under our present circumstances, must provisionally exist, both in Germany and in England. I never saw Riehm, but can easily believe that, with his "liebenswerthe Persönlichkeit," he was incapable of such an heroic act of faith as De Wette with his cooler or rather more composite nature. Nor do I deny the relative excellence of Riehm's work both as a critic and as an interpreter of criticism. Compare him with Delitzsch and with Orelli, and his services appear in a specially favourable light. He has, I am sure, done better critical work than either, and been more effective in clearing up the views of orthodox students. His two posthumous works are specially valuable from the consideration which the author gives to the views of other critics, and I can well believe that some of the best of our coming theologians have been trained in his lecture-room. Among his other critical writings I may mention his early work, *The Legislation of Moses in the Land of*

Moab[1] (1854), and his articles in the *Studien und Kritiken*, especially the criticism of Graf's theory[2] (1868), and the papers entitled respectively, "The so-called 'Grundschrift' of the Pentateuch" (1872), and "The Conception of Atonement in the Old Testament" (1877). Nor must I omit his exegetical work on the Epistle to the Hebrews (1858-59; ed. 2, 1867), his edition of Hupfeld's *Psalms* (already mentioned), and his contributions to the *Dictionary of Biblical Antiquity*, edited by him in 1875—1884.

Eduard Reuss, the Nestor of Old Testament students in our own time, died quite recently (April 15, 1891), but was born as long ago as July 18, 1804 ("29 Messidor, xii."). His home, from youth to age, was at Strassburg. There he began his philological and theological studies, but according to the laudable custom of continental students, he sought further

---

[1] The Deuteronomic law-book is here assigned by Riehm to the second half of Manasseh's reign. In his posthumous *Introduction* the date is thrown even further back—to the time shortly before or at the beginning of the reign of Hezekiah (against both views, see Kuenen, *Hexateuch*, p. 219). I do not understand how Westphal can date the advent of historical Pentateuch criticism from the appearance of this book (*Les sources du Pent.*, ii. Pref. p. xxiv).

[2] To some extent this criticism is decisive against Graf, as that candid critic himself acknowledged (Merx's *Archiv für wissenschaftliche Erforschung des A. T.*, i. 467). It appears however from a letter of Graf, printed by Kuenen (see *Hexateuch*, Introd. p. xxxiii), that it was really a friendly criticism of Kuenen that led Graf to revise his theory, and to admit that the ritual laws could not be separated from the narratives of the "Grundschrift."

guidance at other seats of learning—first at Göttingen and Halle (1822—1826), and then (as was natural) at Paris (1827-28), where De Sacy reigned supreme among Arabic scholars. He then returned to Strassburg, and after proving his capacity as a lecturer, became in 1834 extraordinary and in 1836 ordinary professor of theology. So famous a Biblical critic and theologian hardly needs to be characterized. For his devoutness, none the less genuine because it finds a modern expression, it is enough to refer to his *Addresses to Students of Theology* (1878); for his capacity for hard work to his monumental edition of Calvin. Both these features in his character betoken his German origin, while his clear and sometimes witty style is explained by his long French connexion. To his residence in Elsass we may also attribute the width of his range as a theologian and the comprehensive character of many of his works. Protestantism in Elsass needed the infusion of a vigorous but not pedantic scholarship, and the great country to which that border-land was (till 1871) united deserved such religious help as a man like Reuss could give. This was why he edited (with Colani) the *Revue de théologie*, and (with Baum and Cunitz) the first twenty volumes of the works of Calvin; this was why he wrote in a clear and incisive style, sometimes in French, sometimes in German, such works as the *Geschichte der heil. Schriften N. T.* (1842; ed. 5, 1874), the *Histoire de la théologie chrétienne au siècle apostolique* (1852; ed. 3, 1864), the *Histoire du canon des saintes Ecri-*

tures (1862 ; ed. 2, 1863), the new French translation of the Bible with commentary (1874—1880), and the *Geschichte der heil. Schriften A. T.* (1881—1890).

There was a time when Eduard Reuss narrowly missed becoming a hero of Old Testament criticism. It was in 1834, the year before Vatke's *Biblical Theology* and George's *Die jüdischen Feste* made a sensation in the theological world. Reuss (not as yet appointed a professor) was lecturing on Old Testament introduction at Strassburg. He had already come to results which were so much opposed to those generally received that he dared not put them forward systematically. But what he did divulge then or afterwards fastened itself in the memory of two Alsatian students who were present—K. H. Graf and August Kayser. The germs grew, and we have the results in Graf's important work on the historical books of the Old Testament (1866) and Kayser's on "the pre-Exilic book of Israel's primitive history and its expansions" (1874). And what was the germ-idea deposited by Reuss in the minds of his students? It came to him, he informs us, rather as an intuition than as a logical conclusion, and it was nothing less than this—that the prophets are earlier than the Law, and the Psalms later than both. From the first, we are told, his principal object was to find a clue to the development of Israelitish religious culture, so as to make its historical course psychologically conceivable. His early youth had seen the extravagant rationalistic exegesis of Paulus. But the most startling of all miracles, viz. the existence of the complete Levitical system in the first stage of the religious education of Israel, together with the absence of any sign that the greatest prophets, such as Samuel and Elijah, were acquainted with it, seemed to mock at explanations. The prevalent critical theories appeared in many points to run directly counter to psychology, nor should it be overlooked that among the young critic's difficulties were some connected with the Davidic authorship of psalms. The autobiographical passage in which Reuss has recorded all this will be found in the preface to the *History of the Old Testament Scriptures* (1881), and the twelve theses in which in 1833 he formulated his conclusions in a volume of his great Bible-work (*L'histoire sainte et la loi*, 1879, pp. 23, 24).

That Vatke's difficult work produced no effect upon a lover of clearness like Reuss, is not surprising. It was Graf's book, together with Kuenen's *Religion of Israel*, which stimulated him long afterwards to supplement and systematize his old ideas. The fact, however, that Reuss anticipated both Vatke and Kuenen is of some significance. For he was not a Hegelian philosopher like the one, nor did he take his starting-point in the historical books like the other. It was by studying the legal portions of the Pentateuch that the young Strassburg critic sought a way of escape from the unnatural hypotheses of the day. Three such men as Reuss, Vatke, and Kuenen (to mention no more), reaching the same result by different paths, are not likely to have been entirely mistaken. And now to return to Reuss's early studies. Later on, no doubt, he completed the detailed criticisms which for a time he broke off. But he completed them rather for himself than for the great world of critics :—upon the whole, we cannot say that Reuss has left a deep mark on the critical movement. What he has effected for the Old Testament is to sum up and popularize with a master's hand advanced critical results. No French student can afford to dispense with his great work on the Bible, and if German students (or English students who know German) can afford to disregard his critical history of the Old Testament Scriptures, they must be very clever indeed. His judgments may not always commend themselves to us (he puts Joel and the Song of Songs early),[1] but less than any one except Kuenen can he be called a rash and inconsiderate critic. His *History* is unique, and a necessary companion to Kuenen's masterly *Inquiry*.

[1] For instance, he makes Joel, Job, and the Song of Songs pre-Exilic, and sees no need for disintegrating either Micah or Isa. xl.—lxvi. His hypothesis on the Psalms, though right in some of its main features, seems not to presuppose much detailed criticism. It should be added that Reuss denied the existence of Davidic psalms as early as 1839 (in a Halle periodical). Also that in 1888 he published a tasteful translation of the Book of Job, with a brief introduction, both well adapted for the wider public.

The moral affinities of Reuss are rather with Kuenen than with Delitzsch. It was sad to see how despondent the latter became at last, and how regretfully he looked back to the days of his youth. The concessions which he made to criticism were wrung from him by a sense of duty, and he seems to have had not much hope that his own synthesis of Church doctrine and modern criticism would be widely accepted. Reuss on the other hand had a keen sympathy with the younger generation; he had nothing to "concede," for he had himself always been progressive. I saw him in the summer of 1890 in his country home near Strassburg full of life and hope, though preparing to put off his armour. He believed that truth was sure to win, and looked forward with hope to the constant expansion of our knowledge. In this faith and hope Kuenen too lived and died, and it contributed to his remarkable serenity. Of a still greater scholar, though a less notable " higher critic " of the Old Testament, **Paul de Lagarde**, we cannot venture to say as much. He was not (to judge from appearances) happy, save in his work, which indeed was colossal. It was well for him that his more special work was linguistic and textual—studying languages and editing texts from manuscripts. As soon as he turned his eyes away to behold mankind and its perversities, he became subjective, and both conceived and excited numberless antipathies. He could not even register his linguistic facts and theories without falling into sarcasm and railing (see for instance that brilliant treatise, published in 1889, the *Survey of the Formation of Nouns in Aramaic, Arabic, and Hebrew*); much less could he avoid this in speaking of things which lay even nearer to his heart—religion and the science (*Wissenschaft*) of religion. This being the case, it is not surprising that in his opinions both on the history of doctrine and on "higher" critical problems there is an unusually strong subjective and even eccentric element. He could not take much account of the opinions of others; in the subjects referred to he may even appear to have rejected the scientific methods of others. How is this to be accounted for? Lagarde was too great, too self-denying a man for us to impute anything like a mean motive, and his services to that "lower criticism" which is so essential to Biblical study (not now to mention his brilliant intuitions in "higher criticism") are so important that we could not excuse ourselves for passing such painful facts over altogether.

The true explanation may be that which has been earnestly advocated by the pro-Rector of Göttingen University. Lagarde's self-consciousness was abnormal; he felt and spoke as a prophet, in that wide sense of the term according to which our own Carlyle is admittedly a prophet. "He was often a *vox clamantis in deserto*; but he did not allow this to disturb him. He belonged to the class of those who penetrate more deeply than others into the essence of all that they see, but who are tied to one point of view. Such men are powerful but subjective natures; they awaken strong sympathies and antipathies. In all, there remains, the more closely we observe them, 'ein Erdenrest, zu tragen peinlich.' In all, the point of view from which they regard the universe is in reality religious; and—let us be frank—the moral standard, which is valid for others, is incommensurable for the prophets. *They are seldom happy;* 'der Blick der Schwermut ist ein fürchterlicher Vorzug.' They have a keener eye for the hurts and pains of humanity; therefore they call for a radical change: but as a compensation, they look through the mists of earth into the region of the sun and of eternal truth."[1] There are many pages of Lagarde which must be read in the spirit of these words, if we are to think of him as highly as we could wish. With all his peculiarities there was an idealism in him which deserves veneration; and exaggerated as much of his writing on religion may be, there is often a kernel of truth in it which cannot safely be disregarded. He did well to emphasize the truth that now, as in the days of Luther and Calvin, Biblical criticism was a great reforming agency for theology and for the Church.

Lagarde was born at Berlin, Nov. 22, 1827; he died at Göttingen, Dec. 1891. He studied at Berlin in 1844—1846, and in Halle in 1846-47. From 1855 to 1866 he carried on the deepest linguistic studies in the intervals of scholastic work; at last, on Ewald's

[1] *Rede gehalten am Sarge des Professors Dr. Paul de Lagarde am 25 Dec.* 1891, *von Ulrich von Wilamowitz-Moellendorff*, p. 6.

decease, he was appointed to a chair at Göttingen. How much he was to his pupils in Semitic philology, more than one of our best known Hebraists can testify; he was, to prepared disciples, a great teacher. Was he under similar obligations himself to others? Certainly not, so far as theology proper is concerned. He found a way for himself to the "original Gospel." But to some great scholars and teachers he owed much—to Friedrich Rückert his love for Eastern studies, to Jacob Grimm his patriotic romanticism, to Karl Lachmann his philological tastes and methods. What the last-mentioned scholar undertook for the text of the New Testament, Lagarde aspired to do for the Old. It was by far the harder task of the two; it involved "the brave worker in those labours on the Septuagint text, in which, when struck by fatal sickness, he still persisted."[1] Much else he did by the way; but this was his life's work. By this, as well as by much Hebrew philology, Lagarde well deserves to be styled a "founder of Old Testament criticism."[2]

Lagarde's judgments on points of "higher criticism" will be found chiefly in the *Symmicta* (1877—1880), the *Semitica*, i. (Critical Notes on the Book of Isaiah, &c., 1878), the *Purim* (1887), and the *Mittheilungen* (4 vols., 1884—1891). I content myself with quoting

---

[1] The last part of his *Septuaginta Studien* was published after his death by Dr. Rahlfs.

[2] In the *Contemporary Review* for March 1889 (p. 393, &c.) Prof. Driver has given a full and instructive account of some of Lagarde's more recent philological works.

an utterance of Lagarde on the origin of the Hexateuch, which proves (as Kuenen remarks [1]) that he "had reached important points of agreement with the Leiden critics independently of their help"; or to put it shortly, that, equally with Vatke and the others, he is one of the founders of the newer Hexateuch criticism. "I am convinced (and the conviction has stood the testing of years) that not a few portions of the Old Testament arose in the age of Ezra, who with incomparably better right than Moses may be called the creator of Judaïsm. I consider the Elohist, whose activity extends beyond the Pentateuch (as my pupils were aware as early as 1864), identical with the editor of the Pentateuch, and to be either Ezra himself or a priest of the second temple working under his direction. The abstract is everywhere later than the concrete; therefore Elohim (as a singular) is later than Yahwé, and indeed Elohim by itself (without suffix and without an accompanying Yahwé) occurs as good as never in prophets of admitted antiquity to designate the Supreme Being. Those Israelites who wrote the earlier Elohistic portions of the Old Testament, especially the Elohistic psalms composed during the Exile, are the spiritual fathers of those who pronounced Adonai where the text had Yhwh. If this 'perpetual Q'ri' is a late expression of a false piety, so too is that dread of pronouncing the name of Yahwé

---

[1] See *Hexateuch* (transl. Wicksteed), Introd. p. xxxiii. Kuenen also mentions similar statements of Merx. *Prot. Kirchenzeitung* for 1865, No. 17.

(transformed into the one God of the world). I have always been surprised that no one has yet thought of the parallel between 2 Kings xxii. 8, &c., and 2 Esdr. viii. 1, &c. If the former passage means that our Deuteronomy was written in the time of Josiah, the latter can only mean that the Tora as a whole proceeds from Ezra. Besides, the Pentateuch, or rather the Hexateuch (for the work includes the Book of Joshua), has its only *raison d'être* in the idea of instructing the Jewish colony assembled under Ezra in the conditions of its reoccupation of the promised land. Those conditions are the same under which its ancestors had formerly conquered it; hence too these ancestors are feigned to have had the same disposition —especially with regard to the 'conubium'—which Ezra so rigorously exemplified in his community. The works of the Yahwist, a writer of the prophetic school, whose spirit doubtless agreed with that of the speech of Stephen (Acts vii.); of the older Elohist, presumably contemporary with the Elohistic psalms; and of the Deuteronomist; together perhaps with other isolated passages, were worked up together in his own spirit by the younger (hitherto designated the older) Elohist, Ezra. Thus, for instance, we can explain the beginning of the Pentateuch as intended to contradict the Persian cosmogony."[1]

Kuenen, the last of this group of critics, resembles

[1] *Symmicta*, i. 55, 56. For Lagarde's developed views on the latter point, see his *Purim* (p. 44), and cf. my *Origin of the Psalter*, p. 283, note ᶜᵉ.

Lagarde in little except in his love of truth and his want of sympathy with traditional forms of Christian theology. His character was so pure and noble that I ask permission to dwell upon it; if such are the fruits of criticism, we need not perhaps augur so much evil from its increased prevalence. To have known him, is a privilege; and it is right to give the student (who alas! cannot now see him in the flesh) some faint idea of what he was. He was born, Sept. 16, 1828, at Haarlem, where his father was an apothecary.[1] At the age of fifteen, upon his father's death, his studies were interrupted; but friends were at last found to restore him to his school, and in the autumn of 1846 he was already qualified to enter the university. It was Leiden which he then made his academic home, and at Leiden he remained to the day of his death. The names of Dutch theologians are less known in England than they ought to be, but that of Scholten the dogmatic theologian is not unfamiliar to students of the Fourth Gospel.[2] To Scholten the young student was more indebted than to any other member of the theological faculty; through him Kuenen became a theologian, and not merely an exegete like van Hengel or an Orientalist like Juynboll. I have ventured to

---

[1] These facts are from C. P. Tiele's *Levensbericht van Abraham Kuenen* (Amsterdam, 1892), and P H. Wicksteed's beautiful sketch in the *Jewish Quarterly Review*, July 1892. For a critical estimate of Kuenen's work, see Prof. Toy in the *New World*, March 1892.

[2] See Scholten, *Het Evangelie naar Johannes* (1864; in German, 1867); and cf. Watkins, *Bampton Lectures*, p. 264, &c.

say elsewhere that one of Kuenen's many merits is that he *was* a theologian: not altogether baseless was the dislike expressed by Delitzsch for a purely critical theology. We must remember however that the Scholten of those days was not, either in New Testament criticism or in dogmatic theology, as radical as he afterwards became: Scholten and his pupil went on developing side by side. In Semitic philology Kuenen was equally indebted to another luminary of that day—Juynboll. For his doctor's thesis (1851) he presented an edition of part of the Arabic version of the Samaritan Genesis (chaps. i.—xxiv.), and was soon after appointed to succeed Dozz as " adjutor interpretis legati Warneriani." The next result of his researches in the Leiden library was an edition of the whole of Genesis, Exodus, and Leviticus in the same version (1854).

But Kuenen's pleasant position on the Warner foundation was but like a temporary fellowship: his life's work as a teacher had yet to begin. In 1853 he became extraordinary professor of theology (retaining his "fellowship" till 1855). His inaugural lecture (on the theological importance of the study of Hebrew antiquity) contained this remarkable passage—

"Nor do I myself believe that the opinions of von Bohlen, Vatke, and others concerning these books can be reconciled with the utterances of Jesus and the apostles. But—to say nothing of the fact that their ravings have already been rejected by all the critics of any note, to a man—the abuse of a thing should not prohibit us from using it."[1]

In 1855 Kuenen was appointed to an ordinary professorship, and that same year he married. Kuenen, like Lagarde, had a close intellectual companionship with his wife, and his bold venture in starting from the prophets of the eighth century in his researches into the religion of Israel was partly due to Mrs. Kuenen's sympathy. Henceforth there are few events to chronicle in this modest scholar's life. He took part in all academic and civic movements, preached (though but seldom), and lectured with ability (though, like Vatke, not with uniform success). In 1882 he visited England to deliver the Hibbert Lectures. In 1883, the year of the Oriental Congress at Leiden, he lost his wife; in 1886, his attached and ever-helpful sister. These blows told upon him, and when in 1887 he was attacked by a distressing disease, he had great difficulty in resisting it. In 1891 he was again seized with painful illness, and on December 10 he departed this life suddenly but peacefully at the age of sixty-three.

Let me mention some of the moral qualities which distinguished Kuenen as a scholar. Love of truth, thoroughness in work, freedom from vanity and personal ambition, generosity in praise, considerateness in censure, willingness to reconsider opinions—all these can be traced in Kuenen's writings. Nor was

---

[1] Quoted by Wicksteed in his sketch.

his religion of a commonplace type. Though not fervid like that of Delitzsch, his faith was firm, serene, and most truly reverent. Reverence indeed was one of his leading characteristics. In his most controversial work, he asserts the claims of the prophets to our reverence, and in reviewing Steinthal's *Ethics* he regrets the omission of reverence in that philosopher's definition of the religious sentiment.[1] Turning now to his three critical works, I notice first of all that, when rightly understood, he is not so alien in spirit to progressive Church theologians as has been represented. "Take the first edition of that monument of critical scholarship, the *Historico-critical Inquiry* (1861—1865), and see how moderate its results are. And now compare the second (part 1, 1885—1887; part 2, 1889). Can it be said that there is any real extremeness in his conclusions? No; Kuenen is still as moderate and as circumspect as ever, but his eye for facts has become keener. I know that he opposed the old supernaturalism, and that he himself admits that his theological convictions may have reacted on his criticisms; but I know that he also assures us that neither his method nor his main results were the outcome of his theological principles. It was through critical exegesis that he came to the conviction that a dogmatic supernaturalism was untenable, and the canons of critical exegesis are independent of theological dogma."[2]

[1] *Theologisch Tijdschrift*, 1886, p. 307.
[2] From my notice of Kuenen, *Expositor*, Jan. 1891.

Nor can it be said that Kuenen's second great work, the *Religion of Israel* (published in Dutch in 1869-70) is in any bad sense "naturalistic." No doubt he considered on critical grounds that the religion of Israel was but one among other religions (*Religion of Israel*, i. 5). But he would have fully admitted that the difference in their respective degrees of spiritual nobility between the higher religion of Israel and the best of the other religions of antiquity was so great as to amount practically to a difference of kind. All that was good both in the religion of Israel and in the other religions he would have ascribed to the same divine source. If this is to be a "naturalist," then Kuenen may be so called. I should myself have preferred to call him a psychologist, and with him I cannot help grouping such respected Church theologians as Lightfoot and Westcott, Bruce and Davidson, who are unqualified psychologists in exegesis, whatever may be their attitude towards the results of the psychological method in criticism.

I am not however writing as an apologist of this able book. As a whole, it is simply unique as a specimen of the right historical method in such studies. But in details one may often differ from it. Thus, Kuenen's explanation of the rise of spiritual prophecy seems to others besides Matthew Arnold inadequate. But Kuenen was perfectly justified in offering it. He also appears to me deficient in insight into the higher religious ideas of the Israelites; one may still turn for stimulus from the *Religion of Israel* to Ewald on the Prophets and on the Poets. And if we pass to Kuenen's third work (which owes its inception to the late Dr. John Muir), called *The Prophets and Prophecy in Israel* (1877), the same incomplete comprehension of religious ideas is visible. As a controversial treatise, however, the work has merits of the highest order. The only question is, whether the doctrine which he opposes might not have been left to fall of itself, or rather to be superseded by something far higher and deeper, to which no progressive theologian would withhold his assent. More than this I cannot say here. Nor can I venture to discuss either the **Hibbert** Lectures for 1882[1] or the long series of articles (both critical investigations and reviews of books) contained in the *Theologisch Tijdschrift*. The Lectures show how lightly Kuenen bore his learning, while the articles show how utterly removed from rashness he was, and (so far as they deal with the opinions of others) how mild and gracious he could be to those from whom he differed. One delights to think of the latter characteristic. Fairness one expects from an opponent, but graciousness—how nearly unknown is this Christ-like temper among critics!

Lastly, as to Kuenen's place in the critical movement. There is in many respects a striking contrast between the first edition of the *Inquiry (Onderzoek)*

---

[1] A competent estimate of the *Hibbert Lectures* has been given by Prof. Tiele in his short life of Kuenen, and by Prof. Toy in his article on **Kuenen** in the *New World*.

and the second.[1] In Pentateuch criticism in particular Kuenen's position changed greatly between 1861 and 1885. Upon the whole, in 1861 he adhered to what was then the prevalent school of criticism. He found in the Pentateuch three independent writers, all pre-Exilic, though he admitted post-Deuteronomic revision of the Levitical legislation, and he doubted whether the Levitical laws were written down by the same hand which penned the connected narratives. But in 1862, the year after the publication of Kuenen's first volume, appeared Part I. of Bishop Colenso on the Hexateuch, and the detailed criticism of the data of the *Grundschrift* contained in that work led Kuenen to re-examine his own just published critical theories. It was not the only cause, but it was not the least important one, of a complete change in Kuenen's opinion.[2] Another attack on the *Grundschrift* (with special regard to Ex. xxxv.—xl.) was made in 1862 by the Jewish scholar Dr. J. Popper, and again a third in 1866 by K. H. Graf in his "epoch-making" work on the historical books. In 1868 appeared a dissertation by W. H. Kosters of Leiden, which showed inductively that the Deuteronomist was not acquainted with the priestly narratives. In 1869-70 Kuenen thoroughly com-

---

[1] Of the three portions already published, only one is accessible in English (*The Hexateuch*, by P. H. Wicksteed); all have however appeared in a German version by C. Th. Müller.

[2] See *The Hexateuch*, Introd. p. xiv, &c., *Theol. Tijdschrift*, 1870, p. 398, &c.

mitted himself in the *Religion of Israel* to a Grafianism revised by its author at the instance of Kuenen, and subsequently, in the *Theologisch Tijdschrift*, published a series of papers, which are models in their kind, on special points or aspects of the new theory. Finally, in 1885 appeared the first portion of the new edition of the *Inquiry*. This was as great an event as the publication of the *Religion of Israel*. Many who, like myself, were fascinated with the view of Jewish literature and history given in the latter work must have felt, with me, that there were unexplained difficulties in Kuenen's theory. In the revised form of his views given in the second edition of the *Inquiry* these difficulties were much less striking, and through Kuenen and Wellhausen together it became possible even for cautious English critics to come over to the "advanced" school.

Of the second edition of this critical masterpiece three portions have as yet appeared. The changes of opinion indicated in the second and third of these are less striking than those in the first, but careful students will notice Kuenen's great increase of critical sensitiveness in dealing with the prophetic literature. A survey of the results of the third portion (called Part II.) has been given by Mr. Montefiore in the *Jewish Quarterly Review*, 1890, pp. 311—321. I have a keen regret in learning that the fourth portion (part 3), dealing with the gnomic and lyric poetry, was not fully prepared by Kuenen for the press. The *Religion of Israel* is disappointing in its treatment of this section of the Old Testament, and Kuenen's revised opinions, with the full justification which he would have given to them, would have been of the greatest interest. On the Psalter particularly one could have wished for the counsel of this wise scholar. Nor can one help deploring that there can now be no revised and corrected edition of his noble work on the religion of Israel. *Pendent opera interrupta.*

Kuenen, more than any one else of his own generation, pointed the way for future inquiry. In particular, he saw, first of all, the right order in the stages of Israelitish religion, and secondly, the necessity of digging deeper foundations of criticism in archæological research. Wellhausen and Robertson Smith (leaders and representatives of Kuenen's juniors) have therefore lost more than can be said in this prince of critics. But at this point I must break off. Gladly would I have treated, even if less fully, of Dillmann, and of the younger German and Dutch scholars. But time and space are wanting.

CHAPTER IX.

COLENSO — KALISCH — S. DAVIDSON — ROWLAND WILLIAMS—PEROWNE—A. B. DAVIDSON (1862) —RUSSELL MARTINEAU.

WE have already seen that at the end of the eighteenth century a Cambridge professor (H. Lloyd) attempted to obtain episcopal and academical sanction for a translation of Eichhorn's *Introduction to the Old Testament*. To his great surprise (but not to ours) the attempt failed. We will not be hard on the simple-hearted professor's rude episcopal correspondents; they did but carry out the policy of restriction which then prevailed in all departments of life, and which had many and various causes. But we may regret the consequences, one of which was the failure of Lowth and Kennicott to produce a succession of eminent Hebrew scholars. What, in fact (so all but a few born linguists would feel), was the good of profound researches into the text of the Old Testament, when historical and theological inferences were precluded? And though contact with German thought began the regeneration of

English theology long before 1862, yet neither Hare, nor Arnold, nor Jowett, nor even Stanley, could (for want of Hebrew scholarship and other things) be the predestined champion of reform in the study of the Old Testament. At length, in 1862, the hour came, and the man; and, strange to say, the champion was a bishop—and though neither a great Hebrew scholar, nor a critic trained in historical investigations, he was at any rate free from the influences adverse to history which proceeded from the philosophy of Coleridge. It was John William Colenso who reopened the suspended intercourse between the critical students of England and the continent; for I shall hardly be called upon to admit that the timid adhesion of Dr. Samuel Davidson in 1859 to the critical analysis of the Pentateuch in some not very clearly defined form entitles him to a higher title (at least in the present connexion) than that of precursor. How a South African bishop was enabled to become more than this, is a matter of history. I must, however briefly, record the striking facts. It would be unjust to pass over this brave man, who in the teeth of opposition made himself a genuine critic, and who won his battle more completely for others than for himself.

We owe this iconoclast, reformer, and critic to Cornwall: he was born at St. Austell's, Jan. 24, 1814. It would have been strange if he had not been religious; from first to last no cold, sceptical breath ruffled the surface of his soul. Early difficulties awakened a sense of responsibility and strengthened his moral energy. Through friends (whose help he repaid) he entered Cambridge university, where he took all but the very highest mathematical honours, and in 1837 became fellow of St. John's College. From 1836 to 1841 he filled the post of mathematical master at Harrow (under Longley), and then returned to his college as tutor. In 1841—1843 he brought out his very successful treatises on algebra and arithmetic, and in 1846 retired to the village-cure of Forncett St. Mary's, Norfolk, where he divided his time between his parishioners and his pupils. In 1853 he was appointed first Bishop of Natal, and shortly before his consecration dedicated a volume of village-sermons to F. D. Maurice, avowedly doing so as a protest against the blows levelled at his friend by the *Record*. It may be well to quote the words in which Maurice expressed his thanks.

"I should convey a very inadequate impression of my own feelings of the generosity and courage which your words manifest, and of the strength and hope which they imparted to me. I could have wished that you had stifled all your regard for me rather than run this risk. Nevertheless, I do so thoroughly and inwardly believe that courage is the quality most needed in a bishop, and especially a missionary bishop, that I did at the same time give hearty thanks to God that He had bestowed such a measure of it upon you."[1]

---

[1] *Life of Maurice*, ii. 185.

To send such a "strong, simple-hearted" Cornishman as Colenso to Natal might seem wise to the Colonial Secretary of that day, and the Bishop's devoted educational work among the Zulus might appear to justify the appointment. Colenso however had a deep repugnance both to oppression and to formulæ (whether of thought or of action), and here lay one of the possible germs of difficulty in his relations to others. Soon afterwards came the disputes respecting Kafir polygamy, which I refer to here, because the state of things with which Colenso had to deal helped to give him a historic sense of some primitive usages in ancient Israel. In a published letter to the Archbishop of Canterbury he took a comprehensive survey, from a historical, Biblical, and practical point of view, of the question of the position of polygamists with regard to Christian baptism. He argued with great force in favour of toleration. The laws of the Church and the sayings of Christ Himself ought, he said, to be interpreted, and their letter if need be transgressed, in accordance with Christ's spirit. This view was opposed by Canon (afterwards Bishop) Callaway, who considered Christianity to be a "sacred deposit of doctrine," and the Church to be a "divine corporation with explicit regulations which cannot be modified." Bishop Colenso made up his mind after he had been only ten months in the colony. This rapidity in forming a conclusion was characteristic. Colenso was, as his subsequent opponent Bishop Gray said, "impetuous," but he was not incapable of revising his decisions (as his Pentateuch criticism proves), and his opinion of Kafir polygamy was at any rate supported by the high authority of Mr. (since Sir Theophilus) Shepstone.[1]

The deep questions suggested to Colenso by his Zulu friends followed. "To these poor lads the Bishop was emphatically Sobantu, the 'father of the people,' but as he was their teacher and guide, so in turn he was stimulated by their questions to the most momentous inquiries." "He was now translating the Book of Genesis for human beings with the docility of a child, but with the reasoning powers of mature age, and he was met at every step by the point-blank question, 'Is all that true?' 'My heart,' he says, 'answered in the words of the prophet, Shall a man speak lies in the name of the Lord? I dared not do so.' These questions had set him free."[2]

It is easy to scoff at Colenso for giving way to a Zulu—easy, upon condition that we know all that the Bishop learned through his Zulu, and ought to have been taught long ago by his professors at Cambridge; easy, upon condition that we do not realize the deep gulf which at that time existed between English and German theologians. But even the scoffers must admire the energy with which the Bishop set himself to study Biblical criticism in a

---

[1] Comp. my article, "Polygamy in Relation to Christian Baptism," *Mission Life*, April 1880.
[2] Sir G. W. Cox, Bart., in *Dict. of Nat. Biography*, art. "Colenso."

distant colony. For him it was no merely academic question, but one of intense practicalness, and he cherished the belief that those who taught the Bible in our towns and villages would more readily listen to a working clergyman like himself than to an academic recluse. He cannot, I think, have fully counted the cost at first, but he never withdrew from the work because of its increasing magnitude, and the obloquy which it brought upon him. He continued his examination of the Hexateuch, and between 1862 and 1865 came to conclusions which, though from one point of view startlingly negative, were yet from another moderate even to a fault.

These earlier results of Bishop Colenso are contained in Parts I.—V. of his great work.[1] The sensation which they produced is now a thing of the past, and one can do full justice to Colenso without being harsh to his adversaries. Looking back upon the controversy one can see that he had greatly the advantage in dignity of bearing; Colenso never lost his temper. On the other hand, there was much both in the facts which he made known, and in the suddenness and utter frankness with which he published them, that could not help irritating so prejudiced a body as the Anglican clergy of that day. It was probably unwise in Colenso to bring out the first part of his

---

[1] A reply to Part V. was published by Dr. Kay under the rather absurd title *Crisis Hupfeldiana* (1865). Kay was a learned man and an able Hebraist, but did not know the superiority of Hupfeld.

work separately; it would have caused but a brief delay to have combined with it a portion of his more technical criticism, which was already in the press. He might thus have strengthened his case with many fair-minded readers, and stopped the mouth of many objectors. But iconoclasm seemed to Colenso the more immediately necessary course, and it may be questioned whether a born reformer such as Luther would not have justified him. This policy cost him however the good opinion of many friends (including even Maurice), who did not feel the necessity of negative as a preliminary to sound positive criticism, and as the Bishop of Natal was famous for his arithmetic, the materials for many a caustic gibe lay ready to hand. It is now time, however, to speak frankly and seriously respecting Colenso's work. To critics of this generation Parts II.—V. present little of special interest; the details may be had elsewhere in a better and more critical form, and the positive conclusions, always too moderate and in some points eccentric, are now antiquated. But Part I. will remain historically important, because it directed the attention of the most progressive critic of the day to difficulties in the prevalent theory which he had failed to reckon with. Colenso, as Kuenen somewhat bluntly expresses it, "showed that the very documents which most expressly put themselves forward as authentic, and make the greatest parade of accuracy, are in reality the most unhistorical of all. In other words, it is just the narratives of the 'Grundschrift' or 'Book of

Origins' which turn out to be the most helpless before his criticism. . . . Colenso himself did not perceive the legitimate inferences that flowed from his demonstrations; for in Parts II.—V. he accepts the current opinion as to the date and character of the 'Grundschrift.'"[1]

Colenso's sixth part appeared in 1871, and the seventh in 1879. In these he takes his place as a critic side by side with the continental scholars, whose works in distant Natal he sedulously but critically studied. In the former he definitely adopts the theory of Graf, assigning the Levitical legislation to the post-Exilic period, while still regarding the "Elohistic narrative" as a work of the age of Samuel, if not written by Samuel himself. In the latter he examines the origin of a large part of the Old Testament outside the Hexateuch, and considers the bearings of the results on the question of the Canon. It cannot however be said either that the author has entirely thrown off the weaknesses which marked his early attempts at critical analysis, or that he shows a high degree of capacity for special historical criticism.[2] He is a genuine but not an eminent critic, and misses the truth on that very important point, on which

---

[1] *The Hexateuch*, Introd. pp. xv—xvii.

[2] Cf. Maurice, *Life*, ii. 510: "It should be observed that Colenso has not the least studied under Niebuhr. He belongs... to the later and merely negative school of Sir G. C. Lewis, who scorned Niebuhr for supposing that any discoveries could be made about the history of a nation, unless there were contemporary, or nearly contemporary, testimony."

Graf himself finally gave way—the unity of the laws and narratives of the *Grundschrift*.[1] And yet, as we have seen, he helped Kuenen at a turning-point in his path. Must we not remember Lessing's fine saying that, if by an error he has led another to the discovery of a truth, he has deserved as well of the cause of truth as the discoverer himself?

Of the brave Bishop's later history I need not say much. Though by no means a negative critic, he was not qualified to do thoroughly sound constructive work either in historical criticism or in theoretic theology. Let us be thankful for all that he did in breaking up the hard soil, and not quarrel with him for his limitations.[2] To have borne so many burdens at one time would have overpowered any one but this impetuous and yet long-enduring Cornishman. For he had not only upon him the cares of a reformer of Bible-study in England, but those of a missionary bishop. To the last he protected the interests of his Zulu friends, and by his zealous and conscientious advocacy, in the cases of Langalibalele and Cetshwayo, of a policy which was unpopular in the colony, he lost many of those whom his simple, noble character and earnest piety had brought to his side among the colonists. But at last all these cares

---

[1] In Part VII. Preface, p. xxxi, however, he expressly reserves his final judgment in graceful deference to Kuenen.

[2] Among his other works his work on Romans (1861), and his *New Bible Commentary Critically Examined* (1871—1876), have a claim to be mentioned. Also a pamphlet entitled *Wellhausen on the Composition of the Hexateuch* (Lond. 1878).

and anxieties (especially those which have just been mentioned) began to tell upon the strong man. After a brief illness, he passed away at Bishopstowe, Natal, June 20, 1883, in the same faith in which he had lived—a faith which could not be shaken by any discoveries of criticism, because it was directed to the great spiritual realities.

It was one of Colenso's deficiencies as a historical critic that his insight had not been quickened by philosophical study. For his special work as a reformer this may indeed have been no disqualification; he approached a "momentous" subject with a plain, practical, characteristically English mind. That was not the case with an eminent scholar, who by long residence had become English, but who could never (even had he wished it) have disowned his German training, **M. M.** Kalisch. In the preface to Part I. of his *Leviticus* this writer expresses the hope "that he has aided in supporting by arguments derived from his special department of study the philosophical ideas which all genuine science at present seems eager to establish," and, so far from wishing to become a popular reformer, dissuades all who cling to theological prejudice from reading his books. That Kalisch has helped to "found" criticism in England cannot however be doubted. As a learned Jew, he commanded the respect of many who disparaged the self-trained Colenso, and he has undoubtedly promoted the naturalization of foreign critical theories. We may claim him therefore as to some extent an

English scholar, and the fine qualities of his character may make us even proud to welcome him. **And who was Kalisch? That he** came to this country as a political refugee in 1848, that his literary labours, **facilitated** by the munificence of the Rothschilds, were bravely continued to the last amidst the drawbacks of impaired health, and that he died in 1885 at the somewhat early age of fifty-seven, **are** the only facts of his outward life known to me. But his inner life is revealed to us in his books. We see there that he was more than a scholar, more than a Jewish theologian—that he studied deeper questions than the criticism of the Pentateuch, and had wider interests **than** those even of his own Œcumenical Jewish Church. This is especially clear in the latest of his books (*Path and Goal*), published in 1880, which, in the form of a conversation between friends, discusses the old problems of the "highest good." To a student the value of *Path and Goal* is great from its sympathetic exhibition of opposing points of view.

No object was so dear to Kalisch as the growth of mutual respect and sympathy among religionists of different schools, and we cannot doubt that the host at whose house the interlocutors of the conversation assemble, and who appreciates and adopts all their highest thoughts, represents Kalisch himself. He is therefore not a "dry, cold rationalist," as one of the newspapers in 1885 described him, but has an ideal akin to that which Prof. Max Müller describes at the close of his eloquent *Hibbert Lectures*.[1] Such a man cannot be altogether an unsympathetic commentator on the Old Testament.

Kalisch had a mind sensitive to all intellectual influences, and passed through several stages of development as an exegete. His *Exodus* (1855) would now be reckoned orthodox and conservative; his *Genesis* (1858) distinctly recognized the principles of analytic criticism. The latter work in particular displays a fine sympathetic spirit towards the narratives of Genesis which reminds one of Eichhorn and Ewald. In his *Leviticus* however (2 vols., 1867—1872) Kalisch took up the most "advanced" position both in criticism and in theology. With his later theology I have here no concern, but on the critical questions I may say with Kuenen that he shows "great vigour and independence." His conclusion is expressed thus:—

"We trust we have succeeded in demonstrating that the laws of Leviticus in reference to every particular subject are of later origin than the corresponding enactments of Deuteronomy. We have at least spared no pains to establish this point; for upon it hinges the true insight, not only into the composition of the Pentateuch, but into the entire history of Hebrew theology. . . . In every case, Leviticus, as compared with Deuteronomy, manifests a most decided progress in hierarchical power and

---

[1] Cf. *Expositor*, 1885 (2), pp. 390--393.

organization, in spiritual depth and moral culture; but it manifests on the other hand a no less decided decline in freedom and largeness of conception. . . . Therefore Leviticus must be placed later than the seventh century—the date which critics almost unanimously assign to Deuteronomy."

"The laws which Ezekiel, in delineating the restored commonwealth, propounds with respect to the rights and duties of priests, the sacrificial service, and the festivals, are greatly at variance with those of Leviticus. . . . If, in the prophet's time, the commands of Leviticus had existed, or had been known as a part of the holy "Book of the Law," he would assuredly not have ignored and overthrown them by substituting others devised by himself. We must therefore conclude that the Book of Leviticus did not exist, or had at least no divine authority, in the earlier years of the Babylonian captivity."

"The destruction both of the northern and of the southern kingdom, and the misery of the people scattered in the countries of the Euphrates and the Tigris, are in one of the last chapters (xxvi.) vividly and most accurately described. This part of the book therefore leads us on to an advanced period of the Babylonian rule."

"The contemporaries of Nehemiah (about B.C. 440) were unacquainted with the Law of Moses. When the people heard it read, they wept, exactly as about 200 years before, King Josiah had wept when portions of Deuteronomy were read to him; and they were grieved for the same reason—because they had not lived in accordance with the precepts of that Law."

"Leviticus contains ordinances respecting several institutions, the existence or full development of which cannot be proved until long after the captivity —such as the sin-offerings and the high-priesthood, the Day of Atonement and the Year of Jubilee, institutions of all others the most characteristic or most important. Now . . . the Day of Atonement was unknown in the time of Nehemiah; and as the Year of Jubilee was associated with the Day of Atonement, the compilation of the book must fall later than that date; and we shall probably be near the truth if, considering the spirit of the concluding chapter on votive offerings and tithes, we place the final revision of Leviticus and of the Pentateuch at about B.C. 400." [1]

It seemed only fair to give this record of a modest scholar who is in some danger of being overlooked, partly because he was an Israelite, and partly because his style of philology is not altogether that to which we are accustomed.[2] As a companion I will give him **Dr. Samuel Davidson**, who has also had his phases of opinion, and is not perhaps now estimated according to his deserts. This venerable scholar (born in 1807) has been severely handled by a recent

---

[1] *Leviticus*, Part II., pp. 637—639.
[2] Kalisch's other works are his well-known Hebrew Grammar, and his *Bible Studies on Balaam* (1877) and *Jonah* (1878).

writer, whose contention is that Dr. Davidson's change of critical position was the unfortunate effect of his expulsion from his professorship.[1] I confess I do not see why Davidson, like Kuenen and like Delitzsch, should not, upon sufficient cause, change his opinions, and the charge of bias seems to me one which might reasonably be retorted against all who hold any educational office, for no bias perhaps can be greater than that insensibly produced by the endeavour to enter sympathetically into the minds of pupils. So much in defence of one whom as a writer I certainly cannot admire, and in whom as a researcher I cannot see that independence which, as I imagine, is among the signs of a first-rate critic.[2] But Dr. Davidson has in times past been so able a theological interpreter between Germany and England, and to an advanced age has shown such zeal for truth, that I cannot omit his name or ignore his services. If in his later years he has felt the bitterness of isolation, I would rather give him pity than censure. Of his earlier work on the *Old Testament*, Mr. (now Bishop) Westcott wrote thus to the author (in 1857?): "No one can question the great value of your Introduction. I know no English work on the subject which can be compared with it; and I doubt

---

[1] Watkins, *Bampton Lectures*, p. 272, &c.

[2] Among Dr. Davidson's works are, *The Text of the Old Testament Considered; with a Treatise on Sacred Interpretation and a brief Introduction to the O. T. Books and the Apocrypha*, 1856 (ed. 2, 1859), and *An Introduction to the Old Test., critical, historical, and theological*, 3 vols., 1862-63.

whether any German Introduction is equally complete."[1]

We have now almost reached what I may call the modern age in English Bible-study, but a few names of men and books seem still to require mention. First, that of **Rowland Williams** (1817—1870), whom Ewald, as we have seen, visited at Broadchalke. The story of the life of this eminent divine is " the history of an epoch in English thought," and it is noteworthy that the chief literary production of his later years is a work on the Hebrew prophets (2 vols., 1866—1871), which, in its object, as Ewald remarked in reviewing it,[2] was up to that time quite unparalleled in English literature. That object was, not merely to give a better translation, but to ascertain the period of each separate prophetic writing, and to study the prophetic ideas, with which it may fairly be said that he had a natural affinity. The author's rearrangements are chiefly due to Ewald, but he has now and then striking critical ideas of his own ; in philology, he is weak. Of **Dr. E. H. Perowne**, on the other hand, it may be said that his excellent translation of the Psalms with commentary (first ed., 1864—1868) is more advanced in its philology than in its criticism ; how indeed should it have been otherwise at that date ? I trust that no subsequent critics will forget the debt which England owes to Dr. Perowne, **not only for**

---

[1] See the passage in full, *Facts, Statements, and Explanations*, by **Samuel** Davidson, D.D., 1857, pp. 123-4.
[2] *Gött. gel. Anzeigen*, Jan. 23, 1867.

this useful student's book, but for his timely criticisms of Pusey's *Book of Daniel* (*Contemporary Review*, Jan. 1866), and in more "modern" times for his defence of a moderate Pentateuch-criticism (*Contemporary Review*, 1888), of which indeed he had himself in Smith's *Bible Dictionary* given a fragmentary suggestion. Recognition is also due to this scholar's learned and critical but inconclusive article "Zechariah" (*Bible Dictionary*), in which more than once the Exilic origin of Isa. xl.—lxvi. is assumed. **Mr. A. B. Davidson**, author of vol. i. of a learned philological commentary on Job (Edinb. 1862), deserves grateful recognition; the reader will meet him again. Lastly, **Mr. Russell Martineau**, by his (too few) critical articles in the old *Theological Review* and in the translation of Ewald's *History* showed his acumen and fine scholarship, and contributed to prepare the way for the modern period.[1]

---

[1] Dean Stanley can alas! only be mentioned in a footnote. It was his main work to excite an interest in the picturesque accessories, and permanent moral interest, of Biblical history. In doing this he availed himself largely of Ewald's results. Even his most original work, the *Sinai and Palestine* (1856), has numerous references to this great scholar.

CHAPTER X.

THE MODERN PERIOD—ROBERTSON SMITH—A. B. DAVIDSON—BRIGGS—TOY—[SCHRADER]—SAYCE—KIRKPATRICK — RYLE — FRANCIS BROWN—MOORE—WHITEHOUSE—G. A. SMITH—DUFF—FRIPP—ADDIS—MONTEFIORE—BEVAN.

THE modern period may be opened here with the name of **W. Robertson Smith**, who from the first gave promise of becoming the most brilliant critic of the Old Testament in the English-speaking countries. Aberdeen university never turned out a keener intellect, and with admirable forethought his friends there bade him complete his training under A. B. Davidson (recently appointed professor) at the Free Church College at Edinburgh, and under the most learned and exacting of professors, Paul de Lagarde at Göttingen. Physical science however long strove with theology for this able student, and perhaps it was only the definite offer of a professorship of Oriental Languages and the Old Testament at the Free Church College at Aberdeen that prevented him from being finally enrolled among Scottish academical teachers of physics. At any rate, it was a great advantage for **Robertson Smith both as** a special Biblical critic and as a theologian to have **obtained** so good an insight into the methods of physical science, and among other things into the right use of hypothesis according to such men as Thomson **and** Tait. Bold, but wisely bold, were those who appointed so young a man (he was then twenty-four) to a professorship. But our Scottish friends know when to be bold, and when cautious. The young professor came of a good stock; attachment to evangelical religion might safely be presumed in his father's son. It was true that he could not have passed under the influence of Albrecht Ritschl at Göttingen without having modified some of his ideas as to what constituted orthodoxy, nor under that of Lagarde (who said that he "accepted everything that was proved, but nothing else") without having become increasingly strict in criticizing traditional narratives. But the directors of the Free Church colleges were aware of the necessity of strengthening the scientific (*wissenschaftlich*) portion of Scottish theology, and a policy of generous trust in the rising generation supplanted that of obscurantism and distrust. The Bible needed to be reexamined in the light of historical research (here Lagarde's training would show itself), **and** both dogmatics and apologetics required reinterpretation and revision (here the profoundly positive Ritschl would not be unhelpful). In other words, not Hengstenberg but Tholuck was the model of these liberal-conservative directors—Tholuck, whom another Free Church student heard say shortly before his death, "The more liberal view of inspiration can be safely introduced among the laity, only on condition that the theologians first show that they can hold it without losing the power and purity of their religious life."

From 1870 to 1881 Prof. Robertson Smith worked at Aberdeen. Those years of his life now appear so far off, and the evidence relative to the activities which filled them has become so historical, that I can venture to speak of them. As a lecturer, he not only benefited his students intellectually, but "settled them in the Bible, in their faith, in their doctrines"; as a helper in popular education, he won the grateful regard of young men in business; as a preacher, he confirmed his hearers in evangelical religion. This was not his whole work, however. In 1875 he began writing for the ninth edition of the *Encyclopædia Britannica*. The first of his articles is headed "Angel"; the second "Bible." The former shows his mastery of the historico-exegetical problems of Biblical theology; the second, the comprehensiveness of his learning and his deep critical insight. The composition of the articles "Canticles" and "David" also comes into this period—the latter of which in particular is a model of sympathetic Biblical criticism. Nor must I forget contributions to the *British Quarterly* and the *British and Foreign Evangelical Review*, and to the old series of the *Expositor*, all of which impress one with the singular steadiness and rapidity of this scholar's development, and, not least, with the security of his theological position. In fact were we to name a scholar of this period who was qualified to be professor both of Old Testament subjects and of theology in its broadest aspects, it would be Prof. Robertson Smith.

In 1878 this very scholar was charged with serious offences against sound doctrine with regard to the Scriptures. It was a historical event of no less moment than the proceedings against Bishop Colenso in England. Into the various phases of the trial (which was of course a purely ecclesiastical one) I will not enter.[1] They were followed with keen interest by the friends and foes of criticism both in the English-speaking countries and in Germany. It is said that Delitzsch, though not as far advanced critically as Robertson Smith, heartily wished him success. But the wish was not to be gratified. The Professor won his battle for others, but not for himself. Undisturbed by this, he determined to appeal to the Scottish laity, and in the winter of 1880 delivered introductory popular lectures on Old Testament criticism to large audiences at Edinburgh and Glasgow. These lectures were then published in a volume, of which in fifteen months 6,500 copies were sold. In the following winter the experiment was repeated with the

---

[1] The various publications connected with the trial are, to a great extent, of permanent interest. See especially the Professor's *Answer to the Form of Libel now before the Presbytery of Aberdeen* (Edinb., David Douglas, 1878).

same success, and these lectures too appeared in book-form. Need I say that these two volumes are those well-known books, *The Old Testament in the Jewish Church* and *The Prophets of Israel*, the former of which has lately (1892) been republished in a second, enlarged edition?

It is probable that the trial instituted in 1878 was not wholly unconnected with the appearance in the same year of that brilliant and incisive but, as English readers cannot help thinking, here and there irreverent book, Wellhausen's *Geschichte Israels* (vol. i.). However that may be, it is no secret that the two writers, Robertson Smith and Wellhausen are (in spite of their different idiosyncrasies) close friends,[1] and that they have exchanged many suggestions which have borne abundant fruit. In Hexateuch criticism, no doubt, the indebtedness is chiefly on the side of Robertson Smith, who has been (if I may say so) the most brilliant exponent of his friend's theory, not of course because it is Wellhausen's theory, but because it is truth. It ought however to be remembered that, taking this scholar's work as a whole, with all the minute details often stowed away in notes or in special journals (like the *Journal of Philology*), it is distinctly original work of a high class. When Robertson Smith began to devote himself more especially to Arabic studies, it was for the immediate present (not in the long run) the greatest possible loss

---

[1] The preface to the English edition of Wellhausen's book was written by Prof. W. R. Smith.

to our native Biblical criticism. He has but given us specimens of what he can do. Excellent as the *Encyclopædia* articles are, they are but very full summaries, and the two volumes of lectures are after all in the main popular introductions. That well-deserved eulogy which a conservative writer in the *Church Quarterly Review* (Oct. 1892) has given to one of the latter would certainly not be repeated, were Prof. Robertson Smith to publish a work of minute research, from the point of view actually reached by advanced critics.

Still, in spite of the regrets which I have expressed, we must all congratulate Cambridge on its adoption of so eminent a scholar. It was in 1883 that Robertson Smith became the colleague of Wright as a professor of Arabic, at the same time continuing the editorial labours on the *Encyclopædia Britannica* which he began in 1881. Apart from his Biblical articles in this work (note especially "Messiah," 1883; "Psalms," 1886; and the latest of all, "Zephaniah," 1888), the results of his studies are mainly embodied in two important books, which prove not only his interest in Semitic research in general, but also his sense that future Old Testament studies will be largely affected by archæological investigations. These works are—*Kinship and Marriage in Early Arabia* (1885), and *Lectures on the Religion of the Semites* (first series, 1889). It would carry me too far to discuss the theories of these brilliant and original volumes. From the point of view of an Old Testament scholar, who has not made the same special studies as the author and Wellhausen, what has to be said has been put forward with due modesty by Karl Budde in a review of the latter work.[1] If the author has sometimes based a bold theory on evidence of uncertain value, this cannot obscure the many results which are in a high degree probable, and if he now and then gives us a glimpse of his own theological system, those who believe in the undying importance of a sound theology, and in its close connexion with historical facts, cannot blame him for this. Nor can I criticize him severely for taking no account of Assyriological researches. It was best to attack the subject from the side of non-Assyriological Semitic study; here the author was at home, and his necessary onesidedness can in due time be corrected. It is of course quite another thing when, as in the *Prophets of Israel* (pp. 377, 401), Prof. Robertson Smith betrays a degree of distrust of Assyriology which further study of the subject would even in 1882 assuredly have dissipated.[2]

[1] *Theol. Literaturzeitung*, Nov. 1, 1890; cf. the review (by Mr. Lang?) in the *Speaker*, No. 1.

[2] "Perhaps with an extreme of scepticism" is too gentle an expression to use of Gutschmid's attack on the Assyriologists, considering the elaborate and conclusive reply of Schrader (*Keilinschriften und Geschichtsforschung*, 1878). Nor is it reasonable to doubt the correctness of Schrader's Assyriological explanation of the names of deities in Am. v. 26. We may of course, with Wellhausen (*Die Kleinen Propheten*, 1892), obelize the verse, but if the passage is genuine, the northern Israelites in the time of Amos worshipped Assyrian deities. We may suppose that they sought to appease the anger of those powerful gods, comparing Isa. x. 4 (if Lagarde's reading be adopted).

It was a great satisfaction to receive in June 1892 one's old favourite, *The Old Testament in the Jewish Church*, in a revised and enlarged form. The additions are most conspicuous in that part of Lecture V. which treats of the historical books; a new lecture (XIII.) is also introduced, containing a general sketch of the results of Hexateuch criticism, and the greater part of the lecture on the Psalter has been rewritten. Besides this, there are two fresh appended notes of much interest,—one relating to the text of 1 Sam. xvii., the other to the question of Maccabæan psalms in Books I.—III. of the Psalter. The first of these I shall pass over, referring to a record of my first impressions on reading the note in the *Expositor*, Aug. 1892, pp. 156-7. On the second, I venture to offer some criticisms, because in my work on the Psalter (1891) I professed myself unsatisfied with the theory put forward to account for psalms like the 44th in the very able article "Psalms" (*Enc. Brit.*) which is reproduced in Lect. VII. of this volume.

I am, I think, in no danger of being an unfair critic of Prof. Robertson Smith's theories on the Psalms, for two reasons.[1] First, because in my own conclusion as to the period of the Psalms, I have to a large extent his support. Secondly, because supposing that his theory of Pss. xliv., lxxiv., and lxxix. is correct, I am thereby enabled to strengthen my own

---

[1] The following criticisms are taken, with but little alteration, from my art. in the *New World*, Sept. 1892.

published view[1] as to the date of Isa. lxiii. 7—lxvi. Let me then heartily recommend, not only Lect. VII., but also Note D on pp. 437—440, in which the theory is again advocated that Pss. xliv., lxxiv., and lxxix. were written during the oppression of the Jews by Artaxerxes Ochus (about 350 B.C.). According to Professor Robertson Smith, this oppression included one important event of which no direct record has survived, viz. the burning of the temple (see Ps. lxxiv. 7, and cf. lxxix. 1). He remarks that our notices of Jewish history during the Persian period are extremely fragmentary, and that Josephus, though he does not mention the burning of the temple (as indeed he does not speak of the Jewish captivity under Ochus), certainly does mention a "defilement" of the temple by Bagôses under (as it seems) Artaxerxes II. (*Ant.* xi. 7, 1). Professor Robertson Smith says: "It seems to me that the objection to placing these psalms in the reign of Ochus comes mainly from laying too much weight on what Josephus relates about Bagôses. That Bagôses forced his way into the temple, and that he laid a tax on the daily sacrifices, is certainly not enough to justify the language of the psalms. But for this whole period Josephus is very ill informed, . . . and the whole Bagôses story looks like a pragmatical invention designed partly to soften the catastrophe of the Jews, and partly to explain it by the sin of the High Priest.

---

[1] See "Critical Problems of the Second Part of Isaiah," part 2, in the *Jewish Quarterly Review*, October 1891.

The important fact of the captivity to Hyrcania stands on quite independent evidence, but comes to us without any details. The captivity implies a revolt, and the long account given by Diodorus (xvi. 40 ff.) of Ochus' doings in Phœnicia and Egypt shows how that ruthless king treated rebels. In Egypt the temples were pillaged and the sacred books carried away (*ibid.* c. 51). Why should we suppose that the temple at Jerusalem and the synagogues fared better? Such sacrilege was the rule in Persian warfare; it was practised by Xerxes in Greece and also at Babylon. I have observed in the text that a rising of the Jews at this period could not fail to take a theocratic character, and that the war would necessarily appear as a religious war. Certainly the later Jews looked on the Persians as persecutors; the citation from Pseudo-Hec. in *Jos. c. Ap.* i. 22, though worthless as history, is good evidence for this; and it is also probable that the wars under Ochus form the historical background of the Book of Judith, and that the name Holophernes is taken from that of a general of Ochus, who took a prominent part in the Egyptian campaigns" (p. 439).

It will be seen that three assumptions are made here. The first is that Bagôses is the same as Bagôas,—the name of the ruthless general of the not less ruthless king, Artaxerxes Ochus. (This is a very easy one, though the character of Josephus's Bagôses does not agree with that of Bagôas.) The second is that Josephus almost completely transforms the true story of the events, out of regard for the prejudices of the Jews, who could not understand how God could have permitted His own faithful people to fall into such misery, and His own temple to be a second time polluted and burned by a heathen enemy. The third is that the rising of the Jews (the reality of which is, I think, disputed by Professor S. R. Kennedy only) had a "theocratic character" and a religious sanction. A few remarks may be offered on these assumptions. It is too strong a statement that "sacrilege was the rule in Persian warfare," and the Jewish temple had no images in it to irritate a faithful worshipper of Mazda. I admit, however, that the second and third Artaxerxes were "reactionary kings," who, both morally and religiously, "compromised the purity of Mazda-worship" (*Bampton Lectures*, p. 292); and if I am right in assigning a number of persecution psalms (such as vi., vii., x., xi., and xvii.) to the period of Persian oppression under one or the other of these kings, it is not a great step further to assign Pss. lxxiv. and lxxix. to that dark time. Even the consciousness of legal righteousness in Ps. xliv. is perhaps not much keener than that in Pss. vii. and xvii. It is true that in Isa. lxiv. 5—7 (which very probably comes from the same period) the very deepest contrition for sin is expressed, but the great confession of sin to which this passage belongs may have been written in a greater depth of misery than these psalms. To the references to Pseudo-Hecatæus and to Judith not much weight can be attached; but on other grounds I think it not impossible that after glutting his revenge on Sidon, Ochus sent his general Bagôas to chastise the Jews (cf. Judeich, *Kleinasiatische Studien*, p. 176), and that the temple was not only desecrated but destroyed. I should be inclined at present to hold out as regards Ps. xliv., for I can scarcely believe the Jews had taken so prominent a part in the general rebellion as to account for Ps. xliv. 9. But as regards Pss. lxxiv. and lxxix., the objection to the theory of Ewald (ed. 1) and Professor Smith, which I expressed in *Bampton Lectures*, pp. 91, 92, 102, has grown much feebler.

It may be said that Professor Smith's theory is bold and imaginative. So it is; but it is not on this account to be rejected. Unimaginative critics like Hupfeld are also very insipid, and do not greatly promote a vivid comprehension of the meaning of the Psalms. It cannot of course be proved, and Hitzig's view (suggested by a passage in *Solinus*, xxxv. 6, Mommsen) that it was Jericho, not Jerusalem, which suffered so much under Ochus, is not unworthy of attention. But it would be a great boon to be able to explain Ps. lxxiv. 7, lxxix. 1, and Isa. lxiv. 12, without having to suppose that the liturgical poems to which these passages belong were written to commemorate more than one catastrophe. On Professor Smith's other critical remarks (directed against theories of my own) I may be brief.[1] He appears to me to be too much a prey to the love of

---

[1] Comp. *Expositor*, Aug. 1892, p. 159.

simplicity; why psalms of the Greek age should not have found their way into Books I.—III. is not to me obvious, in spite of Professor Smith's remark (p. 437) on my "complicated hypothesis." That my view of Pss. xlii., xliii. is "fanciful," should be no objection to a historical student like the author. There are, as Milton has told us, two kinds of fancy: the nobler kind some of us prefer to call "imagination." Professor Smith, as we have seen, is himself not devoid of this priceless gift, without which there is no piecing together the scattered fragments of history, no vivifying the lifeless conclusions of a cold criticism. And surely it is hardly right to dismiss a critical theory too positively if you have no better substitute to propose. I myself cling less to my own views on Pss. xlv. and lxxii. than to many other parts of my system. But I cannot see much force in the prejudiced arguments brought against them; nor can I believe that Ps. lxxii. can be "a prayer for the re-establishment of the Davidic dynasty under a Messianic king according to prophecy" (why not call it at once a purely imaginative royal psalm?); nor that Ps. xlv. is most easily viewed "as a poem of the old kingdom." Nor can I see my way to explain Ps. lxviii. of the hopes created by the catastrophe of the Persian empire. Verse 30 seems clearly to show that when the psalmist wrote, Egypt was a powerful empire, from which danger to Palestine might be reasonably apprehended.[1] These however are but minor points,

---

[1] For my own present view of the passage, see *Journal of*

compared with those large ones on which this scholar, more completely and definitely than Prof. Driver, is on my side. And Prof. Robertson Smith cannot go back, he is still in the vanguard of critics.

Of **Prof. A. B. Davidson** this can perhaps hardly be said; and yet no one has done more to "found" criticism, at least in Scotland, than this eminent teacher. It is a noble but a difficult position—that of a professor of Biblical study in one of the great Scottish schools of theology,—noble, because he has access to the keenest and most inquisitive theological students in our island, and difficult, because until of late evangelical warmth has in Scotland been combined with singularly strong dogmatic prejudices. If conservative reviewers will permit me to say so, I venture to think that Dr. Davidson was specially prepared by nature and by training for this great position. Of his natural gifts, I will not speak now, because my small personal acquaintance with him, though enough to give me a special interest in all that he writes, is not sufficient for me to do so as I could wish. Moreover, one of Prof. Davidson's pupils, who has since gone to a higher school, has already given a delicate psychological study of his old master, and to this I can refer the reader.[1] But I am glad to have been able to verify to some slight extent much

---

Biblical Literature (Boston, U.S.A.), June 1892, and cf. *Aids to Study of Criticism*, p. 341. A possible historical situation is suggested by Jos., *Ant.*, xii. 3, 3.

[1] See Elmslie's study, *Expositor*, Jan. 1888

of what Elmslie has said. I see that modesty, that sense of the many-sidedness of truth and of the difficulties inherent in all systems, that disintegrating criticism, that latent heat which corrects the criticism, that love of great spiritual ideas. I see too—and I delight to see—that Prof. Davidson has a theology; it is not indeed any one of the current theologies, it is not systematic, nor shut up in formulæ, but it colours his thinking, and if all his too few sermons are like the single one which I have read (not heard), I can believe that he can sway the souls of all who are not mere church-goers but in earnest like himself. Prof. Davidson is evidently a great teacher, and the effect which he has produced proves that he has been seconded by generations of great-minded students.

These Scottish students, who have owed so much to their teacher, have, as it seems, partly repaid their debt. What else can be the reason of the strange fact which I am about to mention? His early unfinished work on Job (1862) showed a thorough philology and a power of dramatic presentation which justified the highest hopes. But not until 1881 did Prof. Davidson give any help to critical students at large (I refer to the article "Job" in the *Encyclopædia Britannica*), and not until 1884 did he publish his excellent volume on Job in the modest Cambridge Bible-series. Then, as it would appear, he became bolder, and felt sure enough about some solutions to express them in notices of books (see the now extinct theological review published by Free Church students, and the very useful *Critical Review*, edited by Prof. Salmond). And only last year we have received a commentary on Ezekiel in the same series, which is a worthy companion to its predecessor. Must we not, to some extent, thank the students of New College (from Robertson Smith's time onwards) for this diminished suspense of judgment? It was clearly impossible for such a teacher to let himself be distanced by his pupils. His pupils, in fact, had, to adopt Niebuhr's figure, become his "wings."

That in his hesitativeness Prof. Davidson has been true to his nature, I do not doubt. But it is scarcely possible for all of us to accept the justification of his teacher which Elmslie has given at one point of his sketch.[1] From a "higher critic's" point of view, Prof. Davidson sacrifices too much to the Philistines in that humorous and somewhat cavalier declaration which Elmslie quotes on p. 42 of his sketch. There is not a little of the Philistine in every untutored student even at New College, and those teachers who are more sensitive than Prof. Davidson to the less conspicuous data of criticism may be pardoned for regretting a gibe which in almost any other person they would meet with as dry and cavalier a retort. There is however much to be said in favour of the book on Job as a whole. The commentary is as thorough as under the limitations of the series to which it belongs it could well be, and the introduction,

[1] See *Expositor*, pp. 41—43.

in dealing with "higher criticism," puts forward, in an excellent form, some of the best suggestions which have been made. The objection which I shall have to raise, in speaking of Prof. Driver's views of Job, does not in the least affect my general estimate of the book. And similarly high praise is due to the *Ezekiel*. Both works are based upon accurate philology, though the text critical element may be hardly advanced enough for some. In the *Ezekiel* however the writer shows his grasp of a subject which, though closely connected with, is theoretically separate from the "higher criticism," viz. Biblical theology. And upon the whole, we may say that the best results of modern study have been passed through a cool and critical mind, and have come out in a form such as all students can appreciate. There can be no harder book than Ezekiel for the commentator, and if the last three pages of the introduction do but graze the surface of difficult critical problems, this is of course justified by the nature of the commentary. One only asks why this able scholar has not sought more opportunities of helping forward critical study. He is himself the loser by his excessive caution. For how can that introduction to Biblical theology, which we are eagerly expecting from him, be produced without the aid of a wisely bold "higher criticism"?[1]

---

[1] Prof. Davidson's other works are—*Outlines of Hebrew Accentuation* (1861); *An Introductory Hebrew Grammar* (ed. 1, 1874); *The Epistle to the Hebrews* (a dry but very able work ;

Another eminent **Biblical** theologian, who may justly **claim to** be moderate in the use of the "higher criticism," is **Prof. C. A. Briggs.** A more eager worker than Prof. Davidson, he fills (one may believe) a place specially marked out for him in his own land. We on this side of the Atlantic may however be allowed to adopt him, since his books appeal in part to a British public, and he contributes to the Oxford-printed Anglo-American Hebrew Lexicon. His two best-known books—*Biblical Study* (1883) and *Messianic Prophecy* (1886)—display a grasp of the religious as well as historical significance of the Old Testament, for the want of which no learning or critical keenness could atone. And with him I am bound to group another American critic of another school, **Prof. C. H. Toy,** author of *Judaism and Christianity*, and of some fine critical articles on the early traditions of Israel and cognate subjects in the *Journal of Biblical Literature*. Both these are Berlin students, and worthily promote the cause of international **Bible-criticism.**

Of individualities there is happily no end. This is the pledge to Old Testament critics that their science will constantly renew its youth. How different is **Gesenius** from Ewald, Davidson from Robertson Smith, **Schrader** from Sayce! Of the

---

1882). I may add that Prof. W. R. Smith has also written articles on Hebrews in the old *Expositor*. See also Prof. Davidson's articles in the *Expositor* on Hosea (1879), the Second Isaiah (1883-84), Amos (1887), **and** Joel (1888).

two latter I have now to speak; for Sayce needs a companion, and I can find none of English race. Both are eminent Assyriologists, though the scrupulous sobriety of the former hinders him from the often happy divinations of the latter. And lastly, both have been compelled to drop behind as Old Testament critics, so eager and rapid has been the advance of recent criticism. In **Schrader's** career two stages may be noticed. Like Dillmann, he was a scholar of Ewald, and was early drawn to the study of Ethiopic, on which he printed a prize dissertation in 1860. In 1863, at the age of twenty-seven, he succeeded Hitzig at Zurich, and published some valuable critical studies on Gen. i.—xi. After this the second stage begins. From Ethiopic studies he not unnaturally passed to Assyrian. In 1869 he brought out a revision of De Wette's Old Testament Introduction, and the accuracy of his statements respecting Assyrian matters was not less a special feature of that work than his development of the older Hexateuch criticism. In 1870 he passed to Giessen, and in 1873 to Jena, as professor of theology. But his zeal for Assyrian studies could not be restrained. In 1872 he replied convincingly to Alfred von Gutschmid's attack upon Assyriology, and in 1875 had the proud distinction of becoming the first professor of that subject in Germany, passing to Berlin university as the colleague of Dillmann. His best known work, *Die Keilinschriften und das Alte Testament* (ed. 1, 1872; ed. 2, 1883), has been translated by Prof. Whitehouse, whose introduction contains a full account of Schrader's former critical theories on the Hexateuch.

Of such an old friend as **Prof. A. H. Sayce** I could not speak in the tone of criticism, but for serious reasons. In the past I, like many others, have derived much stimulus from him, and in obtaining a working acquaintance with Assyrian philology his advice was invaluable. His high merits are incontestable. He has been an Assyriologist from his youth, and though he is ten years younger than Schrader, he was able in 1871-72 to discuss with him on equal terms the question of the name of the besieger of Samaria.[1] He is probably unsurpassed in his knowledge of the data of the inscriptions, and I am sure that no living scholar can excel him in his imaginative sense of history, and in his use of the imagination as the handmaid of discovery. For the latter habit I have heard him blamed, but it would be not less futile to blame Schrader for his sobriety. If Sayce's intuitions are hasty, they are also brilliant. His most daring hypotheses have again and again in various degrees pointed the way to truth, and when this has not been the case, he has generally corrected his own error. And yet I fear that there is one important point on which, not for the first time, I must remonstrate with him. It is too frequently his habit to appeal, not to Cæsar, but to the people.

[1] See articles by Sayce and Schrader, *Theol. Studien und Kritiken*, 1871-72.

In his historical inferences from the inscriptions he often stands, for good or for evil, alone. In spite of this, he constantly popularizes his results, without indicating whether they are peculiar to himself or not, and through the attractiveness of his style and the concessions which he makes to traditional Biblical orthodoxy, these results have obtained such a currency in the English-speaking countries that they are at present practically almost incontrovertible. The consequence is that our popular literature on the Old Testament is (as it seems to me) becoming an obstacle to progress. Bad as the old books on the Hebrew Scriptures were, they at any rate did not lay claim to any special degree of archæological accuracy. Now however all this is changed. I hear of Prof. Sayce everywhere as a pillar of traditional views of the Bible. Not to quote the American *Sunday School Times*, the *Newbery House Magazine*, the *Expository Times*, and the publications of the Religious Tract Society, I find it confidently stated that Prof. Sayce's Assyriological discoveries on the one hand and Prof. Margoliouth's Hebraistic and metrical "discoveries" on the other, were "recognized at every hand at the late Church Congress" (of 1892) as having brought about "a complete turn of the tide against the views of the higher critics."[1]

Now I do not for a moment accept the parallelism put forward in this quotation. To compare his

---

[1] Letter by W. W. Smyth, *Spectator*, Oct. 15, 1892.

results in the mass with those of Prof Margoliouth's inaugural lecture and subsequent essays, is absurd. The present Laudian Professor is a Hebraist from whom brilliant results may be expected, but these are as yet in the future, whereas Prof. Sayce can look back upon a long series of services to the study of the Bible. It is a pleasure to feel that one is at all a fellow-labourer with him—a pleasure to express a general assent to much that he has lately written (see *e.g.* his article in the *Contemporary Review*, Sept. 1890). But one must regret, not less for his own sake than for the cause of progress, that he should popularize so many questionable theories, and that in doing so he should make so many concessions to a most uncritical form of traditional theology. There was a time when he was not ashamed to be called a friend by the unpopular Bishop Colenso;[1] a time when he tried his skill on problems of the "higher criticism"; a time, not so far distant, when he delivered the Hibbert Lectures. Now however I find him coupled as an orthodox apologist with one of the most uncritical of living theologians. Now too I find him repudiating any favour for the long-tested methods of "higher criticism," and adopting that unfortunate error of conservative theologians which identifies the "higher criticism" with the conclusions of this or that writer, perhaps even of one who lived many years since. This course Prof.

---

[1] See Colenso, *The Pentateuch*, &c., Part VI., Pref. p. xxxii.

Sayce has taken, for instance, in two articles in a journal which discharges in many respects useful functions, the *Expository Times* (Dec. 1891, Oct. 1892). He may tell me that he was not writing for scholars, but he *was* writing for those who may yet become scholars, who at any rate claim to express an opinion, and have it in their power to hinder progress.

I may seem to be too fond of qualifying; but positive and peremptory assertions, even when speaking *pro domo*, are not to my taste. I fully admit that until Schrader and Sayce arose, Old Testament critics did not pay much attention to Assyriology. This however was not because they held a narrow theory of criticism. From the time of Graf (1866) onwards the necessity of archæological detail-criticism has been fully admitted by Hexateuch critics, and this admission implies a gradual change in the habit of mind of Old Testament critics in general. Not that literary analysis is in the least disparaged, but the time has come, as even Colenso, quite apart from Graf, dimly felt in 1862, for a greater infusion of historical "realism" into the critic's work. Since 1866, every ten years has shown an increase of this spirit, and though a vast amount of work remains to be done (we want the help of friendly and critical archæologists), a good beginning has been made. No single worker has helped so much as Prof. Robertson Smith (working on Wellhausen's lines), and if Prof. Sayce had more time, and could and would co-operate with the "higher critics," he might himself give invaluable assistance. In 1873-74 he was still friendly to critical analysis, though he very rightly desired the analysts to revise and, if necessary, modify their results in accordance with Assyriological data. He himself offered provisional critical conclusions with regard to Isa. xxxvi.—xxxix., and the Deluge-narratives and the " Ethnological Table " in Genesis.[1] I fear that his suggestions on Gen. x. have not been considered by the analysts (at least in any published work), while those which he put forward on the two other passages have failed to win acceptance. And Prof. Sayce himself has no doubt by this time given up his old view on the date of the Hebrew Deluge-stories.

What Prof. Sayce should, in my opinion, have done in the semi-popular articles referred to, was to place himself frankly where he stood in 1873-74, and admit once more that Assyriology "demonstrated the untenability of the traditional view of Genesis," and "confirms the [main] conclusions of scientific criticism." If he had further said that some critics needed to be stirred up to greater zeal for archæology, —that Kuenen for instance had not given enough attention to Assyriology, and that Wellhausen and Robertson Smith had in former years (like other Semitic scholars) displayed an excessive distrust of that study, I should have had no objection. But to bring such unfair charges against the "higher critics," and

[1] See *Theological Review*, 1873, pp. 15—31, 364—377 ; 1874, pp. 59—69.

to speak so disparagingly of their (supposed) methods, and moreover to make such ill-founded statements as to the relation between Assyriology and the Book of Genesis as he has of late years done, conduces to the spread of theological prejudice and historical error.

To oppose Prof. Sayce (not indeed as an Assyriologist, nor as an archæological student, but as a popularizer of questionable theories and unfair accusations) is at present, I know, a difficult task, so far as England and America are concerned. Not merely for theological reasons, but because the archæological interest among us has become so strong. As Prof. Sayce knows, I have always been on the side of archæology. But I conceive that one ought not to favour archæology at the expense of criticism. Old Testament criticism is a genuine historical movement, and those who have produced it have gone on constantly widening their range and improving their methods. To speak as disparagingly of Old Testament critics as Prof. Ramsay has lately done of Homeric critics,[1] is, I venture to submit, highly unjust, and calculated to produce a quite unnecessary partisanship. That very able explorer may or may not be altogether right in drawing a line between the non-archæological Homeric criticism of the past and the archæological of the future. But even if he be right, there is no true analogy between this case and that of Old Testament criticism.

[1] See his art., "Mr. Gladstone on Homer," *The Bookman*, 1892; cf. Gardner, *New Chapters in Greek History* (1891).

Much evil has been wrought by the mistaken use of analogy, and for the sake of historical truth let those who read Prof. Sayce be on their guard.

Let me take a crucial instance. "Recent discovery," says Prof. Ramsay, "is bringing home to us the possibility that after all Agamemnon may once have lived.... We may prefer to explain the origin of the 'tale of Troy divine' in some other way, and not as the history of actual events; but we must now treat the view that it is a fundamentally true tale as conceivably right; and there is a widely-spread and growing feeling that in the immediate future the attitude towards the Homeric poems which is least erroneous and most likely to lead to further discovery is that they preserve a picture of a period of history which did once exist." It would be natural for an unwary student to assume that the same possibility or probability exists in the case of the story of Abraham. Prof. Sayce, in his well-known work *Fresh Light from the Ancient Monuments* (pp. 53—59), even speaks as if those details in the story to which he refers were, beyond doubt, strictly historical, and as if "the whole account" of the campaign of Chedorlaomer and his allies, and the surprise of the invaders by Abraham and his confederates, were "extracted from the Babylonian archives." He also gives "an approximate date for the rescue of Lot by Abraham, and consequently for the age of Abraham himself." Still more recently he has even assured us that "in every point the history of Melchizedek in

Gen. xiv. receives confirmation."[1] I confess that I am astonished at this. So far as regards the facts mentioned in *Fresh Light*, pp. 55-56, they have long since been absorbed by Old Testament critics, by moderate critics like Dillmann in one way, by advanced critics like Kuenen in another.[2] And what difficulty need be caused by the facts derived by Prof. Sayce from the priceless Tell el-Amarna tablets? A distinction must however be drawn between the certain and the uncertain facts. The reported "discovery of transcendent importance" relative to Gen. xiv. 18 sinks upon examination into

---

[1] *Expository Times*, Oct. 1892, p. 18; cf. also *Records of the Past*, v. 60—65, and articles by Sayce in *Hebraica* and the *Newbery House Magazine*. The *Guardian*, in a review of Fripp's *Genesis* (Nov. 16, 1892) unsuspiciously adopts Prof. Sayce's results and inferences. I have no controversial *animus*, and simply desire a critical treatment of the facts. Comp. Winckler's translations in *Zt. f. Assyriologie*, Sept. 1891. Comp. also Halévy, *Recherches bibliques*, last fascicule, p. 727; Morris Jastrow, *Zt. f. Assyriologie*, 1892, heft 3, and *Journal of Biblical Literature*, 1892, Part I. (regretting that this distinguished "scholar" should be "doing a mischief of incalculable extent").

[2] Dillmann is of opinion that the narrative in Gen. xiv. (*vv.* 18—20 excepted) contains facts derived from a foreign source. But this must be qualified by what he says of the Abraham of Genesis elsewhere (see introd. to Gen. xii. &c.). The Melchizedek-story is a justification of the practice of paying tithes to the priestly tribe, but the figure of Melchizedek is probably derived from some popular legend. Kuenen thinks that Gen. xiv. is a fragment of a post-Exilian version of Abram's life, a *midrash*, such as the Chronicler likewise had among his authorities (2 Chron. xxiv. 27), and adopts E. Meyer's view that the historical facts of the setting of the story were obtained by the author of the *midrash* in Babylon. Cf. Cheyne, *Origin of the Psalter*, pp. 42, 165, 270.

an interesting and valuable fact about Jerusalem which is of no direct importance for Genesis-criticism. I do not think that we can at present grant that Uru-Salimmu was anciently shortened into Salimmu, nor (though I inclined to this view myself in 1888)[1] that Salimmu is the name of a god, much less that his priest was the king of Jerusalem. But in any case there is ample room both in Dillmann's theory and in Kuenen's (which is my own) for these facts, if proved. I am afraid that Prof. Sayce's defence of the narrative in Gen. xiv. is not very successful. And neither by him, nor by any one else, has it yet been made probable that there was a historical individual among the ancestors of the Israelites called Abram, or that the picture of "the times of Abraham" in Genesis is (to adopt Prof. Ramsay's phrase) a "fundamentally true tale" (except indeed so far as it reflects the times of the narrators).

Another chapter of Genesis, the historical characters of which Prof. Sayce is popularly supposed to have vindicated against the "higher critics," is Gen. xxiii. Was there, as he himself stated in 1888, a "Hittite population" in the south of Palestine, "which clustered round Hebron, and to whom the origin of Jerusalem was partly due"?[2] It is at any rate proved by the Tell el-Amarna tablets, which Prof.

---

[1] The present writer himself favoured this view before Sayce had published either his views on Melchizedek or even his *Hibbert Lectures* (see Cheyne, *Book of Psalms*, p. 213).

[2] *The Hittites* (R.T.S.), p. 13.

Sayce and others are studying, that the Hittites made conquests in Canaan in the fifteenth century B.C., and even threatened Jerusalem. But this admission does not carry with it the historical character of the narrative in Gen. xxiii., which states that Abraham brought a "field" and a sepulchre of "the people of the land, even the children of Heth" (Gen. xxiii. 7). The historical fact of the Hittite conquest has come down to the writer symbolized as P in a meagre and scarcely recognizable form, and has become the setting of a tradition of uncertain date. There is much more that might be added. How strange it is that even Prof. J. Robertson refers quite seriously to Prof. Sayce's theories on the names of Saul, David, and Solomon.[1] One could wish that Franz Delitzsch were still alive, to write another powerful protest[2] against the audacities of a free lance.

I am aware that Prof. Sayce guards himself now and then against being supposed to be a pure conservative. He declines (in *Expository Times*) to make any concession to the "historical" theory of the narratives in Daniel, he believes (unlike M. Halévy) that there are documents in Genesis,[3] and even that

---

[1] *Early Religion of Israel*, pp. 178-179. So a reviewer of my *Aids to the Devout Study of Criticism* (letter in *Guardian*, Oct. 5, 1892) not less seriously appeals to Prof. Sayce as a critical authority. Against Sayce, see Tiele's review of the *Hibbert Lectures* in the *Theologisch Tijdschrift*, 1890, p. 96.

[2] *Zt. f. kirchliche Wissenschaft*, 1888, pp. 124—126.

[3] For Halévy's opinions, see his strange review of Kautzsch and Socin's *Genesis, Revue critique*, 14—21 sept. 1891.

a good deal of the Old Testament **in its present form is composite in character,** though nothing definite beyond that has been established.[1] But these concessions to criticism cannot obtain the same wide currency as his other statements, and even were it otherwise, they come far short of justice. From a layman they would be an interesting proof of the gradual filtration of critical views, **but from one who** is well known to have been long interested in theology they are only an additional obstacle to progress. I cannot help deploring this state of things. **Need it continue? Why** should not this "versatile and Protean **scholar"** (as Prof. Ramsay calls him), who has, by his own admission, "not paid much attention of late years to Biblical criticism," and speaks of "the school of Wellhausen" from hearsay, repair this omission, **and** seek the assistance of the critics in questions on which he and they are equally concerned? To the services of Assyriology they are by no means blind; why should not he on his side once more recognize them as fellow-explorers with himself of the dark places of antiquity? It is at any rate as such an explorer that I venture to include him among English "founders of criticism."

Last, not least, **in the** present group is another colleague of the writer, **Prof. S. R.** Driver. His **merits however are too great** to be dealt with adequately in the space which remains in this chapter.

[1] *Christian Commonwealth,* Oct. 22, 1891 (a report of Prof. Sayce's opinions which has evidently been carefully corrected).

I will therefore reserve this subject, and pass on to some younger scholars who are now winning their way to the front. **Prof. A. F. Kirkpatrick**, in his handbooks to 1 and 2 Samuel (*Cambridge Bible*, 1880-81), showed himself a careful Hebraist and an able teacher, but his point of view was non-critical. Since then, in *The Divine Library of the Old Testament* (1891) and in his commentary on Book I. of the Psalms (same series, 1891), he has shown that he has come over to the critical side. The moral and intellectual energy presupposed by this step deserves cordial recognition. One can only welcome so true, so earnest, so reverent a scholar. His two earliest critical or semi-critical works are deficient (naturally enough) in maturity of judgment and in grasp of the large and complicated questions before him. But he has time yet to spare, and if he should prefer rather to follow Davidson than Robertson Smith—rather to be an exegete and a Biblical theologian than a historical critic, one can but rejoice, assuming that he too has an equally friendly feeling towards those who, for the sake of exegesis and Biblical theology, feel bound to prosecute a keener criticism.[1] Nor can one hope anything less from his younger colleague, **Prof. H. E. Ryle**. This scholar appears to have specialized rather late, and to this we may attribute a certain hesitatingness in his thoughtful and learned handbook on the Canon (1891). But he too is a careful Hebraist (as his own and Mr. James's work, *The*

[1] His *Warburton Lectures* have not as yet appeared (Nov. 1892).

Psalms of the Pharisees, proves), and his popular studies on the Early Narratives of Genesis (1892) show that he is assimilating the best results of literary and archæological criticism. His expected (November 1892) volume on Ezra and Nehemiah (*Cambridge Bible*) will no doubt confirm this view of his capacities and attainments. Very much light has been thrown upon these books by recent study, and no one can adapt this new knowledge to English wants better than Prof. Ryle.

Nor must one overlook two rising American scholars, who, by their linguistic training and early adhesion to the critical point of view, justify the highest hopes—**Prof. Francis Brown** and **G. F. Moore.** The former has given special attention to the relations between Assyriology and Old Testament studies, the latter to critical exegesis; and both seem to be more completely at home in the "higher criticism" than their Cambridge colleagues. Circumstances and individualities differ, nor must we complain if America should for a short time surpass Great Britain in the maturity of its "higher critics." Prof. Moore's articles in American and German periodicals are models in their kind, and one looks forward with eagerness to a philological commentary from his pen. Prof. Brown's promised handbook to the contemporary history (*Zeitgeschichte*) of the Old Testament in Clark's new International Library will fill a gap which is every day more painfully felt. His lecture on the use and abuse of Assyriology in

Old Testament study (1885), and his articles on the Hittites and on Babylonian religion (*Presbyterian Review*, 1886, 1888), will repay an attentive perusal. Above all, the Hebrew Lexicon, of which he is the principal editor, will, when completed, ensure a sound basis for Old Testament criticism for many a long day. An Episcopalian scholar, Dr. J. P. Peters, a trained Hebraist and Assyriologist, should also be mentioned with honour.

The name of Prof. Francis Brown naturally suggests that of **Prof. Owen C. Whitehouse**, a careful student of Assyriology, who has translated Prof. Schrader's important work, *The Cuneiform Inscriptions*, with learned additions. This scholar has moved but slowly from a more conservative critical point of view as regards the Hexateuch. In 1888 he attempted to revive the theory of Ewald that the "Grundschrift" dated from the time of Solomon;[1] from more recent articles I gather that he has seen reason to give up this view, but that he has not yet obtained many fixed points in Old Testament criticism. **Prof. G. A. Smith** was probably trained in a freer atmosphere. Of his popular exposition of Isaiah (1889-90) I have often spoken with no lack of warmth. Why I cannot assent to his views on the dates of the later portions of Isa. xl.—lxvi., I have explained elsewhere.[2] **Prof. Archibald Duff's** *Old Testament Theology*, vol. i. (1891), is a work conceived

---

[1] *Expositor*, 1888 (1), p. 144.
[2] *Ibid.* 1891 (1), pp. 150—160.

in a free, evangelical spirit, and carried out with delicate insight and a sometimes almost too ingenious scholarship. Both Duff and G. A. Smith have suffered somewhat as writers from the effects of over-much preaching, but if by their books preachers can be induced to study the root-ideas of Biblical religion in their historical development, the Church at large will be the gainer. But has pure criticism been neglected? Certainly not. The year 1891 saw the appearance of two new writers, **Mr. E. J. Fripp** with his truly practical edition of Genesis according to advanced criticism (not without some more or less original views of his own), and **Mr. W. E. Addis** (a ripe theological and Semitic scholar and follower of Kuenen and Wellhausen) with the first volume of his translation and chronological arrangement of the documents of the Hexateuch. The latter book has useful notes, and an introduction as lucidly expressed as it is full of matter. Mr. Addis was already known to specialists by his brave attempt to familiarize Roman Catholic readers with the facts revealed by the "higher criticism" of the Old Testament. His work, being based on more prolonged studies, has a scholarly ripeness which Mr. Fripp's work, bright and keen as he is, can hardly possess. **Mr. C. G. Montefiore's** *Hibbert Lectures* for 1892 have not yet (November 1892) appeared, but his articles in the *Jewish Quarterly Review* sufficiently prove how steadily and surely he is ripening into a fine critic.

Returning to America, one chronicles with pleasure

Mr. B. W Bacon's *The Genesis of Genesis* (1892). This, as the title-page tells us, is a study of the documentary sources of the first Book of Moses in accordance with the results of critical science, illustrating the presence of Bibles within the Bible. It is, as Prof. G. F. Moore says in his introduction, the fruit of long and thorough study of the text, and of intimate acquaintance with the literature of recent criticism. Mr. Bacon strikes me as the ablest of our younger critics of the Hexateuch; his articles in *Hebraica* and in the *Journal of Biblical Literature* well deserve to be studied. Nor is he the only contributor to these two periodicals who would have a claim to recognition in a more complete record than this. From the editor himself (Prof. Harper) we may expect some solid work in Prof. Haupt's expected translation of the Old Testament.

The last of the younger English critics whom I can mention at present [1] is **Mr. A. A. Bevan.** It is true that he has been chiefly attracted by the linguistic side of the Old Testament. His emendations [2] of the text of Isaiah and of Daniel may not commend themselves to one's judgment, but they are evidence of his critical acumen. His *Short Commentary on the Book of Daniel* (1892), though critically

---

[1] Scholars like Prof. Bennett, Prof. A. R. Kennedy, Prof. Davison, and Dr. John Taylor (author of *The Hebrew Text of Micah*) will pardon me if I wait for published evidence of what I do not in the least doubt, their ability to deal from their respective points of view with critical problems.

[2] See *Journal of Philology*, and *The Book of Daniel*.

incomplete, aims at a high philological standard, not without success, and the frankness with which he adopts and defends the best current solution of the problem of Daniel, without looking about for a compromise, deserves high praise. It is, I confess, the spirit of compromise that I chiefly dread for our younger students. Many of them are now in influential posts, and are listened to with respect. But under present circumstances it is perhaps difficult for them to avoid extending the sphere of compromise from education to scientific inquiry. May they have firmness and wisdom to meet their ofttimes conflicting responsibilities!

CHAPTER XI.[1]

DRIVER (1).

THE much fuller adhesion of **Professor Driver** to the still struggling cause of Old Testament criticism is an event in the history of this study. That many things indicated it as probable, can doubtless now be observed; but until the publication in the *Contemporary Review* (February 1890) of a singularly clear and forcible paper on the criticism of the historical books, it was impossible to feel quite sure where Dr. Driver stood. Up to the year 1882, he was known through various learned publications (notably that on the Hebrew Tenses) as an honest and keen-sighted Hebrew scholar, but in matters of literary and historical criticism he had not as yet committed himself, except of course to the non-acceptance of any such plainly unphilological view as the Solomonic authorship of Ecclesiastes.[2] In 1882, to the great benefit of Hebrew studies, he succeeded Dr. Pusey at Christ Church, and began at

---

[1] Chaps. xi.—xiii. originally appeared in the *Expositor* for Feb., March, and April 1892. They have however been carefully revised, and in some parts expanded, condensed, or otherwise modified.   [2] *Hebrew Tenses*, § 133 (ed. 2, p. 151).

once to improve to the utmost the splendid opportunities of his position both for study and for teaching. He now felt it impossible to confine himself within purely linguistic limits, however much from a conscientious regard for the "weak brethren" he may have desired to do so. It is true that in his first published critical essay, he approached the "higher criticism" from the linguistic side (*Journal of Philology*, 1882, pp. 201—236), but there are evidences enough in the pages of the *Guardian* and of the *Expositor* that he was quietly and unobtrusively feeling his way towards a large and deep comprehension of the critical and exegetical problems of the Hexateuch. Nor must the old lecture-lists of the university be forgotten. These would prove, if proof were needed, that his aspirations were high, and his range of teaching wide, and that the sketch of his professorial functions given in his excellent inaugural lecture was being justified. To the delightful obligation of lecturing on the Hebrew texts, we owe a singularly complete and instructive volume on the Hebrew of Samuel (1890), the earnest of other volumes to come. And that Dr. Driver did not shrink from touching the contents of the Old Testament, the outsider may divine from a small and unostentatious work,[1] which forms an admirable popular introduction to the reverent critical study of

[1] *Critical Notes on the International Sunday School Lessons from the Pentateuch for* 1887 (New York: Charles Scribner's Sons, 1887).

certain chapters of Genesis and Exodus. In 1888 came the excellent though critically imperfect handbook on Isaiah (in the "Men of the Bible" Series), which very naturally supersedes my own handbook published in 1870.[1] In 1891 we received the valuable introduction which forms the subject of this notice, and some time previously we ought, I believe, to have had before us the articles on the books of the Pentateuch which Dr. Driver had contributed to the new edition of Smith's *Dictionary of the Bible*.

So now Dr. Driver's long suspense of judgment is to a great extent over. The mystery is cleared up, and we know very nearly where he now stands. If any outsider has a lingering hope or fear of an imminent counter-revolution from the linguistic side, he must not look to Dr. Driver to justify it. The qualities which are here displayed by the author are not of the sensational order, as a brief summary of them will show. First, there is a masterly power of selection and condensation of material. Secondly, a minute and equally masterly attention to correctness of details. Thirdly, a very unusual degree of insight into critical methods, and of ability to apply them. Fourthly, a truly religious candour and openness of mind. Fifthly, a sympathetic interest in the difficulties of the ordinary orthodox believer. Willingly do I

[1] It is only just to myself to say that this work is in no sense, as a hostile writer in the *Guardian* states, "a *youthful* production," but was written at an age when some men nowadays are professors, and both was and is respectfully referred to by German critics.

mention these points. Dr. Driver and I are both engaged in a work

"Too great for haste, too high for rivalry,"

and we both agree in recognizing the law of generosity. But I must add that I could still more gladly have resigned this privilege to another. For I cannot profess to be satisfied on all really important points with Dr. Driver's book. And if I say what I approve, I must also mention what I—not indeed disapprove—but feel obliged to regret. But why should I take up the pen? Has not the book had praise and (possibly) dispraise enough already? If I put forward my objections, will not a ripe scholar like Dr. Driver have an answer from his own point of view for most of them? Why should I not take my ease, and enjoy even the less satisfactory parts of the book as reflections of the individuality of a friend? And the answer is, Because I fear that the actual position of Old Testament criticism may not be sufficiently understood from this work, and because the not inconsiderable priority of my own start as a critic gives me a certain vantage-ground and consequently a responsibility which Dr. Driver cannot and would not dispute with me. I will not now repeat what I have said with an entirely different object in the introduction to my *Bampton Lectures*, but on the ground of those facts I am bound to make some effort to check the growth of undesirable illusions, or, at any rate, to contribute something to the formation of clear ideas in the popular mind.

I must here beg the reader not to jump to the conclusion that I am on the whole opposed to Dr. Driver. As I have already hinted, the points of agreement between us are much more numerous than those of difference, and in many respects I am well content with his courage and consistency. The debt which Dr. Driver owes to those scholars who worked at Old Testament criticism before him he has in good part repaid. He came to this subject theologically and critically uncommitted, and the result is that, in the main, he supports criticism with the full weight of his name and position. There is only one objection that I have to make to the *Introduction*. It is however threefold: 1. the book is to a certain extent a compromise; 2. the (partial) compromise offered cannot satisfy those for whom it is intended; 3. even if it were accepted, it would not be found to be safe. Let us take the first point. My meaning is, that Dr. Driver is free in his criticism up to a certain point, but then suddenly stops short, and that he often blunts the edge of his decisions, so that the student cannot judge of their critical bearings. I will endeavour to illustrate this from the book, and, in doing so, never to forget the "plea" which Dr. Driver so genially puts in to be "judged leniently for what he has *not* said" (Preface, p. ix). At present, to clear the ground for future "lenient" or rather friendly criticisms, let me only remark that I am not myself opposed on principle to all "stopping short," *i.e.* to all compromise. In June and August 1889, I submitted to those whom it concerned a plan of reform in the teaching of the Old Testament, which included a large provisional use of it.[1] My earnest appeal was indeed not responded to. Even my friend Dr. Sanday passes it over in a well-known work,[2] and praises the waiting attitude of our more liberal bishops. But I still reiterate the same appeal for a compromise, though I couch it differently. It is not at all hard to find out what results of criticism are most easily assimilated by thinking laymen, and most important for building up the religious life. Let those results be put forward, with the more generally intelligible grounds for them, first of all for private study, and then, with due regard to local circumstances, in public or semi-public teaching. To *practical* compromises I am therefore favourable, but this does not bind me to approve of *scientific* ones. The time for even a partly apologetic criticism or exegesis is almost over; nothing but the "truest truth" will serve the purposes of the best contemporary students of theology. This indeed is fully recognized in the preface of the editors of the "Library" to which this book belongs, the object of which is defined as being "adequately (to) represent the present condition of investigation, and (to) indicate the way for further progress."

I regret therefore that Dr. Driver did not leave the task of forming a distinctively Church criticism (of

---

[1] See *Contemporary Review*, August 1889.
[2] *The Oracles of God* (1891).

which even now I do not deny the value for a certain
class of students) to younger men,[1] or to those
excellent persons who, after standing aloof for years,
now begin to patronize criticism, saying, " Thus far
shalt thou come, but no farther!" I heartily sympathize with Dr. Driver's feelings, but I think that there
is a still " more excellent way " of helping the better
students, viz. to absorb the full spirit of criticism
(not of *irreligious* criticism), and to stand beside the
foremost workers, only taking care, in the formulation
of results, frankly to point out their religious bearings,
of which no one who has true faith need be afraid.
I know that this might perhaps have involved other
modifications of Dr. Driver's plan, but I cannot help
this. I do not feel called upon to sketch here in
outline the book that might have been, but I could
not withhold this remark, especially as I am sure
that even Dr. Driver's very "moderate" textbook
will appear to many not to give hints enough
concerning the religious value of the records criticized.
And forcible, judicious, and interesting as the preface
is, I do not feel that the author takes sufficiently high
ground. I am still conscious of an unsatisfied desire
for an inspiring introductory book to the Old Testament, written from the combined points of view of a
keen critic and a progressive evangelical theologian.

Next, as to the second point. Can this com-

---

[1] A popular semi-critical book on the origin of the Old
Testament Scriptures might be of great use for schools and
Bible-classes.

promise (or, partial compromise) satisfy orthodox judges? It is true that Dr. Driver has one moral and intellectual quality which might be expected to predispose such persons specially in his favour—the quality of caution. The words "moderation" and "sobriety" have a charm for him; to be called an extreme critic, or a wild theorist, would cause him annoyance. And this "characteristic caution" has not failed to impress a prominent writer in the most influential (Anglican) Church paper. The passage is at the end of the first part of a review of the *Introduction*,[1] and the writer hazards the opinion that, on the most "burning" of all questions Dr. Driver's decision contains the elements of a working compromise between the old views and the new. But how difficult it is to get people to agree as to what "caution" and "sobriety" are! For if we turn to the obituary notices of the great Dutch critic, Abraham Kuenen, we find that he strikes some competent observers as eminently cautious and sober-minded, not moving forward till he has prepared the way by careful investigation, and always distinguishing between the certain and the more or less probable. And again, it appears from the recent Charge of Bishop Ellicott that this honoured theologian (who alas! still stands where he stood in earlier crises) sees no great difference between the critical views of Kuenen and Wellhausen on the one hand, and those

---

[1] *Guardian*, Nov. 25, 1891.

of Dr. Driver and "the English Analytical School" on the other. If the former have "lost all sense of proportion" and been "hurried" to extreme results by an "almost boundless self-confidence," the latter have, by their "over-hasty excursions into the Analytical," prepared the way for "shaken and unstable minds" to arrive at results which are only a little more advanced.[1] And in perfect harmony with Bishop Ellicott's denial of the possibility of "compromise," I find a writer of less sanguine nature than Dr. Driver's reviewer warning the readers of the *Guardian* that the supposed *rapprochement* will not "form a bridge solid enough to unite the opposite sides of the chasm" between the two schools of thought.[2]

This is in my opinion a true saying. Some of those to whom Dr. Driver's compromise is addressed will (like Bishop Ellicott) be kept aloof by deep theological differences. Others, whose minds may be less definitely theological, will place their hope in a critical "counter-revolution" (see p. 250), to be effected either by an induction from linguistic facts, or by means of cuneiform and archæological discovery. I do not speak without cause, as readers of popular religious journals will be aware. The limits of Dr. Driver's work did not permit him to refer to this point; but considering the avidity with which a

---

[1] *Christus Comprobator* (1891), pp. 29, 59. I cannot help respectfully protesting against the title of this work.
[2] *Guardian*, Dec. 2, 1891.

large portion of the public seizes upon assertions backed by some well-known name, it may soon become necessary for him and for others to do so. Upon a very slender basis of reason and of facts an imposing structure of revived and "rectified"[1] traditionalism may soon be charmed into existence. We may soon hear again the confident appeal to the "common sense" of the "plain Englishman"—that invaluable faculty which, according to Bishop Ellicott, is notably wanting, "*if it be not insular prejudice to say so*," in all recent German critics of the Old Testament. Critical and historical sense (which is really the perfection of common sense, trained by right methods, and assisted by a healthy imagination) may continue to be treated with contempt, and Dr. Driver's book may receive credit, not for its substantial merits, but for what, by comparison, may be called its defects. These are real dangers; nay, rather to some extent they are already facts which cannot but hinder the acceptance of this well-meant compromise.

And, lastly, as to the third point. Is even a partial compromise like this safe? I am afraid that it is not. It implies that Biblical criticism must be pared down for apologetic reasons. It assumes that though the traditional theory of the origin and (for this is, in part, allusively dealt with) the historic value of the Old Testament books has been over-

---

[1] I borrow the word from Bishop Ellicott.

thrown, yet we must in our reconstruction keep as close to the old theory or system as we can. This, at the present stage of intellectual development, is unsafe. Dr. Driver's fences are weak, and may at any moment be broken down. Nothing but the most *fearless* criticism, combined with the most genuine spiritual faith in God, and in His Son, and in the Holy Spirit, can be safe. I do not of course judge either friends or foes by their expressed theories. If it should be made decidedly the more probable view that St. John did *not* originate the Fourth Gospel as it now stands, I am sure, in spite of Dr. Sanday's recent words,[1] that all truly religious students would believe, with heart and with head, as strongly as ever in the incomparable nature and the divine mediatorship of Jesus Christ.[2] They would do so on the ground of the facts which would still be left by the historical analysis of the Gospels, and on the correspondence between a simple Christian view of those facts and the needs of their own and of the Church's life. And so I am sure that without half so many qualifications as Dr. Driver has given, the great facts left, not to say recovered, by advanced Old Testament criticism are quite sufficient to justify the theory of Hebrews i. 1, which is, I doubt not, of permanent importance for the thinking Christian.

Before passing on, let me crave permission to make

---

[1] *Contemporary Review*, Oct. 1891, p. 530.
[2] See Hermann's article, "The Historical Christ the Foundation of our Faith," in the *Zt. f. Theol. u. Kirche*, 1882, p. 232.

two remarks, which may perhaps take off any undue sharpness from previous criticisms. The first is, that in criticizing the author, I am equally criticizing myself. There was a time when I was simply a Biblical critic, and was untouched by the apologetic interest. Finding that this course cramped the moral energies, I ventured to superadd the function of the "Christian Advocate" (of course only in the modern sense of this indispensable phrase). **The plan to which I was led was to *adapt* Old Testament criticism and exegesis to the prejudices of orthodox students by giving the** traditional view, in its most refined form, the benefit of the doubt, whenever there was a sufficiently reasonable case for doubt. This is what **the** Germans call *Vermittelung*, and **I** think that as late as ten or twelve years ago *Vermittelung* was sorely needed. But now, as it seems to me, we have got beyond this. *Vermittelung*, when practised by the leaders of study in works of a scientific character, will prove a hindrance, not only to the progress of historical truth, but to the fuller apprehension of positive evangelical principles. The right course for those who would be in the van of progress seems to be that which I have faintly indicated above, and too imperfectly carried out in my more recent works. A perfectly free but none the less devout criticism is, in short, the best ally, both of spiritual religion and of a sound apologetic theology.

The second is, that in Dr. Driver's case the some- **what excessive caution** of his critical work can be accounted for, not merely by a conscientious regard to the supposed interests of the Church, but by his peculiar temperament and past history. In the variety of temperaments God has appointed that the specially cautious one shall not be wanting; and this, like all His works, is no doubt "very good." Caution, like other useful qualities, needs to be sometimes represented in an intensified degree. And Hebrew grammar in England urgently needed a more cautious, more exact treatment. This Dr. Driver felt at the outset of his course, and all recent Hebrew students owe him a debt of gratitude. But what was the natural consequence of his long devotion to the more exact, more philological study of the Hebrew Scriptures? This—that when he deliberately enlarged his circle of interests, he could not see his way as far nor as clearly as those critics of wider range, who had entered on their career at an earlier period. Indeed, even apart from the habits of a pure philologist, so long a suspension of judgment on critical points must have reacted somewhat upon Dr. Driver's mind, and made it at first very difficult for him to form decisions. These have been real hindrances, and yet to what a considerable extent he has overcome them! How much advanced criticism has this conscientious churchman—this cautious Hebraist—been able to absorb? And how certainly therefore he has contributed to that readjustment of theology to the general intellectual progress which is becoming more and more urgent!

I now proceed to such a survey of the contents of the work as my limits render possible. The preface states, in lucid and dignified language, though not without an excess of caution, the author's critical and religious point of view, which is that of all modern-minded and devout Old Testament critics. Then follows an introduction on the Old Testament Canon according to the Jews, which gives *multum in parvo*, and is thoroughly sound. It was desirable to prefix this because of a current assertion that critical views are in conflict with trustworthy Jewish traditions. So now the student is free, both in a religious and in a historical respect, to consider the proposed solutions of the literary problems of the Old Testament, and the accompanying views respecting the objects of the several records. The books are treated in the order of the Hebrew Bible, beginning with those of the Hexateuch, and ending with Ezra, Nehemiah, and Chronicles. To the Hexateuch one hundred and fifty pages are devoted—a perfectly fair allotment, considering the great importance of these six books. The plan adopted here, and throughout the composite narrative books, appears to be this: after some preliminary remarks, the particular book is broken up into sections and analyzed, with a view to ascertain the documents or sources which the later compiler or redactor welded together into a whole.[1] The grounds of

[1] Note especially the care bestowed on the composite narrative of Korah, Dathan, and Abiram in Num. xvi.-xvii. (p. 59), and cf. Robertson Smith, *The Old Testament in the Jewish Church* (ed. 2), pp. 402-3.

the analysis are given in small print, without which judicious arrangement the book would have outrun its limits. A somewhat different plan is necessary for Deuteronomy, which is treated more continuously, special care being taken to exhibit the relation of the laws to the other codes, and to trace the dependence of the two historical retrospects in chapters i., iii., and ix.-x. on the earlier narrative of " J E." Then follows a very important section on the character and probable date of the "prophetical"[1] and the "priestly" narratives respectively, followed by a compact synopsis of the priestly code. As regards the analysis of the documents, it would be difficult, from a teacher's point of view, to say too much in praise of the author's presentation. *Multum in parvo* is again one's inevitable comment. The space has been utilized to the utmost, and the student who will be content to work hard will find no lack of lucidity. No one can deny that the individuality of the writer, which is in this part very strongly marked, fits him in a special degree to be the interpreter of the analysts to young students. One only asks that the cautious reserve,

[1] On the so-called "Book of the Covenant" (*i.e.* Ex. xx. 22—xxiii. 33) excellent remarks are given (p. 33). Cornill, Budde, and Baentsch have lately given much attention to the study of this record, and its position in the "Mosaic" legislation. There is, as Baentsch shows, no trace of a Mosaic kernel in the Book of the Covenant, nor of its owing anything to the attempt to adapt Mosaic ordinances to a later time. It has however been much edited. Originally, it may only have contained the so-called "judgments," which may (cf. Gen. xxxi. 38—40) have once been fuller than they are now.

which is here not out of place, may not be contrasted by that untrained "common sense," which is so swift to speak, and so slow to hear, with the bolder but fundamentally not less cautious procedure of other English or American analysts. Such remarks will, I am sure, be disapproved of by the author himself, who willingly refers to less reserved critics. And Dr. Driver's fellow-workers will, on their side, have nothing but respect for his helpful contributions. It should be added that whatever is vitally important is fully granted by Dr. Driver. The documents J, E, D, and P are all recognized; and if the author more frequently than some critics admits a difficulty in distinguishing between J and E, yet this is but a formal difference. Moreover, no one doubts that J and E were combined together by an editor or (Kuenen) "harmonist," so that we have three main records in the Hexateuch—the prophetical (J E), the Deuteronomic (D), and the priestly (P). On the limits of these three records critics of different schools are practically agreed.[1]

And now, will the author forgive me if I say that neither here nor in the rest of the Hexateuch portion does he, strictly speaking, verify the description of the object of the "Library" given by the general editors? The book, as it seems to me, does not, upon the whole, so much "represent the present condition of investigation, and indicate the way for future progress,"

[1] On Klostermann's original, not to say eccentric, contributions to Hexateuch criticism, see Driver, *Expositor*, May 1892.

as exhibit the present position of a very clear-headed but slowly moving scholar, who stands a little aside from the common pathway of critics? For the many English students this may conceivably be a boon; but the fact (if it be a fact) ought to be borne in mind, otherwise the friends and the foes of the literary study of the Old Testament will alike be the victims of an illusion. There is a number of points of considerable importance for the better class of students on which the author gives no light, though I would not impute this merely to his natural caution, but also to the comparative scantiness of his space. For instance, besides J, E, D, P, and, within P, H (*i. e.* the "Law of Holiness," Lev. xvii.—xxvi.), I find now and then recognized both D^2 and P^2, but not J^2 and E^2, though it is impossible to get on long without these symbols, which correspond to facts. Nor do I find any mention of the source and date of Genesis xiv., upon which so many contradictory statements have been propounded.[1] Nor is there any constructive sketch of the growth of our present Hexateuch, though this would seem necessary to give coherence to the ideas of the student. It would however be ungracious to dwell further on this. On the dates of the documents J and E, Dr. Driver is unfortunately somewhat indefinite. It is surprising to learn that "it must remain an open question whether both (J and E)

---

[1] See above, p. 238. On no question would a few clear and frank statements of facts, and of the critical points which are really at issue, be more useful than on this.

may not in reality be earlier" (*i. e.* earlier than "the early centuries of the monarchy"). I can of course understand that, had the author been able to give a keener analysis of the documents, he would have favoured us with a fuller consideration of their period. But I do earnestly hope that he is not **meditating a step backwards** in deference to hostile archæologists. One more startling phenomenon I seem bound to mention. On p. 27 we are told that "probably the greater part of the Song is Mosaic, and the modification, or expansion, is limited to the closing verses; for the general style is antique, and the triumphant tone which pervades it is just such as might naturally have been inspired by the event which it celebrates."

I greatly regret this. To fall behind Ewald, Dillmann, and even Delitzsch and Kittel,[1] is a misfortune which I can only account for on the theory of compromise. I hesitate to contemplate the consequences which might possibly follow from the acceptance of this view.

This naturally brings me to the pages on the authorship and date of Deuteronomy. There is here very much which commands one's entire approbation, especially with an eye to English readers. Candour is conspicuous throughout, and whenever one differs

---

[1] See, besides the works cited by Dr. Driver, Lagarde, *Semitica*, i. 28; Kuenen, *Hexateuch*, p. 239; Wellhausen, *Prolegomena*, p. 374 [352]; Cornill, *Einleitung*, pp. 68, 69; Kittel, *Geschichte*, i. 83, 187; and my *Bampton Lectures* (which give my own view since 1881), pp. 31, 177.

from the author, it is reluctantly and with entire respect. The section begins thus—

"Even though it were clear that the first four books of the Pentateuch were written by Moses, it would be difficult to sustain the Mosaic authorship of Deuteronomy. For, to say nothing of the remarkable difference of style, Deuteronomy conflicts with the *legislation* of Exodus-Numbers in a manner that would not be credible were the legislator in both one and the same" (p. 77). And in particular "when the laws of Deuteronomy are compared with those of P such a supposition becomes impossible. For in Deuteronomy language is used implying that *fundamental institutions of P are unknown to the author*."[1] Sufficient specimens of the evidence for these statements are given with a reference for further particulars to the article "Deuteronomy" in the belated new edition of Smith's *Dictionary*. I look forward with eagerness to the appearance of this article, and meantime venture to state how I have been struck by the author's treatment of the question of *date*. Whatever I say is to be taken with all the qualifications arising from my high opinion of the author, and demanded by a fair consideration of his narrow limits.

In the first place, then, I think that on one important point Dr. Driver does not quite accurately state the prevailing tendency of recent investigations. No one would gather from p. 82, note 2, that criticism is

---

[1] Here, as always in quotations, the italics are those of the author.

more inclined to place the composition of the original book in the reign of Josiah than in that of Manasseh. Such however is the case. Delitzsch himself says regretfully, "It will scarcely be possible to eradicate the ruling critical opinion that Deuteronomy was composed in the time of Jeremiah."[1]

If this view of the tendency of criticism is correct, it would have been helpful to state the grounds on which the reign of Josiah has been preferred. May I venture to put them together briefly thus? Let the student read once more, with a fresh mind, the famous narrative in 2 Kings xxii., which I for one do not feel able to reject as unhistorical. He can hardly fail to receive the impression that the only person who is vehemently moved by the perusal of "the law-book" (more strictly, "the book of *tōrāh*") is the king. How is this to be accounted for? How is it that Hilkiah, Shaphan, and Huldah display such imperturbability? The easiest supposition is that these three persons (to whom we must add Ahikam, Achbor, and Asaiah) had agreed together, unknown to the king, on their course of action. It may be thought strange that all these, except Hilkiah and Huldah, were courtiers. But they were also (as we partly know, partly infer) friends of the prophet Jeremiah, and therefore no *mere* courtiers. Huldah, moreover, though the wife of a courtier, was herself a

---

[1] Preface by Delitzsch to Curtiss's *Levitical Priests* (1877), p. x. The latest introduction (that of Cornill) verifies this prognostication.

prophetess. We must suppose, then, in order to realize the circumstances at once historically and devoutly, that to the priests and prophets who loved spiritual religion God had revealed that now was the time to take a bold step forward, and accomplish the work which the noblest servants of Jehovah had so long desired. The "pen of the scribes" (Jer. viii. 8) had been recently consecrated to this purpose by the writing down of the kernel of what we now call Deuteronomy. This document consisted of ancient laws adapted to present purposes, and completed by the addition of recent and even perfectly new ones, framed in the spirit of Moses and under the sacred authority of priests and prophets, together with earnest exhortations and threatenings. It had apparently been placed in a repository beside the ark (comp. Deut. xxxi. 9, 26),[1] and there (if we may so interpret the words "in the house of Jehovah") Hilkiah professed to Shaphan "the secretary" to have "found" it. One of these seeming "chances" which mark the interposing hand of God favoured

---

[1] Deut. xxxi. 9 belongs to the main body of Deuteronomy, whereas ver. 26 (as a part of *vv.* 24—30) belongs to the editor. According to Dillmann, however, *vv.* 24—26*a* (down to "Jehovah your God") originally stood after *vv.* 9—13, and belong to Deuteronomy proper. But in any case it is certain that the editor *rightly interpreted* the "delivering" of the Torah to the "Levitical priests," when he made Moses say, "Take this law-book, and put it beside the ark." For of course the persons addressed were to carry both the ark and the "bag" or "box" (*argâz*, see 1 Sam. vi. 8, 11, 15) which contained the most sacred objects of religion.

the project of Hilkiah. Repairs on a large scale had been undertaken in the temple, and with his mind set on the restoration of the material "house of God," Josiah was all the more likely to be interested in the re-edification of His spiritual house. So Shaphan reported the "finding," and read the book in the ears of the king. **The** king recognized the voice of Moses; this was not one of those law-books which Jeremiah ascribed to "the *lying* pen of scribes." The result is matter of history to all at any rate but the followers of M. Maurice **Vernes.**

It may doubtless be urged against this view of the circumstances that we have enlisted the imagination in the service of history. But why should we not do so? Of course, we would very gladly dispense with this useful but dangerous ally, but is there a single historical critic, a single critical historian, who is not often obliged to invite its help? Certainly in the case of 2 Kings xxii., which is an extract from a larger and fuller document,[1] it is impossible not to endeavour to fill up *lacunæ* with the help of the imagination. The alternative view—that **the** "law-book" was written in the reign of Manasseh—is not one which commends itself to the historic sense. Even supposing that some ardent spirit conceived the idea of a reformation by means of **a** "law-book," yet **there is a** gulf between such an idea and its successful accomplishment. **No** prophecy pointed to the advent **of** a reforming king

[1] **This has,** I think, **not been** sufficiently considered by Prof. Ryle in his work on the Canon, when referring to 2 Kings xxii.

(1 Kings xiii., as consistent critics agree, is of very late origin); we cannot therefore appeal to the analogy of Ezekiel's ideal legislation. The hopeful and practical spirit which pervades the book is inconsistent with a time of reaction, when it seemed to a prophet that the "good man" had "perished out of the earth," and that there was "none upright among men" (Mic. vii. 2). I admit that the prophecy from which I have just quoted (Mic. vi. 1—vii. 6), and which was probably written under Manasseh, reminds us somewhat, at the outset, of Deuteronomy, but the gloomy and indignant tone which predominates in it is entirely alien to the great "law-book." The assertion that the date of Deuteronomy must be pushed up a little higher to allow time for literary style to sink to the level of Jeremiah is a doubtful one. Certainly Jeremiah's style *is* less pure than that of Deuteronomy (as Kleinert has well shown). But who would maintain that in all the different literary circles of Jerusalem at the same period an equally pure style was in vogue? Proverbs i.—ix. is placed by critics, with whom Dr. Driver (p. 382) seems inclined to agree, in the reign of Josiah, and here at least we have an elevated, oratorical diction, with very little Aramaism. Jeremiah himself was too emotional to be either a purist or an artist. What is the most obvious conclusion from all the facts and indications? Surely this—that while the heathenish reaction under Manasseh, by knitting the faithful together and forcing them to meditate on their principles and on the

means of applying these to practice, created some of the conditions under which alone "**Deuteronomy**" could arise, and while it is not impossible that a Deuteronomic style began to form itself a little before the time of Josiah, the reign of Manasseh is nevertheless not the period in which the Book (*i. e.* its kernel) can have been composed. Instead of saying, "not later than the reign of Manasseh" (p. 82), it would have been truer to the actual state of critical study to say (against M. Vernes), "by no possibility later than the eighteenth year of the reign of Josiah."

Indeed, the sole advantage of Dr. Driver's present theory is that it will enable popular writers to defend Hilkiah the more easily from the charge (which conservative scholars sometimes imagine to be involved in the other theory) of complicity in a "forgery."[1] But may it not be questioned whether even for popular writers it is not best to approach as near as they can to the truth? The test of a forgery suggested by Mr. Gore, viz. to find out whether the writer of a particular book could have afforded to disclose the method and circumstances of his production, can be successfully stood by the writer of

---

[1] I quite enter into the dislike of reverent Bible-readers for the theory of "pious fraud." I think that dislike an exaggerated one. No student of Oriental life and history could be surprised at a pious fraud originating among priests. But I do not adopt that theory to account for 2 Kings xxii., and have sought to be somewhat clearer and more explicit than my friend Prof. Robertson Smith in his *Old Testament in the Jewish Church*.

Deuteronomy. Hilkiah, as representing this writer,[1] could well have afforded to make such a disclosure to literary students familiar with the modes of thought of priestly and prophetic writers. But was Josiah such a student, and even if he were, was this a time for any such minute explanation? Practical wisdom required that the account given to Josiah should be the same which would have to be given to the people at large. The Book *was* "the *tōrāh* of Moses," and the basis of the legal portion of it (viz. the "Book of the Covenant") had no doubt been kept in the temple archives. What, pray, could be said of it, even by a *religious* statesman, but that it had been "found in the house of Jehovah"? Such conduct as that of Hilkiah is, I maintain, worthy of an inspired teacher and statesman in that age and under those circumstances. It is also not without a distant resemblance to the course of Divine Providence, so far as this can be scanned by our weak faculties. Indeed, if we reject the theory of "needful illusion," we are thrown upon a sea of perplexity. Was there no book on Jeremiah bringing home the need of this theory to the Christian conscience, to which Dr. Driver could have referred?

But no doubt the student will here ask, How can

---

[1] Hilkiah may possibly (in spite of Deut. xviii. 6—8) have had to do with the composition of the book. He was certainly concerned in its publication, and, as Baudissin remarks, was probably above the narrow class-feelings of his corporation. To say that he was "the forger of Deuteronomy" is of course a gross misrepresentation of my opinion.

the kernel of the Book of Deuteronomy be justly described as the "*tōrāh* of Moses"? Dr. Driver devotes what space he can afford to this most important question (see pp. 83—85). He begins by drawing the distinction (on which great stress is also laid by Delitzsch) that "though it may seem paradoxical to say so, Deuteronomy *does not claim to be written by Moses*. Wherever the author speaks himself, he purposes to give a description *in the third person* of what Moses did or said. The true 'author' of Deuteronomy is thus the writer who *introduces Moses in the third person;* and the discourses which he is represented as having spoken fall in consequence into the same category as the speeches in the historical books, some of which largely, and others entirely, are the composition of the compilers, and are placed by them in the mouths of historical characters. . . . An author, therefore, in framing discourses appropriate to Moses' situation, especially if (as is probable) the elements were provided for him by tradition, could be doing nothing inconsistent with the literary usages of his age and people."

This hardly goes far towards meeting the difficulties of the student. In a footnote (p. 84) there is a list of passages of Deuteronomy describing in the third person what Moses did or said, which closes with Deuteronomy xxxi. 1—30. I do not forget the demands on Dr. Driver's space, but in this closing passage there occur two statements, "And Moses wrote this *tōrāh*" (ver. 9), and "When Moses had made an end of writing the words of this *tōrāh* in a book, until they were finished" (ver. 24), which demanded special consideration. Let us listen to the candid and devout Delitzsch. "If the statement, 'And Moses wrote,' were meant to be valid for the whole of Deuteronomy as it stands, Deuteronomy would be a pseudepigraphon" (*Genesis*, p. 23). In the sequel Delitzsch communicates his own explanation of the difficulty. Now should not Dr. Driver have given two or three lines to a mention of the difficulty, and a particularly full reference to the sentences in Delitzsch's *Genesis*, which contain that scholar's solution, if he was not prepared to give one of his own? What Dr. Driver tells us in the text is, that ancient historians (including those of Israel) habitually claimed the liberty of composing speeches for the personages of their narratives. But where, it may be replied, is there any instance of this liberty being used on such a large scale as in the discourses of Deuteronomy? If indeed Ecclesiastes had been introduced by the words, "And Solomon said," and inserted in the Book of Kings, an Old Testament parallel would not be wanting. But Ecclesiastes bears no such heading, and was presumably designed by the unknown writer for the narrow circle of his friends or disciples. The licence appealed to by Dr. Driver will hardly bear the weight which he puts upon it. Josiah certainly did not conceive that it was used in the composition of the Book, which he received with alarm as the neglected law-book written of old by Moses. As for the statement that the elements of the discourses in Deuteronomy were provided for the writer by tradition, if it means that the writer reproduces the substance of what Moses really said, somewhat as the writer of the Fourth Gospel is held to reproduce sayings or ideas of the Lord Jesus, I should think this, historically, a very difficult position. This does indeed appear to have been the belief of Delitzsch, but the principles which underlie it are not those which Dr. Driver would, as I think, deliberately desire to promote.

Dr. Driver's second argument in justification of the writer of Deuteronomy relates to the legislative portion of the book. He says, "It is an altogether false view of the laws in Deuteronomy to treat them as the author's 'inventions.' Many are repeated from the Book of the Covenant; the existence of others is independently attested by the 'Law of Holiness': others, upon intrinsic grounds, are clearly ancient. . . . The new element in Deuteronomy is thus not the laws, but their *parenetic setting*. Deuteronomy may be described as the prophetic re-formulation and adapatation to *new needs of an older legislation*."

Dr. Driver does almost too much honour to a view which is only worthy of some ill-instructed secularist lecturer. The statement that "the laws in Deuteronomy" are "the author's inventions," is, of course, utterly erroneous. But Dr. Driver's statement of his own opinion may possibly bear amendment. He at any rate appears to identify himself with the view of Kleinert that Deuteronomy consists of "old statutes worked over and adapted to later circumstances,"[1] and as an instance of a law which has an ancient kernel, he proceeds to adduce the so-called "law of the kingdom" (Deut. xvii. 14—20). But the former view seems to have been refuted by Kuenen, and on the latter I may appeal to Dillmann's judgment that "the law is *new and purely Deuteronomic.*" It seems to me even possible that Kleinert and Stade may be right in regarding this law as a later Deuteronomistic insertion. Dr. Driver refers next to the "law of the central sanctuary" (Deut. xii. 5, &c.). He states distinctly that it "appears, in its exclusiveness, to be of comparatively[2] modern origin," but seems to weaken the force of this remark by saying that "it only accentuated the old pre-eminence [of the sanctuary where the ark for the time was placed] in the interests of a principle which is often insisted on in J E, viz. the separation of Israel from heathen influences." Surely the important thing to know is that the law itself is not old but new, and that even Isaiah does not appear to have conceived the idea of a single sanctuary. "The one and essential point," says Dr. G. Vos, "which we wish the higher criticism to estab-

---

[1] *Das Deuteronomium und der Deuteronomiker*, p. 132.

[2] I understand the qualification. But in view of the want of any confirming evidence from Isaiah, one may, with Stade, doubt whether Hezekiah did indeed formally and absolutely abolish all the local sanctuaries throughout his kingdom, as 2 Kings xviii. 4 *appears* to state.

lish, is this, that the (Deuteronomic) Code does **not** fit into the historical situation, by which, according to its own testimony, it was called forth."[1] Dr. Driver should, I think, have had some regard to this, even though he was not directly speaking of the date of the law-book. And in order more fully to represent the strictly critical point of view, he should (if he will excuse me for seeming to dictate to him) **have** mentioned other laws besides that of the central sanctuary, which, even if more or less developments of ancient principles, are held by consistent critics to be of modern origin.[2]

Upon the whole I desiderate a larger theory to account for, and therefore to justify, the statements in Deuteronomy, "And Moses said," "And **Moses wrote."** May we perhaps put the whole matter thus? The book is at once legal, prophetic, and historical. Under each of these aspects a fully instructed Israelite might naturally call it " Mosaic." In so far as it was legal, it could be said that the author belonged to the " Mosaic," **or,** as we may describe it (in opposition to certain " lying pens," Jer. viii. 8), the " orthodox" school of legalists. **Its** priestly author claimed, virtually at any rate, the name of Moses (just **as the** school of the prophet-reformer Zarathustra, not only virtually, but actually, called itself by its founder's name), because he " sat in Moses' seat," and continued the development of the antique decisions of

[1] *The* Mosaic Origin of the Pentateuchal Codes (1886), p. 90.
[2] Cf. Dillmann, *Num.-Deut.-Jos.*, p. 604.

the lawgiver. That Deuteronomy xii.—xxvi. was intended as a new edition of the old "Book of the Covenant," admits of no reasonable doubt. It was possibly in the mind of the author a "legal fiction," like similar developments in English, and more especially in Roman law,[1] though this may not have been understood by Josiah. In so far as the book was prophetic, it was a "Mosaic" work, because its author summed up the religious ideas of that prophetic succession of which Moses, as the writer fully believed, was the head.[2] And in so far as it was historical, it was "Mosaic," because the facts which it recorded were based on traditional records which the author believed to have come from Moses or his circle. Yes; even the statement that Moses delivered laws to the people in the fortieth year of the wanderings, has very probably a traditional basis. In JE, as it stands, both the Book of the Covenant (Exod. xx. 22—xxii.) and the Words of the Covenant (Exod. xxxiv. 10—28) form part of the Sinaitic revelation. But Kuenen has made it in a high degree plausible that in the original JE they were revealed indeed at Sinai, but not promulgated by

---

[1] Cf. W. R. Smith, *The Old Testament in the Jewish Church* (ed. 1), p. 385.

[2] See Deut. xviii. 18, "A prophet will I [from time to time] raise up unto them . . . like unto me." Note the emphasis laid upon the truthfulness of the prophet: how could the writer of such a passage be—a "forger"? Even M. Darmesteter holds that the ideas of the Book are derived from the great prophets (review of M. Renan's *Histoire d'Israel* in *Revue des deux mondes*, 1 avril 1891).

Moses till just before the passage of the Jordan. It was, as he has sought in a masterly way to show, the Deuteronomic writer of JE who transposed the scene of the promulgation from Moab to Sinai, thus making room in the narrative of the fortieth year for the new edition (as Kuenen well calls it) of the Book of the Covenant (*i.e.* Deut. xiii.—xxvi. with the "parenetic setting").[1]

Dr. Driver's treatment of the other problems of Deuteronomy shows learning, but no special critical insight. In dealing with the date of Deuteronomy xxxii., no arguments are adduced from the religious contents of the Song. Indeed, it is here once more shown how unsatisfactory it is to treat the lyric products of the old Hebrew poetry *separately*. But let us pass on to the Priestly Code. Here the evidence of date is abundant, though complicated, and Dr. Driver's treatment of it shows him at his very best. I should say that this portion (pp. 118—150) is the gem of the whole book. Here too at any rate there is no deficiency of courage. The author is strong in the confidence that all that orthodoxy really requires is, that the chief ceremonial institutions referred to in P should be "*in their origin* of great antiquity," and that the legislation should be based on legal traditions which, though modified and adapted to new circumstances from time to time,

---

[1] See Kuenen, *Hexateuch*, pp. 258—262, and (especially on Exod. xxiv. 4) cf. Cornill, *Einleitung*, p. 75 ; Montefiore, *Jewish Quarterly Review*, Jan. 1891, p. 280, &c.

were yet in unbroken connexion with Israel's prime. This he believes that a patient criticism can show. He is therefore free to admit (frankly and without reserve) that P in its completed form is later than Ezekiel, who was the first to introduce the radical distinction between priests and Levites which we find in P (see Ezek. xliv. 6—16). The arguments for a later date are so fully and clearly presented, that I can hardly conceive any fresh mind resisting their force. I can only here refer to the linguistic argument. Dr. Driver has, I observe, made progress since 1882, when he subjected the not sufficiently exact philological argument of Giesebrecht (in Stade's *Zeitschrift* for 1881) to a somewhat severe criticism.[1] It is obvious that the writer was still feeling his way in a complicated critical problem, and did not as yet see distinctly the *real value* of the linguistic argument. His criticism of Giesebrecht's details is indeed upon the whole sound, but, for all that, Giesebrecht was right in his general principles. It was Ryssel (in a somewhat earlier treatise, praised by Dr. Driver in 1882) and not Giesebrecht who overrated the value of the linguistic argument, and Giesebrecht has in the article referred to already, put forward what Dr. Driver, in 1891, expresses thus : "The phraseology of P, it is natural to suppose, is one which had gradually formed ; hence it contains elements which are no

---

[1] See reference, p. 249 ; and comp. Kuenen, *Hexateuch*, p. 291. Cornill (*Einleitung*, p. 66) is slightly too eulogistic towards Giesebrecht.

doubt ancient side by side with those which were introduced later. The priests of each successive generation would adopt, as a matter of course, the technical formulæ and stereotyped expressions which they learned from their seniors, new terms, when they were introduced, being accommodated to the old moulds" (p. 148).

It is possible, indeed, that Dr. Driver, writing in 1891, would assert the presence of a larger traditional element in the phraseology of P than Giesebrecht did, writing in 1881. But whatever difference there may now exist between the two scholars must be very small, and not of much importance, except to those who attach an inordinate value to proving the archaic origin of Jewish ritual laws. To Dr. Driver's excellently formulated statement I only desire to add the remark of Kuenen: " Linguistic arguments do not furnish a positive or conclusive argument. But they do furnish a *very strong presumption* against the theory that the priestly laws were written in the golden age of Israelitish literature. As long as P^2 [Dr. Driver's P] is regarded as a contemporary of Isaiah, the ever-increasing number of parallels [to later writers] must remain an enigma. A constantly recurring phenomenon ... must rest on some general basis."

On linguistic arguments I may find space to speak later on. It is, at any rate, not unimportant to know that an "induction from the facts of the Hebrew language" cannot prevent us from accepting a post-

Deuteronomic (*i.e.* post-Josian) date for P, indeed that it furnishes good presumptive evidence in its favour.

I do not, however, forget, nor does Dr. Driver, that the Priestly Code contains many very early elements. Leviticus xi. for instance, which is virtually identical with Deuteronomy xiv. 4—20, is, no doubt, as Kuenen says, "a later and amplified edition of those priestly decisions on clean and unclean animals, which the Deuteronomist adopted."[1] And above all, Leviticus xvii.—xxvi., when carefully studied, is seen to contain an earlier stratum of legislation (known as H, or P^1), which "exhibits a characteristic phraseology, and is marked by the preponderance of certain characteristic principles and motives" (p. 54). That the greater part of this collection of laws dates from a time considerably prior to Ezekiel, may now be taken as granted. But what is the date of the writer who arranged these laws in the existing "parenetic framework"; or, in other words, the date of the *compilation* of H? Dr. Driver replies that he wrote shortly before the close of the monarchy; but this relatively conservative conclusion hardly does justice to the natural impression of the reader that the predicted devastation of the land of Israel is really an accomplished fact. It appears safer to hold that H as it stands was arranged by a priestly writer in the second half of the Babylonian exile. On the

---

[1] *The Hexateuch*, p. 264.

question, When was H absorbed into P? and, indeed, on the larger question of the later stages of our present Hexateuch, Dr. Driver still holds his opinion in reserve. No reference is made to the important narrative in Nehemiah viii., which seems the counterpart of that in 2 Kings xxii.

And now as to the character of the Priestly Narrative. The view of things which this narrative gives seems, according to our author, "to be the result of a systematizing process working upon these materials, and perhaps, also, seeking to give sensible expression to certain ideas or truths (as, for instance, to the truth of Jehovah's presence *in the midst of His people*, symbolized by the 'Tent of Meeting,' surrounded by its immediate attendants, in the centre of the camp)," p. 120.

And in a footnote he says that "it is difficult to escape the conclusion that the representation of P contains elements, not, in the ordinary sense of the word, historical" [*e.g.* especially in his chronological scheme, and in the numbers of the Israelites.—See Numbers i.—iv.].

Similarly, in speaking of P's work in the Book of Joshua, he says that, "the partition of the land being conceived as *ideally* effected by Joshua, its complete distribution and occupation by the tribes are treated as his work, and as accomplished in his life-time" (pp. 108, 109).

Let me honestly say that these views, though correct, present great difficulties to those whose reverence is of the old type; and that in order to understand, and, if it may be, to justify the author or compiler of P, careful historical training is necessary. Dr. Driver's book does not give any of the hints which the religious study of criticism appears at this point to require. But, no doubt, he was hampered equally by his want of space and by his plan.

As to the ascription of the laws to Moses, on the other hand, the author is really helpful. He points out the double aspect of the Priestly Code, which, though Exilic and early post-Exilic in its formulation, is "based upon pre-existing temple-usage" (p. 135). In taking this view he is at one with critics of very different schools, so that we may hope soon to hear no more of the charge that, according to the critics, the translation of P was "manufactured" by the later priests. Dr. Driver would rather have abstained altogether from touching on Biblical archæology, his object (an impossible one) being to confine himself to the purely literary aspect of the Old Testament. But, as Merx long ago said, a purely literary criticism of the Hexateuch is insufficient. To show that there is a basis of early customary law in later legal collections, we are compelled to consider historical analogies. In spite of Kuenen's adverse criticism of Mr. Fenton's explanation of the law of "jubilee" (Lev. xxv. 8—55), I still feel that there may be a kernel of truth in it; and much more certainly the sacrificial laws have a basis of pre-Exilic priestly ordinance. But can those institutions and rites be traced back to Moses? Dr. Driver feels it necessary to satisfy his readers to some extent on this point. What he says is, in fact, much the same as Kuenen said in the *Godsdienst van Israel* in 1870.[1] It is however from an orthodox point of view, startling; and considering that Kuenen became afterwards more extreme in his views,[2] Dr. Driver may fairly lay claim, not merely to courage and consistency, but also to moderation and sobriety. Certainly I fully approve what Dr. Driver has said. It is "sober," *i.e.* it does not go beyond the facts, nor is its sobriety impaired by the circumstance that the few facts at his disposal have had to be interpreted imaginatively. How else, as I have said already, can the bearing of these few precious but dry facts be realized? I am only afraid that some readers will think that Moses was more systematic, more of a modern founder and organizer than he can really have been; but I suspect that a fuller explanation would show that there is no real difference between Dr. Driver and myself. I am in full accord with him when he says (in tacit opposition to Kuenen's later view) that "the teaching of Moses on these subjects (civil and ceremonial precepts) is preserved in its least modified form in the Decalogue and the Book of the Covenant." It becomes any one to differ from Kuenen with humility, but my own historical sense emphatically requires

---

[1] Kuenen, *Godsdienst van Israel*, i. 278—286; ii. 209 (E.T. i. 282—290, ii. 302).
[2] Kuenen, *Onderzoek*, i. 238 (*Hexateuch*, p. 244).

that from the very beginning there should have been the germ of the advanced "ethical monotheism" of the prophets; and if only it be admitted that even the shortened form of the Decalogue proposed by Ewald[1] has probably been modified (we have no right to equalize Moses with Zoroaster),[2] we may not unreasonably suppose that the "Ten Words" are indeed derived from "Moses, the man of God," and that the other similar "decads"[3] were imitated from this one. That Dr. Driver has made no reference in this important passage to Exodus xv. (in spite of his conservative view on the authorship of the Song), deserves recognition.

There is only one other point which I could have wished to see stated. I will express it in the words of Kuenen : "It is Moses' great work and enduring merit—not that he introduced into Israel any particular religious forms and practices, but—that he established the service of Jahveh among his people upon a moral footing."[4]

This surely ought to satisfy the needs of *essential orthodoxy*. For what conservatives want, or ought to

---

[1] Ewald, *Geschichte*, ii. 231 (E.T. ii. 163). Comp. Driver, *Introduction*, p. 31, with the accompanying discussion of the two traditional texts of the Decalogue. A conjectural but historically conceivable revision of Ewald's form of the Decalogue has been given by Mr. Wicksteed, *The Christian Reformer*, May 1886, pp. 307—313.

[2] See my article in *Nineteenth Century*, Dec. 1891.

[3] See Ewald, *Geschichte*, l.c.; and cf. Wildeboer, *Theolog. Studien*, 1887, p. 21.

[4] Kuenen, *Religion of Israel*, i. 292 (*Godsdienst*, i. 289).

want, is not so much to prove the veracity of the Israelitish priests, when they ascribed certain ordinances to Moses, as to show that Moses had high intuitions of God and of morality. In a word, they want, or they ought to want, to contradict the view that the religion of Israel—at any rate, between Moses and Amos—in no essential respect differed from that of "Moab, Ammon, and Edom, Israel's nearest kinsfolk and neighbours."[1] Their mistake has hitherto been in attributing to Moses certain *absolutely* correct religious and moral views. In doing so, they interfered with the originality both of the prophets of Israel and of Jesus Christ, and they have to avoid this in future by recognizing that Moses' high intuitions were limited by his early place in the history of Israel's revelation.

I am most thankful that in this very important matter (which, even in an introduction to the Old Testament literature, could not be passed over) Dr. Driver has not felt himself obliged to make any deduction from critical results. The second chapter is one which makes somewhat less demand than the first on the patient candour of orthodox readers. It may also appear less interesting until we have learned that the narrative books are of the utmost importance for Hexateuch students, as supplying the historical framework for the Hexateuch records. In fact, all the Old Testament Scriptures are interlaced by

[1] Wellhausen, *Sketch of the History of Israel and Judah* (1891), p. 23.

numberless delicate threads, so that no part can be neglected without injury to the rest. Undoubtedly, the criticism of Judg.-Sam.-Kings has not reached such minute accuracy as that of the Hexateuch, and it was a disadvantage to Dr. Driver that he had to write upon these books before the researches of Budde and Cornill (to whom we may now add Kautzsch and Kittel) had attained more complete analytical results. Still one feels that, with the earlier pioneering works to aid him (including Budde's and Cornill's earlier essays), Dr. Driver could have been much fuller, with more space and perhaps with more courage. At any rate, the most essential critical points have been duly indicated, and I welcome Dr. Driver's second chapter, in combination with his work on the text of Samuel, as materially advancing the study of these books in England.[1] A valuable hint was already given in chapter i. (pp. 3, 4). With regard to Judges and Kings we are there told that "in each a series of older narratives has been taken by the compiler, and fitted with a framework supplied by himself"; whereas in Samuel, though this too is a compilation, "the compiler's hand is very much less conspicuous than is the case in Judges and Kings" (pp. 3, 4). Of the

[1] The opening chapter of my own *Aids to the Devout Study of Criticism* (1892), which contains Kittel's analysis of 1 and 2 Samuel (in the German translation of the Old Testament edited by Kautzsch), together with notes on the eleven pairs of "doubtlets," will, I hope, be useful as a supplement to this part of the *Introduction*.

work of the compiler in Kings, we are further told in chapter ii. that it included not only brief statistical notices, sometimes called the "Epitome," but also the introduction of fresh and "prophetic glances at the future" and the "amplification" of already existing prophecies (see pp. 178, 184, 189). He judges historical events by the standard of Deuteronomy, and his Deuteronomizing peculiarities receive a careful description, which is illustrated by a valuable list of his characteristic phrases (with reference to Deuteronomy and Jeremiah). We are introduced, in fact, to what Kleinert calls the *Deuteronomistische Schriftstellerei*, and realize how great must have been the effect of that great monument both of religion and of literature—the kernel of our Deuteronomy.

On the historical value of Judges, the author speaks cautiously, following Dr. A. B. Davidson, who has remarked (*Expositor*, Jan. 1887) on the different points of view in the narratives and in the framework, and who finds in the latter, not, strictly speaking, history, but rather the "philosophy of history." To this eminent teacher the author also appeals as having already pointed out the combination of different accounts of the same facts—a striking phenomenon which meets us in a still greater degree in the first part of Samuel. It was surely hardly necessary to do so. Support might have been more valuable for the ascription of the Song of Hannah to a later period, though here Dr Driver is relatively conservative.

U

The other poetical passages in Samuel have no special treatment. Still a generally correct impression is given of the composition of our Samuel, and the praise given to "the most considerable part which appears plainly to be the work of a single author" (2 Sam. ix.—xx., to which 1 Kings i.-ii. in the main belongs) is not at all too high.

It strikes me however that in this chapter Dr. Driver does not show as much courage as in the preceding one. Not to dwell on the cautious reserve with which he alludes to questions of historicity, I must regret that the duplicate narratives in Samuel are so treated, that some of the chief critical points are missed, and that the true character of the record does not fully appear.

And how strange it is to read of 1 Samuel xxiv. and xxvi., that "whether the two narratives really relate to two different occasions, or whether they are merely different versions of the same occurrence, is a question on which probably opinion will continue to be divided"[1] (p. 171)!

Nor is anything said either of 1 Samuel xvi. 1—13 (the anointing of David),[2] or of the prophecy of Nathan (2 Sam. vii.), except that the latter is included among the "relatively latest passages" (p. 173), where I am afraid that the reader may overlook it. The former passage was no doubt difficult to treat with-

---

[1] See Budde, *Die Bücher Richter und Samuel*, p. 227.

[2] It is less important that nothing is said on the "doublets," 1 Sam. xxxi., 2 Sam. i. 1—16.

out a somewhat fuller adoption of the principles which govern, and must govern, the critical analysis of the Hebrew texts. **Nor can I** help wondering whether there is the note of true "moderation" in the remark on 1 Kings xiii. 1—32, that it is "a narrative not probably of very early origin, as it seems to date from a time when the names both of the prophet of Judah and of the 'old prophet' were no longer remembered" (p. 183). I turn to Klostermann, whom Professor Lias at the Church Congress of 1891 extolled as the representative of common sense in literary criticism, and whose doctrinal orthodoxy is at any rate above suspicion, and find these remarks:—

"The following narrative in its present form comes **in the main** from a book of anecdotes from the prophetic life of an earlier period with a didactic tendency, designed for disciples of the prophets. . . . It is probable that the reminiscence of Amos iii. 14; vii. 16, 17; ix. 1, &c., influenced this narrative, as well as *the recollection of Josiah's profanation of the sanctuary at Bethel*" (2 Kings xxiii.).

So then this narrative is later than the other Elijah narratives; is, **in** fact, post-Deuteronomic. To the original **writer of** 2 Kings xxii., **xxiii.**, it was unknown. Obviously **it** occasioned the later insertion of 2 Kings xxiii. 16—18 (notice the apologetic interest in Lucian's fuller text of the Septuagint of *v.* 18). **Why not** say so plainly?

And why meet the **irreverence of the** remarks of

Ewald and of Wellhausen on 2 Kings i.[1] (an irreverence which is only on the surface, and is excused by manifest loyalty to historical truth) by the something less than accurate statement that this chapter " presents an impressive picture of Elijah's inviolable greatness " (p. 185)?

I know that Dr. Driver will reply that he desired to leave historical criticism on one side. By so doing he would, no doubt, satisfy the author of the *Impregnable Rock of Holy Scripture*, who, if I remember right, tolerates literary, but not real historical, criticism. But Dr. Driver has already found in chapter i. that the separation cannot be maintained. Why attempt what is neither possible, nor (if I may say so) desirable, in chapter ii.? Here let me pause for awhile; the first section of my critical survey is at an end. But I cannot pass on without the willing attestation that the scholarly character of these two chapters is high, and that even the author's compromises reveal a thoughtful and conscientious mind. May his work and mine alike tend to the hallowing of criticism, to the strengthening of spiritual faith, and to the awakening in wider circles of a more intelligent love for the records of the Christian revelation.

[1] See Ewald, *History*, iv. 112; Wellhausen, *Die Composition des Hexateuchs*, &c., pp. 284-5. The fundamental reverence of all Ewald's Biblical work is, I presume, too patent to be denied. He would not have spoken as he did on 2 Kings i. without good cause.

CHAPTER XII.

DRIVER (2).

I venture by way of preface to express the hope that whatever I say here may be read in the light of the introductory pages of chapter xi. The book before us is not only full of facts but characterized by a thoroughly individual way of regarding its subject. This individuality I have endeavoured to sketch with a free but friendly hand. If the reader has not followed me in this, he may perhaps misinterpret the remarks which this part of my study contains. It is only worth while for me to differ from Dr. Driver because at heart I am at one with him, and on many important points we agree. And I am reconciled to a frequent difference of opinion both as a critic and to some extent as a theologian by the thought that in our common studies it is by the contact of trained and disciplined "subjectivities" that true progress is made.

In the first two chapters of the *Introduction*, a part of which I have called "the gem of the book," Dr. Driver takes the student as near as possible to the centre of the problems. I do not think that this is equally the case throughout the remainder of the work. But I am very far from blaming the author for this relative inferiority of the following chapters. His narrow limits, which he refers to in the preface, go a long way towards accounting for this. And if I add another explanation which seems here and there to be applicable, it is not in the spirit of opposition. Let me confess, then, that some problems of not inconsiderable importance are neglected, possibly because Dr. Driver's early formed linguistic habits of mind hinder him from fully grasping the data for their solution. The reader will see what I mean presently.

Let us now resume our survey. Chapter iii. relates to the very important Book of Isaiah. I need not say that it is a very careful and solid piece of work; and yet nowhere, as it seems to me, do the limitations of Dr. Driver's criticism come more clearly into view. How inadequate, for instance, is his treatment of chap. i., the prologue, presumably, of a larger collection of Isaiah's prophecies! Has it, or has it not, more than a literary unity? The question is not even touched. And what is the date of its composition or redaction? Two dates are mentioned, but without sufficient explanation, and no decision between them is made.[1] Is this a laudable "sobriety"

---

[1] The reference (p. 196, foot) to Gesenius, Delitzsch, and Dillmann as having advocated this date is hardly correct. Gesenius says (*Jesaia*, i. 148), "For Jotham I find no grounds adduced."

and "judicial **reserve**"? It would be an illusion to think so. And yet, even here there is an indication that the author has progressed since 1888. The curiously popular reason offered (but "without any confidence") in *Isaiah*, p. 20, for assigning this prophecy to the reign of Jotham is silently withdrawn. And just so (to criticize myself as well as the author) I have long ago ceased to assign **Isaiah i.** to the time of a supposed invasion of Judah by Sargon. I might of course fill many pages were I to follow Dr. Driver through the Book of Isaiah step **by** step. This being impossible, I will confine myself to the most salient points of his criticism. There is much to content even a severe judge; how excellent, for instance, are the remarks on the origin of Isaiah xv.-xvi.! Nor will I blame the author much for not alluding to what some may call hypercritical theories; it is rather his insufficient reference to familiar and inevitable problems which I am compelled to regret. Nothing, for instance, is said of the difficult problem of Isaiah xix. 16—25. It may be urged by the author that Kuenen himself pronounces in favour of the integrity of the chapter,[1] and that such a careful scholar as Prof. Whitehouse has recently expressed

---

Delitzsch (*Jes.*, p. 68), "The date of this first prophecy is a riddle," but at any rate it seems, he thinks, to belong to "the **time after Uzziah and Jotham.**" Dillmann (*Jes.*, p. 2) refers Isa. i. to the Syro-Ephraimitish war, but he states emphatically (p. 63) that though the hostilities began under Jotham, they were not very serious till the reign of Ahaz.

[1] *Onderzoek*, ii. 71, **72**.

his surprise at the continued doubts of some critics.[1] That is true, but it should be added that Kuenen fully admits the strength of the critical arguments on the opposite side, and that Prof. Whitehouse pronounces judgment before he has fully heard the case.

Nor can I help being surprised (in spite of the anticipatory "plea" offered in the preface) at Dr. Driver's incomplete treatment of Isaiah xxiii., and for the same reason, viz. that its problems are familiar ones. I will not here argue the case in favour of the theory of editorial manipulation. But among the stylistic phenomena which point to another hand than Isaiah's I may at least mention מעזניה (v. 11), כשדים and יסדה לציים (v. 13), מכפה (v. 18). And why should the unintelligent ridicule directed against so-called "divination" and "guesswork" prevent me from attaching weight to the impression of so many good critics that Isaiah never (if I may use the phrase) "passed this work for publication"? Verses 15—18 are doubtless a post-Exilic epilogue[2] ("doubtless" from the point of view of those who have already satisfied themselves of the existence of much besides that is post-Exilic in pre-Exilic works). Verse 13 is written by one who has both Isaiah's phrases and those of other writers in his head; it may of course even be an Isaianic verse recast. Verses

---

[1] *Critical Review*, Jan. 1892, p. 10. The case for disintegration is much stronger than this writer supposes, nor are the familiar arguments adduced by him conclusive.

[2] My own original view (in *Isaiah Chronologically Arranged*), from which I ought not to have swerved,

1—12, 14 are too fine (such is my own impression) for Jeremiah, and now that it is certain (see Niese's text of Josephus) that Menander, quoted in Jos., *Ant.* ix. 14, 2, referred to Shalmaneser by name (Σελάμψας) as the besieger of Tyre, there seems good reason to believe that Isaiah really wrote Isaiah xxiii. 1—14, but in a form not entirely identical with our present text.[1]

Thus much on Dr. Driver's treatment of the generally acknowledged prophecies of Isaiah. With a word of hearty praise to the useful criticism of chaps. xxxvi.—xxxix. (in which I only miss a reference to the debate as to the Song of Hezekiah), I pass on to that large portion of the book which is of disputed origin. Here I have been specially anxious to notice any signs of advance, for it is Dr. Driver's treatment of these chapters in his earlier book which prevents me from fully endorsing Dr. Sanday's eulogy of that work in the preface to *The Oracles of God*. First of all, however, I must make some reference to a passage on which I have myself unwittingly helped to lead the author astray. It is one which most critics have denied to Isaiah and grouped with xiii. 1—xiv. 23, but which, following Kleinert, I thought in 1881 might be reclaimed for that prophet by the help of Assyriology—the "oracle on the wilderness by the sea" (xxi.

---

[1] The adaptation of Isaiah's prophecy to post-Exilic readers will be like Isaiah's adaptation of an old prophecy on Moab in chaps. xv., xvi. (if Dr. Driver is right in agreeing with me, p. 203, which is, however, questionable).

1—10). Dr. Driver mentions (p. 205) the chief reasons for thinking that the siege of Babylon referred to in this passage is one of the three which took place in Isaiah's lifetime, and tells us that in his earlier work he followed me in adopting this theory, but adds that it has not found favour with recent writers on Isaiah. With these "recent writers" I myself now fully agree. I adopted Kleinert's (or, more strictly, George Smith's [1]) theory as a part of a connected view of a group of prophecies of Isaiah (including x. 5—33 and xxii. 1—14), and I understood the words "O my threshed and winnowed one" (xxi. 10) to refer to Sargon's supposed invasion of Judah. A change in my view of these prophecies, however, naturally led me to reconsider the date of the prophecy xxi. 1—10, which I now understand as written at the close of the Exile ("Elam" in v. 2 = "Anzan," of which Cyrus was king before he conquered Media). The strange thing to me is that Dr. Driver should ever have agreed with me : 1. because, as I warned the student, there were "reasons of striking plausibility" for not separating this prophecy from the other prophecies on Babylon which were undoubtedly not of Isaiah's age ; 2. because Dr. Driver differed from me as to the reality of Sargon's supposed invasion, and had therefore a much less strong case to offer for the new theory. The truth is that the author was biassed by a false apologetic and an imperfect critical theory. Isa. xxi. 1—10 could hardly refer to the capture of Babylon

---

[1] *Transactions of the Society of Biblical Archæology*, ii. 329.

in 538. Why? Because, "firstly, no intelligible purpose would be subserved by Isaiah's announcing to the generation of Hezekiah an occurrence lying nearly 200 years in the future," &c. (*Introd.* 205). In other words, Dr. Driver quietly assumes (inconsistently, I gladly admit, with his own words on Isaiah xiii. 2, &c.) that Isaiah xxi. 1—10 must be Isaiah's work, or, at least, that any other view is too improbable to mention. And in order to interpret the prophecy in accordance with an isolated part of Kleinert's and of my own former theory, he is forced to interpret "O my threshed **one**" in *v.* 10 as a prediction ("he foresees the sufferings which the present triumph of Assyria will entail upon them," &c., p. 205), whereas the only natural view of the words is that which explains them as descriptive of past sufferings. It is important to add that Dr. Driver seems now inclined **to** retreat from his former position (which was in the main my own), though he does not mention the mixture of Isaianic and non-Isaianic phenomena in the passage. Bishop Ellicott may perhaps be severe on our supposed changeableness. But if he will refer to **my own** *Isaiah* (ed. 3, vol. i. p. 127), he will find these words, " I gladly admit that a further knowledge of the circumstances of the Jews might conceivably enable **us** to reconcile the prophecy with a date at the **close of the Exile.**" Here there was no dogmatism, no determination to treat the point as finally settled. And undue dogmatism is, I am sure, not less abhorrent **to Dr.** Driver than to myself.

Next with regard to the more commonly controverted prophecies in Isaiah i.—xxxix. The remarks on Isaiah xiii. 1—xiv. 23 are excellent. If they appear to any one somewhat popular and obvious, let it be remembered that this section is the first of those which are written from an Exilic point of view. It was therefore specially needful to be popular; I only regret not to find it pointed out that whatever you say about the prophecy, to assign an ode like that in Isaiah xiv. 4—21 to Isaiah is the very height of unreason. Dr. Driver's treatment of the other prophecies shows increased definiteness and insight. Chapters xxxiv. and xxxv. were not expressly dated in the *Isaiah;* they are now referred to the period of the Exile, and grouped with Isaiah xiii. 2, &c., and Jeremiah l., li. This however is not a sufficient step in advance. Long ago (see *Isaiah* i. 194)[1] I ventured to maintain that these chapters are post-Exilic works of the imitative school of prophecy, and ten years have only deepened my convictions. Dr. Driver may indeed claim for his own view the high authority of Dillmann, who thinks that the phenomena of these chapters "bring us at any rate to the close of the Exile," but would it not have been well to give the grounds of that cautious critic's significant qualification (*jedenfalls*)? Let us pass on now to chaps.

---

[1] See *Ency. Brit.*, art. "Isaiah" (1881); *Jewish Quarterly Review,* July 1891, p. 102; Jan. 1892, p. 332; and cf. Dillmann, *Jesaja,* p. 302; Kuenen, *Onderzoek,* ii. 91—93; Grätz, *Jewish Quarterly Review,* Oct. 1891, pp. 1—8.

xxiv.—xxvii.—a dangerous hunting-ground for young scholars in search of distinction, as Mr. W. E. Barnes has lately proved by his elaborate defence of Isaiah's authorship of these chapters against all modern critics (including among these even Delitzsch).[1] Dr. Driver himself, though not a young scholar, was led astray for a time by the same spirit of compromise which has so often injured him as a critic. In 1888 he was "disposed" (as he remarks, p. 209) "to acquiesce in the opinion that it might have been written on the eve of the Exile," a most unfortunate and scarcely critical opinion which **isolated** the author from his **natural** allies. The consequences of this violation of all historical probability has since **then** become visible to the author, who remarks that this prophecy "differs so widely from the other prophecies of this period (Jer. Ezek.) that this view can scarcely be maintained. There are features in which it is in advance not merely of Isaiah, but even of Deutero-Isaiah. It may be referred most plausibly to the early post-Exilic period" (p. 210). Well, perhaps it may—for the present. At any rate, Dr. Driver grants that a post-Exilic writing has found its way into the **Book of Isaiah.** I am not without hope that further **study of the later** prophetic writings and of the post-

---

[1] **Delitzsch**, it is true, had not made himself fully at home in the results of that criticism to which he was so late a convert. He can only satisfy himself that the author is "not Isaiah himself, but a disciple of Isaiah who here surpasses the master." **But he** is not only a disciple of **Isaiah, but of other prophets too** (see Dr. Driver's selection of allusions).

Exilic period in general may convince him that he is still somewhat too cautious, and that the ideas of this singular but most instructive prophecy can only be understood as characteristic of the *later* Persian age. Far be it from any one to disparage this period. The Spirit of the Lord was not suddenly straitened; the period of artificial prophecy (artificial from a literary point of view) was not without fine monuments of faith and hope and religious thought. But to carry this subject further would compel me to enter into the history of religious ideas,[1] and to exceed the limits of this review.

And now we can no longer avoid applying to the author one of the crucial tests of criticism, and ask, How does he stand in relation to the critical problems of Isaiah xl.—lxvi.? That Dr. Driver neither could nor would assign these chapters to Isaiah was indeed well known from his *Isaiah*, nor need I stint my eulogy of the general treatment of Isaiah xl.—lxvi. in that book as compared with most other popular works on the subject. Very heartily do I wish the *Isaiah* a long career of usefulness. For though *unsophisticated* common sense may recognize at once that these chapters can no more have been written by Isaiah than Psalm cxxxvii. can have been written by David, there are still, I fear, not many persons like "my friend A, who, reading more than twenty years ago the Book of the Prophet Isaiah, and passing without

---

[1] Comp. my *Bampton Lectures*, pp. 120, 133, 402, 403.

pause from the 39th to the 40th chapter, was suddenly struck with amazement and the conviction that it was impossible that one man should have written both chapters."[1] In such a brilliantly intellectual paper as the *Spectator* it is still possible to read vehement defences of the unity of authorship, and who can wonder that less literary Bible-students, in spite of their "English common sense," cling to the same belief? It is very necessary therefore for some competent scholar like Dr. Driver to remedy, so far as he can, what may be called the sophistication of our native good sense. Still an older student of Isaiah xl.—lxvi. may be permitted to regret the imperfection of Dr. Driver's work. To treat Isaiah xl.—lxvi. as a "continuous prophecy," written from the same historical and religious standpoint, and dealing throughout with a common theme, is a retrograde policy which I cannot help lamenting. As long as this theory was advocated in a semi-popular work, it was possible to hold that Dr. Driver adopted it from educational considerations. There is, of course, no competent teacher who does not sometimes have to condescend to the capacities of his pupils. It *is* no doubt easier for a beginner to take in the view of what I have heard called the "dual authorship of the Book of Isaiah" than a more complicated, even though a sounder theory. But when the statements of Dr. Driver's *Isaiah* are repeated in a work which aims at

---

[2] From a letter signed "Hope" in the *Times*, Jan. 7, 1892.

"representing the present condition of investigation," it becomes more difficult to account for them. For the progress of exegesis has revealed the fact that there are several striking breaks in the continuity, changes in the tone and the historical situation, modifications of the religious ideas. "Revealed" may seem a strong word, but the truth is that though some early critics had a glimpse of these facts, the knowledge was lost again in a very natural rebound from the pernicious extreme of the fanatical disintegrators. It was Ewald who rectified the new error of Gesenius and Hitzig, and the example of *moderate* disintegration set by him was followed, not of course without very much variety of view, by Bleek, Geiger, Oort, Kuenen, Stade, Dillmann, Cornill, Budde, and in England by myself in 1881, and by Mr. G. A. Smith in 1890. The principal exegetical facts which require disintegration will be found in my own commentary on Isaiah (1880-1881), my own latest explanation of them in two published academical lectures.[1] I have

---

[1] See *Jewish Quarterly Review*, July and Oct. 1891. Budde approaches very near to me, confirming his view by his researches into the "elegiac rhythm" (Stade's *Zt.*, 1891, p. 242). Those who wish for bolder theories may go to Kuenen and Cornill. The gradualness of Kuenen's advance adds special weight to his opinions. I will not deny the plausibility of his arguments, especially in the light of a more advanced view of the date of Job. But I can only write according to the light which I have at the time. [Duhm's masterly treatment of Isa. xl.—lxvi. in his commentary, which has lately appeared, will surely force a reconsideration of the subject, and put an end to the indifference of English critics. Nov. 1892.]

no feverish anxiety to make converts; I am perfectly willing to be converted to other theories by more acute and thorough critics than myself. But what is desirable is this: that the exegetical facts which so many trained critics have noticed should be recognized and critically explained by all earnest scholars, and that some credit both for priority among recent analysts and for caution and moderation should be awarded where it is due. Such remarks as these ought to be impossible in the principal literary organ of Anglican Churchmen: "We think that there is at present in some quarters ['another professor' had been already indicated] a readiness to break up works on utterly insufficient grounds, which is almost wantonly provoking, and we are heartily glad that Dr. Driver gives no countenance whatever to such a proceeding."[1]

The pretension here and elsewhere set up on behalf of Dr. Driver is doubtless most repugnant to that candid scholar, but it is, I fear, his own imperfect exhibition of the "present condition of investigation" which has produced the serious errors and illusions of a conscientious but ill-informed writer.

I will now advance a step. It is in the interests, not only of criticism, but also of that very view of the "prophecy of restoration" which Dr. Driver himself values so highly, that I venture to criticize his treatment of Isaiah xl.—lxvi. For although there is

---

[1] *Guardian*, Dec. 2, 1891 (p. 1953).

much in these chapters which, as conservative scholars admit, may be taken to favour an Exilic date, there are also, as they rightly maintain, other phenomena which seem inconsistent with this date. Dr. Driver has, of course, an explanation for those phenomena which do not altogether suit him, and so, too, have his conservative opponents for those which do not suit them. It is impossible therefore that either side should gain an undisputed victory.[1] Seeing this, the *moderate* disintegrating critics intervene with an *eirenicon;* why should not Dr. Driver join them, and claim for himself a share in the blessing of the peace-makers? There is room enough for the linguistic and the rhythmical keys, as well as for that which I myself chiefly applied to these problems. But I will not dwell longer on this thorny subject.

The next prophets in order are Jeremiah and Ezekiel. On these the "higher criticism" has less to say than on the Book of Isaiah. With regard to Jeremiah x. 1—16, Dr. Driver tells us that either it belongs to the latter part of Jeremiah's career, or it is the work of a prophet at the close of the Exile. But why hesitate? Surely the two theories are not *equally probable,* and interesting as the linguistic remarks on the interpolated Aramaic verse (*v.* 11)

---

[1] Even if it be granted that Isaiah xl.—lxvi. is not Isaiah's work, there is no absolute necessity to adopt Dr. Driver's view. For it may be asked, May not the prophecy be *a work of the restoration-period?* (So not only Seinecke but Isidore Loeb, *Revue des études juives,* juillet-sept. 1891.) My own answer, of course, is ready; but what can Dr. Driver say?

may be, are they not somewhat out of place? **At**
any rate the facts want a little more theory to
illuminate them. Nor are they complete. If אֱרִין
occurs in x. 11 a, is not the ordinary form אֲרֵעָא found
in x. 11 b? And does not the less usual form occur
in the Midrashim (e. g. *Ber. R.* 13)? Moreover,
does not the suffix הוֹם deserve mention? It agrees
with the Aramaic part of Ezra, but not with that of
Daniel[1] (which always gives הוֹן). I do not (as the
reader will see later) undervalue linguistic data; but
would not these particular facts have been more in
place in the great forthcoming Hebrew Dictionary?
And why is there no reference to Mr. Ball's somewhat
elaborate discussion of chap. x. in his contribution to
the *Expositor's Bible?*[2] Consider how much else
has been "crowded out." For instance, though
perhaps enough is said of the two texts of Jeremiah
(Dr. Driver, on the whole, prefers the Hebrew;
Cornill the Greek text), there is no sufficient discussion of the method and plan of Jeremiah's editor,
nor are any hints given with regard to possible interpolations other than those to which the Septuagint
can guide us (*e. g.* xvii. 19—27). Another interesting
question (raised by Schwally) is that of the authorship
of Jeremiah xxv. and xlvi.—li. Though Jeremiah
l.-li. is fully admitted (on grounds which supplement

[1] Mr. Bevan omits to notice this point in his excellent work on Daniel (p. 36).
[2] Mr. Ball's *Jeremiah* has escaped the notice of the author, who takes such pleasure in recognizing English work.

those given in 1885 in my *Pulpit Commentary*) to be Exilic, the larger problem is not referred to. On the contents of Ezekiel, too, much more might have been said. There are difficulties connected with the question of Ezekiel's editorial processes—difficulties exaggerated by a too brilliant Dutch scholar (A. Pierson), and yet grave enough to be mentioned. But of course a difference of judgment as to the selection of material is occasionally to be expected. At any rate, valuable help is given on Ezekiel xl.—xlviii., which, by an instructive exaggeration, some one has called "the key to the Old Testament."[1] It remains for some future scholar to rediscover this great pastor, patriot, and prophet.[2]

The Minor Prophets are by no means all of them either of minor importance or of minor difficulty.[3] In some cases, it is true, the date and authorship are on the whole free from difficulty. Hence in treating of Hosea, Amos, Nahum, Habakkuk, Zephaniah, Haggai, and Malachi, it is the contents and special characteristics of the books to which Dr. Driver mainly directs his attention. Not that there are no critical questions of any moment (*e.g.* the question of

---

[1] J. Orth, *ap.* Wellhausen, *Prolegomena*, p. 447.

[2] Prof. Davidson's *Ezekiel* (in the Cambridge Biblical series) has not yet (November 1892) come into my hands.

[3] I venture to regret that no mention is made of Renan's interesting study on the Minor Prophets in the *Journal des savants*, Nov. 1888. Renan may have great faults, but cannot be altogether ignored. Taylor's *Text of Micah* (1891) might also claim mention. [Wellhausen's small but important work, *Die kleinen Propheten*, has just come to hand, Nov. 1892.]

interpolations or later insertions), but, as a rule, they are of a class in which the author is not as yet much interested. It were ungracious to touch upon them here, except in the case of Habakkuk iii. In omitting all criticism of the heading of this ode, or psalm, Dr. Driver seems to me inconsistent with himself; for though he leaves the authorship of the "Song of Hezekiah" unquestioned, he has no scruple in holding that the psalm in Jonah ii. was not the work of Jonah.[1] In the "present state of critical investigation" it has become almost equally difficult to defend tradition in any one of these cases. Certainly neither the expressions nor the ideas of Habakkuk iii. agree with those of Habakkuk i., ii.; they favour a post-Exilic rather than a pre-Exilic date. The most reasonable view is that both the psalms of Hezekiah and that of Habakkuk once formed part of a liturgical collection (cf. Hab. iii. 19, Isa. xxxviii. 20).[2] Had Dr. Driver omitted the reference on page 283 to a bold conjecture of Prof Sayce,[3] he would have gained more than enough space for some mention of this important critical point. He might also have gracefully referred to Mr. Sinker's *Psalm of Habakkuk* (1890). I venture to add that caution is carried too far when the date of Nahum is

---

[1] On the date of this psalm, cf. my *Bampton Lectures*, p. 127.
[2] So Stade and Kuenen; see also my *Bampton Lectures*, pp. 125 (top), 156, 157, 210, 214, and *Isaiah*, i. 228-9.
[3] For which, besides Dr. Driver's references, see *Babylonian and Oriental Record*, ii. 18—22.

placed between B.C. 664 and 607. The prophecy must, it would seem, have been written either *circa* B.C. 660 (as, following Schrader, Tiele and myself dated it in 1888), or *circa* 623, the date of the first campaign of Cyaxares against Assyria (as recently both Kuenen and Cornill).

The other Minor Prophets are considerably more difficult. Obadiah, for instance, well deserves a closer investigation. Dr. Driver's treatment of the book is, as far as it goes, excellent. On Obadiah 1—9 he adopts the most critical view, viz. that Obadiah here takes for his text a much older prophecy, which is also reproduced with greater freedom in Jeremiah xlix. 7—22. But he makes no attempt to fix the period of the prophecy more precisely. I will not presume to censure him for this. But if the book was to carry out the promises of the programme, I venture to think that the two views which are still held ought to have been mentioned, viz. (1) that Obadiah wrote soon after the destruction of Jerusalem by Nebuchadrezzar (Schrader, Riehm, Meyrick); and (2) that his date is some time after the re-establishment of the Jews in their own land (Kuenen, Cornill).[1] The latter view seems to me to be required by a strict exegesis.

There is also another omission of which I would

---

[1] Schwally's view should also perhaps have been, however briefly, referred to. See his study on Zephaniah, in Stade's *Zt.*, x. 225, note. He makes *vv.* 1—18 Exilic, *vv.* 19—21 post-Exilic.

gently complain. Dr. Driver undertakes to give some account of the contents of the several books. But here he omits one most important feature of Obadiah's description, which I venture to give from a critical paper of my own (printed in 1881) which has escaped the notice of Dr. Driver.

"**One very** singular feature requires explanation. The captives of the northern kingdom are not **to** settle in their old homes; their kinsmen of **the** southern tribes have expanded **too much** for this. They are therefore compensated by the gift of that border-land, which had **never** as yet been thoroughly conquered, 'the cities of the Canaanites as far as Zarephath' (this is the most probable **view** of the first half of $v.$ 20)—they became, in fact, the guardians of the northern marches just as the captives of Judah are the keepers of the southern. Tyre is excepted, for a great future is reserved for Tyre (Isa. xxiii. 17, 18). But in speaking of the captives of Judah we must draw a distinction. The guardians of the 'south-country' (the *Negeb*, or 'dry land') are, not the mass of the captives of Israel, but those 'who are in Sepharad.'"[1]

Now, what is "Sepharad"? If this had nothing to do with the date of the book, Dr. Driver might simply have referred **to a** dictionary of the Bible. But it has very much indeed to do with it, and Prof. Sayce may justly complain of the author for this

---

[1] "**The Book of** Obadiah," *Homiletic Quarterly*, Jan. 1881, pp. 114—117.

neglect of archæological evidences. I am aware of the diversity of opinion which exists among scholars as to the locality of "Sepharad"; the evidence and the arguments lie before me. But it is clear that if the prophecy, as it stands, is post-Exilic, we can hardly help identifying "Sepharad" with Çparda, the name of a province of the Persian empire, which stands between Cappadocia and Ionia in the inscription of Darius at Naksh-i-Rustam.[1] What now becomes the most natural view of the date of the prophecy? When can there have been a captive-band from Jerusalem in Phrygia or Lydia? The earliest possible time known to us is about B.C. 351, when Artaxerxes Ochus so cruelly punished the participation of the Jews in the great revolt. I have remarked elsewhere that this was "the third of Israel's great captivities,"[2] and have referred various psalms to the distress and embitterment which it produced. It is very noteworthy that the prophet nowhere mentions either the Chaldeans or *Babylon*. Also that Joel iii. 6 refers to "children of Judah and of Jerusalem" as having been sold to the "sons of the Javanites" (Ionia was close to Çparda = Sepharad). Now Joel, as Dr. Driver and I agree, is post-Exilic,

[1] See *Records of the Past*, v. 70 (where however "Sparta" is an incorrect identification of "Çparda"). On "Sepharad," Lassen, Spiegel, Oppert, Sayce, but especially Schrader, have learnedly discoursed. See the latter's *The Cuneiform Inscriptions*, &c. (by Whitehouse) on Obad. 20, and his *Keilschriften und Geschichtsforschung*, pp. 116—119.

[2] *Bampton Lectures for* 1889, p. 53; cf. p. 229.

and *appears to refer in ii. 32 to Obad. 17.* Is all this of no importance to the student? I cannot think so, provided that the critic also points out the religious elements which give vitality to this little prophecy.

Here let me remind the reader that I am no opponent of Professor Driver. Most gladly would I have given him unmingled thanks for all the good that is in his book. I am only hindered from doing so by those very serious misapprehensions of the public, which I have endeavoured to combat, and to which, in one respect, the editors of the "Library" have unintentionally contributed. It was perhaps specially difficult for Professor Driver to explain the prevailing tendency of critical opinion on the Minor Prophets because of the attention naturally directed in the Anglican Church to the successor of Dr. Pusey, a scholar who not only worthily summed up and *closed* a philological period, but represented a school of orthodoxy which is still powerful among us. Dr. Driver would not, I believe, say that he has as yet given us all that he hopes to know about Joel. This little book is one of those which suffer most by a separate treatment, and every advance which we make in our study of the other post-Exilic writings must react (as I have shown in one case already) on our view of Joel. But what Dr. Driver does give us is excellent; I only miss the definite statement (which is surely a necessary inference from the facts produced) that the Book of Joel is at any rate hardly earlier than the age of Nehemiah (*i.e.* the second half of the fifth century).[1] It might also have been mentioned that the early Jewish doctors were rather for than against a late date for Joel.[2]

I now come to a book which, by the common consent of sympathetic readers, is one of the most beautiful in the Old Testament Canon—the Book of Jonah. It is also however one of the most controverted, and one cannot but admire the quiet dignity with which Dr. Driver sets forth his own free but devout critical views. In the first place, as to the date. By four (or rather five)[3] arguments unconnected with the extraordinary character of the story, it is shown that the book finds its only natural home in the post-Exilic period. I think myself that we might go further, and that from a fuller study of the literature and history of the post-Exilic period, and also (if I may say so) of *psalm-criticism*, Dr. Driver may obtain a still more definite solution of the critical problem. But the main point has been settled beyond dispute. It remains however to determine 1. What the didactic purpose of the book is, and 2. Whether, or to what extent, the narrative is historical. On the latter point Dr. Driver says that " quite irrespectively of the miraculous features in the narrative, it must be admitted that . . it is not strictly historical," but also that—" No doubt the materials

---

[1] So Merx, Kuenen, Cornill, and Prof. Robertson Smith. On the linguistic argument see further on.

[2] See Rosenzweig, *Das Jahrhundert nach dem bab. Exile*, p. 45.   [3] See Note 1, p. 301.

of the narrative were supplied to the author by tradition, and rest ultimately upon a basis of fact: no doubt the outlines of the narrative are historical, and Jonah's preaching was actually successful at Nineveh (Luke xi. 30, 32), though not upon the scale represented in the book" (p. 303).[1]

May I be allowed gently to criticize the latter statement, which yields too much to stationary thinkers like Bishop Ellicott? The author speaks here as if, whenever the Saviour referred in appearance to historical individuals, He necessarily believed Himself that the persons named were actually historical. This in Sir Philip Sidney's time appears to have been commonly held; for in mentioning the story of the rich man and Lazarus[2] he apologetically refers to "the learned divines" who account the narrative to be a parable. But what necessity is there for this view with regard to Christ's words in Luke xi. 30, 32? Considering how temporary and therefore how superficial the "repentance" of the Ninevites (if historical) must have been, and how completely different was the repentance which Christ demanded, it becomes surely the most natural view that Jesus Christ interpreted the story as an instructive parable. We cannot indeed prove this; and even if He did, with His wonderful spiritual tact, so interpret it, we cannot be sure that He would have communi-

[1] **So Prof.** A. B. Davidson calls this book "a historical episode" (*Expositor*, v. 161).
[2] *An Apologie for Poetrie* (Arber), p. 35.

cated His interpretation to His dull disciples, on whom probably the distinction between history and quasi-historical didactic fiction would have been lost.

I venture also to object that Dr. Driver's reference to the New Testament will give offence to many young men who, without being in the least undevout, desire *to study the Old Testament historically.* He who would guide this best class of students must not even seem to be biassed by a disputable theological theory respecting the knowledge of the Saviour. To me it appears in the highest degree probable that the story of the Book of Jonah is not merely not in all points, but not in any point, historical, and I have on my side such a moderate and orthodox critic as Riehm.[1] The romantic form of literature which flourished among the later Jews must have had a beginning; Tobit cannot have been its first specimen. It also appears to me more than probable that there is a mythic element in the story of Jonah. I do not mean that this story is itself a popular myth, but that, as I showed in 1877,[2] the author of "Jonah" (like the writer of Jeremiah li. 34, 44) adopted a well-known Oriental mode of expression, based upon a solar myth.[3] Bishop Ellicott, whom I meet with

---

[1] Riehm, *Einleitung*, ii. 167 ("eine reine Dichtung").

[2] See *Theological Review*, 1877, pp. 211—219.

[3] The late Prof. Elmslie once expressed the hope that Boehme's theory of the combination in the book of Jonah of divergent versions might be established, and so put out of court the notion that the Book is a pure allegory (*Expositor*, vii. 399). It is, as most good critics agree, a narrative in the style of the

regret as an opponent, thinks this view dishonouring to the Bible. To the younger generation however

---

midrash, attached to the name of the prophet mentioned in 2 Kings xiv. 25. Budde indeed has ably supported the conjecture that it is a fragment of the *midrash* of the Book of Kings, which forms the chief source of Chronicles (Stade's *Zt.*, 1892, p. 37, &c.). My own contribution consists in pointing out the mythic element in the story. I do not mean that the story is itself directly mythical. As H. Zimmern has lately said, the school which professed to discover in every form of early legend the reflection of a natural phenomenon has had its day; Goldziher, I am certain, would now abandon the greater part of his *Hebrew Mythology*. But just as Zimmern maintains that the poet who composed the Blessing of Jacob (Gen. xlix.) utilized material which was ultimately of mythic origin, so I hold that the form of the story of Jonah was partly suggested by a Babylonio-Israelitish expression of mythic origin. That the writer of the Book of Jonah knew the mythic meaning I do not assert. Neither is it at all necessary to suppose that the Second Isaiah and the author of Job knew the meaning of the mythic expressions which they have used.

I venture to refer here to Jer. li. 31, 44, which possibly furnished the author of "Jonah" with the basis of his story, and "supplies a missing link between the Jonah-story and the original myth." "Like the latter, it describes the destroyer as 'the dragon'; like the former, it converts both destroyer and destroyed into symbols" (article "Jonah," *Theological Review*, 1877, p. 217). Israel, in short, is swallowed up by Nebuchadrezzar as by "a dragon." For the Babylonian myth of the Serpent, who in the fight with Marduk devoured the tempest, see *Transactions of Soc. of Biblical Archæology*, vol. iv. part 2, appendix, plate 6; and for a translation of part of it, my *Pulpit-comm.* on *Jeremiah* (1885), ii. 293. Comp. also Smith's *Chaldæan Genesis*, ed. Sayce, pp. 112—114, and my *Job and Solomon*, pp. 76, 77; also H. C. Trumbull, "Jonah in Nineveh," *Journal of Biblical Lit.*, vol. xi. part 1, where the story of Jonah is regarded as providentially arranged so as to seem credible to believers in the fish-god Oannes (= Jonah).

who have felt the fascination of myths, the word which has dropped from the Bishop's pen in connection with myself [1] will appear strangely misplaced. They will be well pleased at the discovery that the story of Jonah (like that of Esther) contains an element of mythic symbol. They will reverence its writer as one of those inspired men who could convert mythic and semi-mythic stories and symbols into vehicles of spiritual truth. Dr. Driver, it is true, is not on my side here. He timidly refers to the allegoric theory, without himself adopting it, and even without mentioning how I have completed the theory by explaining the allegoric machinery. Still, what Dr. Driver does say (p. 302) as to the aim of the Book of Jonah is in itself excellent, and may, without violence, be attached to the mythic-allegoric theory. The story of Jonah did in fact teach the Jews "that God's purposes of grace are not limited to Israel alone, but are open to the heathen as well, if only they abandon their sinful courses, and turn to Him in true penitence." And I think these words may be illustrated and confirmed by a passage from my own discussion of the relation of the Jewish Church to heathen races. "The author [of Jonah] belongs to that freer and more catholic school, which protested against a too legalistic spirit, and he fully recognizes (see Jonah iv. 2) that the doctrine of Joel ii. 12 applies not merely to Israel, but to all nations.

---

[1] *Christus Comprobator*, p. 186.

He is aware too that Israel (typified by Jonah 'the dove') cannot evade its missionary duty, and that its preaching should be alike of mercy and of justice."[1]

There still remain Micah and Zechariah. Both books are treated with great fulness, and with results which fairly represent the present state of opinion. I would gladly quote from both sections, but especially from that on Micah. On Micah iv. 10 the author agrees with me that the words, "and thou shalt go even to Babylon," are an interpolation. This is a brave admission, though the author does not recognize the consequence which follows from this for the criticism of Isaiah xxxix. 6, 7.[2] On Micah vi., vii. (later additions), able as the author's criticisms are, they are lacking in firmness. In the Zechariah section, the great result is attained, that not only Zechariah i.—viii., but also Zechariah ix.—xi., and xii.—xiv., come to us from post-Exilic times. Not that Dr. Driver, like another able philologist, Professor G. Hoffmann,[3] goes back to the old view of the unity of authorship—a plurality of authors is evidently implied

---

[1] *Bampton* **Lectures** *for* 1889, pp. **294-5.** Why is Israel called Jonah? Because Israel's true ideal is to be like, not the eagle, but the dove. See my note on Ps. lxviii. 14 (end), and comp. a beautiful passage in *Links and Clues,* p. 113.

[2] Nothing in Dillmann's note on Isaiah, *l.c.,* affects the main points urged in my own commentary. For my matured opinion **on Micah iv. 10,** and **a** vindication of its essential reverence, see my note in the small Cambridge edition of Micah.

[3] *Hiob* (1891), p. 34, note.

by his remarks; nor yet that he accepts the somewhat radical theory of Stade, published in his *Zeitschrift* in 1881-82. He holds that in Zechariah ix.—xi. we have a post-Exilic prophecy, which was modified in details, and accommodated to a later situation by a writer who lived well on in the post-Exilic period. This is substantially the view which I have already put forward, and to which Kuenen has independently given his high authority. Nor ought I to pass over the fact that though Stade has done more than any one for the spread of a similar view, my own theory was expounded at length by myself in 1879, in a paper read before the Taylerian Society, and briefly summarized in the same year in print in the *Theological Review*.[1] Dr. Driver is so kind as to refer to this paper, which only lately reached publication. For this I thank him. There is too little recognition of work done by Englishmen in darker days, before criticism began to be fashionable. But the greater becomes my regret at Dr. Driver's neglect of similar work of mine, which also stands chronologically at the head of a movement, on Isaiah xl.—lxvi.[2]

---

[1] See *Theological Review*, 1879, p. 284; *Jewish Quarterly Review*, 1889, pp. 76—83. I must add that Professor Robertson Smith said in 1881 that he had long held Zechariah xii.—xiv. to be post-Exilic, and that Stade had convinced him that Zechariah ix.—xii. was of the same period (*The Prophets of Israel*, p. 412).

[2] I ought however to add that my articles receive a bare mention in the addenda to Dr. Driver's second edition.

The remaining six chapters of the *Introduction* relate to the Kethubim or Hagiographa. May they be widely read, and stir up some students to give more attention to these precious monuments of the inspired Church-nation of Israel! Prefixed are some excellent pages on Hebrew poetry, in which some will miss a reference to Budde's important researches on the elegiac rhythm (the omission is repaired on p. 429). After this, we are introduced to the first of the Hagiographa, according to our Hebrew Bibles—the Book of Psalms. Surely there is no book in the Canon on which an Anglican Churchman and a member of a cathedral chapter may more reasonably be expected to throw some light than the Psalter. It must however be remembered that Dr. Driver's space is limited. He has only twenty-three pages— all too few to expound the facts and theories to which the Christian apologist has by degrees to accommodate himself. Let no one therefore quarrel with the author, if on the religious bearings of his criticism he withholds the help which some students will earnestly desire; and let it be also remembered that Dr. Driver is one of a band of scholars who supplement each other's work, and that every good special work on the Psalms which in any large degree deviates from tradition supplies (or should supply) some part of the apologetic considerations which are here necessarily omitted. He had only twenty-three pages! But how full these pages are of accurate and (under the circumstances) lucidly expounded facts!

Nor is this all. His critical argument, though as a whole far less cogent than it might have been, opens up instructive glimpses of the actual condition of investigation. How difficult his task was, I am perhaps well qualified to judge, and the regret which I feel at some undue hesitation in his criticism is as nothing to my pleasure at the large recognition of truth.

For there is in fact no subject on which it is so easy to go wrong as in the criticism of the Psalter. It is to be feared that English scholars in general do not take up the inquiry at the point to which it has been brought by previous workers.[1] Other persons may find, in facts like these, nothing to regret. I confess that I do myself regret them very much. Criticism appears to me a historical and a European movement, and I am sure that this view is endorsed by the editors of this "international and interconfessional" series. But let me hasten to add that I do not feel this regret in reading Dr. Driver on the Psalms. He does not, indeed, tell us much about his method of research; the plan of his work forbade him to exhibit his results genetically. But on pages 360—362 he gives hints of great value to students, on which I will only offer this remark—that with all his love for the Hebrew language he cannot bring himself to say that the

[1] I am thinking of Profs. Kirkpatrick and Sanday, and many recent reviewers. In contrast to these stands Prof. Robertson Smith, whose article "Psalms" (*Enc. Brit.*, 1886) is still the best general introduction to the subject. [This has been reproduced in the new edition of OTJC; see above, pp. 219—224.]

linguistic argument is a primary one (to this point I may return later). One thing at least is certain, that the author is not in that stage represented provisionally by Professor Kirkpatrick, when "internal evidence, whether of thought, or style, or language," seems to be "a precarious guide," and when the student who has become sceptical of the titles of the Psalms feels that he is "launched upon a sea of uncertainty."[1]

But to proceed to details. One of the most important things for Dr. Driver to bring out was the composite origin of the Psalter. At the very outset we are met by the fact that in the Hebrew Bible (comp. the Revised English Version) the Psalter is divided into five books. Four of these books are closed by a doxology, which Dr. Driver explains by the custom of Oriental authors and transcribers to close their work with a pious formula (p. 345). But how strange it is, on this theory, that the Psalter itself is *not* closed by such a formula, but only certain divisions of the Psalter! If the doxologies are expressions of personal piety, the fact that Psalm cl. is a liturgical song of praise constitutes no reason for the omission of a closing doxology. And when we examine the doxologies more closely, we find that they all have a pronounced liturgical character.[2] This is of some consequence for the controversy with traditionalistic writers on the Psalms. Next comes

---

[1] Kirkpatrick, *The Psalms: Book I.*, Introd. p. xxxi.
[2] See *Bampton Lectures for* 1889, p. 457, and cf. Abbott, *Essays on the Original Texts* (1891), p. 222.

the great fact of the existence of internal groups, marked by the headings; Dr. Driver sums up the best that has been said in a small space. On the titles he is somewhat tantalizing; a disproportionate amount of space is given to the demolition of the historical value of the title " To David " as a record of authorship. At least, my own feeling is that the small-print illustrations on pp. 353—355 could have been omitted, and that the author should have trusted to the natural impression of an honest reader of the Psalms. At any rate, no one who has followed Dr. Driver thus far can doubt that, in Prof. Robertson Smith's words, " not only are many of the titles certainly wrong, but they are wrong in such a way as to prove that they date from an age to which David was merely the abstract psalmist, and which had no idea whatever of the historical conditions of his age."

There are three points which I should have been specially glad to see mentioned. First, that the Septuagint differs considerably from the Hebrew text in its psalm-titles. A careful study of the Greek titles would be most illuminative to the ordinary student. Secondly, that in order properly to criticize the ascription of any particular psalm, the student must first of all obtain a historical view of the picture of David in different ages, beginning with that disclosed by a critical study of the Books of Samuel, and ending with that in the Books of Chronicles.[1]

---

[1] To what absurdities an uncompromising defence of the

More especially he must to some extent assimilate a free (but not therefore undevout) criticism of the two former books. Dr. Driver's work does not give as much help as could be wished in this respect, but his results on the "Davidic" psalms really presuppose a critical insight into the David-narratives. And thirdly, something should, I think, have been said about the titles of Psalms vii. and xviii.;—of the former, because conservative scholars maintain that the mention of the otherwise unknown "Cush" proves the great antiquity of the title, or at any rate of the tradition embodied therein,[1] and of the latter, because of its unusual fulness, and because the psalm occurs again in a somewhat different recension with almost exactly the same title near the end of the second Book of Samuel, which latter circumstance has been supposed greatly to increase the probability of the accuracy of the title.[2] With regard to the former title, it ought to be admitted that "Cush" is no Hebrew proper name; there must be a corruption in the text.[3]

---

psalm-titles can lead, will be seen from M. de Harlez's article on the age of the Psalms (*Dublin Review*), July 1891.

[1] So Delitzsch, followed by Prof. Kirkpatrick.

[2] M. de Harlez thinks that "if we choose to look upon the testimony of 2 Kings (Sam.) xxii. as false, then the whole Bible must be a gigantic falsehood, and there is no use troubling ourselves about it" (*Dubl. Rev.*, July 1891, p. 76).

[3] Cornill (*Einl.*, p. 208, proposes to read "Cushi" (following Sept.'s Χουσι); but the episode of "Cushi" (see 2 Sam. xviii.) was surely most unlikely to have been thought of. The corruption must lie deeper. "A Benjamite" certainly looks as if intended to introduce a person not previously known (other-

With regard to the latter, it can hardly be doubted that it comes from some lost narrative of the life of David, which on critical grounds can hardly be placed earlier than the reign of Josiah.[1] (There seems to be no reason for thinking that the editor of the "Davidic" psalter took it from Samuel.)

The result of the argument against the universal accuracy of the title "To David" is thus summed up by Dr. Driver—"Every indication converges to the same conclusion, viz. that the 'Davidic' psalms spring, in fact, from many different periods of Israelitish history, from the period of David himself downwards; and that in the varied moods which they reflect . . . they set before us the experiences of many men, and of many ages of the national life" (p. 355).

It is however scarcely possible to say that this inference is logical. It is, of course, an idea which involuntarily suggests itself at the point which Dr. Driver's argument has reached, but it is not a legitimate "conclusion" from the data which have

---

wise, as Delitzsch remarks, we should have "*the* Benjamite"). But such a person would be sure to have his father's or some ancestor's name given. The Targum substitutes for Cush, "Saul, the son of Kish." But Saul is a well-known person, and elsewhere in the titles has no appendage to his name. Shimei, who reviled David, might be thought of, but he is called (2 Sam. xix. 16) "Shimei, son of Gera, *the* Benjamite." The conjecture adopted in *Bampt. Lect.*, pp. 229—243 alone remains. "Targum sheni" on Esther expressly credits David with a prevision of Mordecai (cf. Cassel, *Esther*, p. 299). I hesitate between this conjecture and the preceding one.

[1] Cf. *Bampton Lect.*, p. 206 (foot).

as yet been brought forward, and to dally with it disturbs the mind, which henceforth has to contend with a conscious or unconscious bias. The author however still strives hard to reason fairly. "The majority of the 'Davidic' psalms," he says, "are thus certainly not David's; is it possible to determine whether any are his?" (p. 355.)

He then examines the evidence respecting David's musical and poetical talents. Here he is less tender to conservatism than I should have expected. He gives no testimony to David's composition of religious poetry earlier than the Chronicler [1] (about 300 B.C.); it is only later on, in connexion with criteria of David's poetical style, that the poems in 2 Samuel xxii. (= Ps. xviii.) and xxiii. 1—7 are referred to. He says, too, that even if David did compose liturgical poems, this would not account for his authorship of more than a very few of the "Davidic" psalms, most of the psalms ascribed to David not being adapted (at least in the first instance) for public worship. This remark seems not very cogent, especially when limited by what is said afterwards respecting the "representative character" of many psalms. What we really want, is something that Dr. Driver could not, consistently with his plan, give us; viz. a statement of the grounds on which psalms similar to those which we possess can (or cannot) be supposed to have existed prior

---

[1] At first I wrongly inferred from this that Dr. Driver regarded the poems in 2 Sam. xxii. and xxiii. as post-Exilic, which is at least a plausible view (see Cornill, *Einl.*, p. 119).

to the regenerating activity of Isaiah and his fellow-prophets (if indeed they can historically be imagined at all in the pre-Exilic period).[1] Prof. A. B. Davidson will, I presume, endeavour to supply the omission in his eagerly expected *Old Testament Theology*.

One group of interesting facts is relegated by the author to a footnote (pp. 356, 357). Among the Jews who returned from Babylon in B.C. 536, the contemporary register (Neh. vii. 44 = Ezra ii. 41) includes 148 (128) "sons of Asaph, singers" (they are distinguished from "the Levites"). On the other hand, there is no allusion whatever to a special class of temple-singers in the pre-Exilic narratives. It seems to follow that the official singers cannot have been very prominent before the Exile. I should like to have seen this more developed; the footnote will be obscure to some readers. But of course the strength of the argument for the late date of the Psalms is wholly apart from "doubtful disputations" respecting pre-Exilic music and singing. I will only add that Jeremiah xxxiii. 11 ought hardly to have been quoted as an evidence for the early existence of a class of singers (for those who blessed Jehovah were not necessarily temple-officers), but in relation to the probable contents of pre-Exilic psalms.

Dr. Driver's remarks on Ewald's *æsthetic* criteria of really Davidic psalms are on the whole very just.

---

[1] That there are no psalms of Jeremiah has lately been shown afresh by W. Campe (1891). Dr. Driver's judgment (p. 360) might be more decided.

But how strange it is that after admitting that we have no tolerably sure standard for David's poetry outside the Psalter except 2 Sam. i. 19—27 and iii. 33, 34, he should close the paragraph thus—"On the whole, a *non liquet* must be our verdict; it is possible that Ewald's list of Davidic psalms is too large, but it is not clear that none of the psalms contained in it are of David's composition."

Surely here Dr. Driver is not untouched by the spirit of compromise. The reader will, I hope, not misunderstand me. I mean that in his desire to help those whose spiritual faith is (unfortunately) bound up with an intellectual belief in Davidic psalms he sometimes sympathizes with them more than is good for his critical judgment, and I wish, not that his desire to help were diminished, but that he could adopt a "more excellent way" of helping. Dr. Sanday works, I imagine, in the same spirit, and consequently "rests for the moment in temporary hypotheses and half-way positions, prepared to go either forwards or backwards as the case may be," and disposed to idealize Dr. Driver's hesitations and inconsistencies as "the combined openmindedness and caution which are characteristic of a scholar."[1] I

[1] *The Oracles of God*, pp. 141, 143. Prof. Sanday explains himself very fully in his little book, *Two Present Day Questions* (1892), pp. 25—35. To much that he says I can apply Goethe's words—

> Ungefähr sagt das der Pfarrer auch,
> Nur mit ein bischen andern Worten.

The archæological stage of the higher criticism began nearly

respect Dr. Sanday very highly, but I have an uncomfortable suspicion that his language helps to foster the "undesirable illusions" to which I referred in chap. xi. I hope that it may not be thought unreasonable if I decline either to "go backwards" or to adopt a "half-way position" until it has been shown that the hypothesis of Davidic elements in the Psalter has any practical value. Unless Books I. and II. date from the age before Amos, any Davidic elements which they contain must have been so modified as to

---

thirty years ago, and there is, as I have said elsewhere, a vast amount of work to be done with the help of archæology. Mr. Joseph Jacobs however has suggested to Dr. Sanday that the Old Testament critics are sadly at fault for want of archæology and "institutional sociology." I have read the article to which Dr. Sanday refers and two other very interesting ones on "junior right" in the Book of Genesis. I welcome Mr. Jacobs' help, but I confess that he is a little too confident both in his criticisms of great scholars, and in his own theories. Mr. Fenton, to whom Mr. Jacobs refers, and whom I have mentioned myself in chap. xi., erred (as Mr. Jacobs would, I fear, be likely to err) from insufficient recognition of critical results. Literary criticism has been carried on so long, and by such eminent persons, that we cannot disregard its results without becoming ourselves unhistorical and insular. It is a singular alliance—that of Prof. Sanday and Mr. Jacobs. Both utter judgments of much interest, though amateur-judgments, which are liable to be unfair or inaccurate. Prof. Sanday, however, from the fact that he is a professed New Testament critic, may do more harm to the cause of international Biblical criticism than Mr. Jacobs. I must ask in conclusion, Is it really true that "the state of New Testament study" in England is "almost wholly hopeful"? There is no doubt much good work being done, but for want of a disposition to learn from the "higher critics" of the Old Testament, it appears to me to be, however fruitful up to a certain extent, singularly onesided.

be practically unrecognizable. To analyze the Psalms with the view of detecting Davidic passages would be the most hopeless of undertakings. David may have indited religious songs; but how far removed was David's religion from that of the Psalms! The Song of Deborah is perhaps not above the highest thoughts of David; but can it be said that the tone of this poem approaches the spirituality of the Psalms? I think therefore that Dr. Driver's verdict is premature. It would have been safer from his point of view to say, "**It is** not clear that some of the psalms may not be pre-Exilic, and that even post-Exilic psalms may not contain unrecognizable Davidic fragments."

But why **all** this eagerness to **rescue a** small Davidic Psalter within the undoubtedly much larger non-Davidic one? Was it David who founded the **higher** religion **of Israel? Surely, as** Professor Robertson Smith in his article on **the** Psalms has **remarked,** "whether any of the older poems really are David's **is a** question more curious than important." For **the** question of questions is, *To what period or periods does the collection of the Psalters within the Psalter belong?* For what period in the religious history **of** Israel may we use the Psalter **as an** authority? This **was** what **I had** chiefly in view when **I** prefixed an inquiry into the origin of the Psalter to a sketch **of** the theology of the psalmist. I **cannot** find that any help is given to the student of this subject in the *Introduction*, and this is one of the points in which this valuable chapter appears to me to fail. Nor can I express myself as satisfied with Dr. Driver's remarks on the means which we have of approximately fixing the periods of the Psalms. I can divine from it that there is much which enters into a full discussion of this subject upon which Dr. Driver and I would at present differ. Nor can I content myself either with the author's neutrality on Psalm cxviii., or with his vague remarks on Psalm cx., that "though it may be ancient, it can hardly have been composed by David,"[1] and that "the cogency of [Christ's] argument (in Mark xii. 35—37) is unimpaired, as long as it is recognized that the psalm is a Messianic one," or with the remark (p. 367) on the

---

[1] These words are from the footnote on pp. 362, 363. In the text it is said that Psalm cx. "may be presumed to be pre-Exilic." I cannot but regret the misplaced moderation of the words "can *hardly* have been composed by David," and the deference to a tradition admitted to be weak in the extreme which expresses itself in the "presumption" that the psalm is pre-Exilic. I can enter into the reasoning so skilfully indicated in the reference to Jer. xxx. 21, but what this naturally leads up to is—not that the psalm refers to an actual pre-Exilic king, but that it is a thoroughly idealistic lyric prophecy of the early post-Exilic period, when both psalmists and prophets devoted themselves largely to the development of earlier prophetic ideas. The author follows Riehm in the stress which he lays on Jer. xxx. 21, but significantly omits Riehm's second reference (*Messianic Prophecy*, pp. 121, 284) to Zech. iii. vi. I must also express my regret at his useless attempt to soften opposition by a necessarily vague description of the contents of the psalm. The whole footnote, in its present form, seems to me out of place; it fosters unfortunate illusions. One result is that Dr. Driver is praised for his weak as well as for his strong points, and another that many theologians will not give a patient hearing to a scholar who cannot adopt Dr. Driver's manner.

accommodation of individualistic psalms to liturgical use by slight changes in the phraseology.[1]

On the other hand I am much gratified to find that Dr. Driver accepts the theory that Psalm li. is "a confession written on behalf of the nation by one who had a deep sense of his people's sin." That he adds "during the Exile" is comparatively unimportant; on the main point he accepts my own view already expressed in *The Book of Psalms* (1888). His arguments are identical with those which I have myself repeatedly urged.[2] The only objection which I have to make relates to his treatment of verse 5, but as I have put it forward already in the *Expositor*, 1892 (2), p. 398, I will here only express the conviction that the Church-nation theory can, without violence, be applied throughout the psalm. I know how much untrained English common sense has to say against it, but I think it quite possible by a few historical and exegetical hints to make common sense agree entirely with the experts. We must however make it perfectly clear that the person who speaks in the 51st and other psalms is not a mere rhetorical collective expression for a number of individuals but that complete living organism of which Isaiah said, "The whole head is sick, and the whole heart faint."[3]

---

[1] Similarly Stekhoven, on whom see *Bampton Lect.*, p. 277.

[2] Most recently in sermon-studies on Ps. li., in *Aids to the Devout Study of Criticism.*

[3] See *Bampton Lect.*, pp. 261—265, 276—278.

CHAPTER XIII.

DRIVER (3).

I SAID in chap. xii. that Dr. Driver would have done well to make his *non liquet* refer, not to Davidic, but to pre-Exilic psalms. There are in fact, as it appears to me, two tenable (though not two equally tenable) views. According to one, we may still have some pre-Exilic psalms (including those which refer to a king, and some at least of the persecution-psalms), a few Exilic (*e.g.* Pss. xxii., li., cii.), and also a considerable number of post-Exilic Psalms (including a few Maccabæan psalms, and at any rate Pss. xliv., lxxiv., lxxix.).[1] This was the view which I adopted not as critical truth but as a working hypothesis, when preparing that commentary on the Psalms (1888)

---

[1] Some of those who have reviewed my *Bampton Lectures* have accused me of having treated the external evidence which has been thought to be adverse to the theory of Maccabæan psalms and the objections drawn from the Septuagint Psalter too slightly. The view which these scholars take of the present position of Psalm criticism is however entirely different from my own and from that taken by competent scholars abroad (see Mühlmann, *Zur Frage der makk. Psalmen*, 1891, p. 3). Nor, so far as I can judge, is it that of Prof. Driver.

which has been so strangely overlooked by nearly all the reviewers of my *Bampton Lectures*. It is the very view now independently adopted by Dr. Driver, which indicates that in his more special study of the Psalms he has now reached the point which I had reached in 1888. At this I rejoice, for I am confident that the view which was only a working hypothesis to me in 1888 is no more than this to Dr. Driver in 1891. He cannot go backward—this were to deny facts; he can only go on to the second of the two views mentioned, viz. that the whole of the Psalter, in its present form, with the possible exception of Ps. xviii., is post-Exilic. Just as Cornill thought in 1881 that the 24th and probably other psalms were Davidic, and that Psalms lxxxiv., lxxxv., xlii., xliii., were of the reign of Jehoiakim, but by 1891 had come to see that the whole Psalter (except perhaps Psalm lxxxix.) was post-Exilic,[1] so it will probably be with Dr. Driver, however much he may modify his view by qualifications.[2] It is the latter theory of which I

---

[1] Cf. his essay in Luthardt's *Zeitschrift*, 1881, pp. 337—343, with § 36 of his *Einleitung* (1891).

[2] I do not think that he will find that much is gained by insisting on an ancient basis which has been obscured by editors. If it helps any one to believe in such a basis, by all means let him do so; it is more harmless than in the case of the Book of Daniel. But the chief object of the criticism of the Psalms is to determine the date when they became known in substantially their present form. It appears to me that in all probability the editors mainly concerned themselves with the omission of passages which had too temporary a reference. In two (presumably) Maccabæan psalms—lxxiv. and cx.—there certainly

have myself for the first time offered a comprehensive justification. Caution and sobriety were as much needed for this as for any other critical task, nor would the want of ability to enter into the feelings of a psalmist (*nachempfinden*) and to realize his historical situation have been at all a helpful qualification. The result is doubtless capable of large improvement in detail, but in the fundamental points can hardly be modified.[1]

Does this latter theory differ essentially, or only in secondary points, from that of Dr. Driver? Only in secondary points. I made no leap in the dark when I prepared my *Lectures*, nor will Dr. Driver be conscious of any abrupt transition, when he finds oppor-

---

seem to be some omissions; in Psalm lxxiv. there may also be a fresh insertion (*vv.* 12—17).

[1] It is difficult to reply as one would wish to a series of criticisms made from a different and perhaps a narrower point of view, especially when such criticisms deal largely with subordinate points which are not essential to the main theory. When the next English dissertation on the origin of the Psalter appears, it will at any rate be compelled to make considerable use of hypothesis, or it will be a failure. Prof. Davison (in the *Thinker*, Feb. 1892) does not seem to recognize this. To him and to Prof. Kennedy (two of the most courteous of my critics) I have given an imperfect reply in the *Thinker* for April; to Prof. Kennedy also in the *Expository Times* for the same month. I am most thankful for any assistance in the work of self-criticism, though English critics, through their unprogressiveness, make it rather difficult for me to learn from them. Among the criticisms to which I have been forced to reply are those of Mr. Gladstone in the *Nineteenth Century*, Oct. 1891 (answered, Dec. 1891), and Mr. J. H. Moulton, in the *Thinker*, May and July 1892 (answered, Aug. 1892). In the interests of progress some reference to these answers seems desirable.

tunity to advance further. The essential of both views is the recognition of the impossibility of proving that any psalm in its present form is pre-Exilic. "Of many psalms," adds Dr Driver, "the Exilic or post-Exilic date is manifest, and is not disputed ; of others it is difficult to say whether they are pre- or post-Exilic" (p. 362). Whichever view be adopted, it must be allowed that even Books I. and II. were put forth *after the Return*. This is not expressly mentioned by Dr. Driver, and, as I have said, it seems to me a regrettable omission. But though not mentioned, it is not, nor can it be, denied. I venture to put this before those theological reviewers who, in their needless anxiety for the ark of God, have hurried to the conclusion that the author has "rejected Dr. Cheyne's sweeping criticism of the Psalms," and that the "net result" set forth by the author on pp. 362, 363 is "very different from that which Dr. Cheyne has given us,"[1] and to express the hope that they may perceive the error into which they have fallen, and begin to suspect that it is not the only one.

We are now come to Proverbs and Job, and nowhere perhaps does one feel more strongly the imperfection of Dr. Driver's plan. It is true, what was most desirable was not yet feasible—a thorough and *comprehensive* study of the contents and origin of the Wisdom-literature, which would furnish results at once surer and more definite than the old-fashioned

[1] See *Church Quarterly Review*, Jan. 1892, p. 343 ; *Guardian* Dec. 2, 1891, p. 1953.

Introductions can give. But I think that more might have been done than has been done to show the threads which connect the products of this style of writing, and to anticipate the results which a critic of insight and courage could not fail to reach. But alas! Dr. Driver has not thrown off that spirit of deference to conservatism which, if I am not mistaken, injures his work elsewhere. At the very outset the tradition respecting Solomon in 1 Kings iv. 29—34 receives no critical examination, and though the headings in Proverbs x. 1, xxv. 1[1] are not unconditionally accepted, Dr. Driver speaks notwithstanding as if some of the Proverbs in two of the greater collections might possibly be the work of Solomon. This is hardly the way to cultivate the critical spirit in young students, and (against the author's will) may foster an unjust prejudice against critics not less careful, but perhaps less compromising than the author. As to the conclusions here offered, I feel that while censure would be impertinent, praise would be misleading. The "present condition of investigation" is only indicated in a few lines of a footnote (p. 381), and the "way for future progress" is not even allusively mentioned. It appears to me that criticism ought to start not from the worthless tradition of Solomonic authorship, but from the fact that the other proverbial books in the Old Testament are with increasing certainty seen to be later than 538 B.C.

[1] Note that Sept. does not give the former heading at all, and has no "also" in the latter.

Now what does Ben Sira tell us about his own work?

> "I, too, as the last, bestowed zeal,
> And as one who gleaneth after the vintage;
> By the blessing of the Lord I was the foremost,
> And as a grape-gatherer did I fill my winepress."
> (Ecclus. xxxiii. 16.)

Who were Ben Sira's predecessors, and when did they live? The writers of Proverbs xxx. and xxxi. 1—9 and 10—31, and of the gnomic sayings (or some of them) in Koheleth may be among them; but surely there were more productive writers or editors than these (so far as we know them from their writings). The force of the arguments against a pre-Exilic date for the final arrangement of our composite Book of Proverbs seems to me to be constantly increasing, and were I to resume the work laid aside in 1887, I feel that my results would be nearer to those of Reuss and Stade (adopted by Mr. Montefiore) than to those of Delitzsch.[1] I am not indeed prepared to give up a large antique basis [2] for chaps. xxv.—xxvii.,

---

[1] In my article "Isaiah" (*Ency. Brit.*, 1889) I expressed the view that the "Praise of Wisdom" is either Exilic or post-Exilic; in my *Job and Solomon* (1887) I dated it earlier. But, as *Bampton Lect.*, p. 365, shows, I have been coming back to my former view of Prov. i.—ix., and taking a survey of Proverbs from this fixed point, I see that the difficulties of Reuss's and Stade's view (when duly qualified) are less than those of my own former and of Dr. Driver's present theory. Comp. Mr. Montefiore's thorough and interesting article on Proverbs, *Jewish Quarterly Review*, 1890, pp. 430—453.

[2] The heading in xxv. 1 reminds one of Assyrian library notes. Isa. xxxviii. 9 may rest on a tradition of Hezekiah's interest in books.

the proverbs in which, as Prof. Davidson has pointed out, differ on the whole considerably in style from those in x. 1—xxii. 16. But not only chaps. xxx. and xxxi., but the passages forming the "Praise of Wisdom," and the introductory verses of the redactor (i. 1—6), are altogether post-Exilic (not of course contemporary), and so too, probably, is much of the rest of the book. Indeed however much allowance is made for the tenacity of the life of proverbs, and for the tendency to recast old gnomic material, one must maintain that in its present form the Book of Proverbs is a source of information, not for the pre-Exilic, but for various parts of the post-Exilic period.[1] I will only add that Dr. Driver may perhaps modify his view of the gradual formation of Proverbs in deference to recent researches of Gustav Bickell.[2]

The chapter on Job is a skilful exhibition of views which are well deserving of careful study. It is evidently much influenced by a book of which I too have the highest appreciation — Prof. Davidson's volume on Job in the Cambridge series (comp. his article "Job" in the *Encycl. Brit.*). If therefore I object to it, it can only be in the most friendly manner, and on the same grounds on which I have already criticized that beautiful textbook.[3] I must

---

[1] In this connexion I may refer to my notes on the Persian affinities of the "Wisdom" of Prov. viii., *Expositor*, Jan. 1892, p. 79.

[2] See the *Wiener Zeitschr. f. d. Kunde des Morgenlandes*, 1891-92 (chiefly important for the metrical study of Job, Proverbs, and Ecclesiasticus). [3] *Academy*, Nov. 1, 1884.

however add that I **think Dr.** Driver should have taken some steps in advance of a book published in 1884. Both he and **Dr.** Davidson **have a way of** stopping short in the most provoking **manner.** At the very outset, for instance, they compromise **rather** more than is strictly critical on the subject of the historical existence of Job.[1] It is true, we ought not, without strong grounds, to presume that the plot of the poem is purely romantic, Semitic writers preferring to build on tradition as far as they can. But to use the words "*history*" and "*historical* tradition" of the main features of the Job story is misleading, unless we are also bold enough to apply these terms to the pathetic Indian story of Harischandra in vol. i. of Muir's *Sanskrit Texts*. No doubt there were current stories, native or borrowed, of the sudden ruin of a righteous man's fortunes; but if we had them, we should see that they were not historical, but simple folk-tales, which, to a student of natural psychologies, are surely better than what we call history. On this however I have said enough elsewhere;[2] so I will pass on to one of the great critical questions—that of the integrity of the book.

Here Dr. Driver is not very satisfactory. It is

---

[1] Among minor matters connected with the Prologue, these may be noted. 1 see no explanation of the name of Job, and for the meaning of the "land of Uz" miss a reference to W. R. Smith, *Kinship in Arabia*, p. 261. A hint might also have been given of the appearance of a legend of "three *kings*" from the East (Job ii. 11, Sept.).

[2] *Job and Solomon*, pp. 62, 290.

true, he thinks it "all but certain" (why this hesitation?) that the Elihu-speeches are a later insertion, which, considering his conservatism on Isaiah xl.–lxvi., is a concession of much value. But he unfortunately ignores even the mildest of those critical theories, of which a wiser critic (in my opinion) speaks thus in an American review [1]—"If we are not mistaken, a much better case could be made out for a theory of many authors than for the theory of one [or of two]. As the name of David attracted successive collections of psalms, and the name of Solomon successive collections of proverbs, why may not the name of Job have attracted various treatments of the problems of suffering righteousness?"

Why not, indeed, if the evidence points, as it does, in this direction? And my complaint is not that Dr. Driver does not adopt this or that particular theory, but that he fails to recognize a number of exegetical facts. He approaches the Book of Job, as it seems to me, with the preconceived idea that it left the author's hand as a finished and well-rounded composition. This idea is no doubt natural enough, but is hardly consistent with the results of criticism in other parts of the Old Testament and in other literatures. As has been well said by the authors of the *Corpus Poeticum Boreale*, "The great books of old time are accretions; our Psalter is such a one, Homer is such a one, the Sagas are such a one." Ewald, who

---

[1] Review of Genung's *Epic of the Inner Life* in *The Nation*, Aug. 27, 1891.

began by believing in the unity of Genesis, found out that this unity was factitious; may it not very naturally be so with a poem, which, like the dialogues in Job, prompted to imitation and to contradiction? Dr. Driver's able forerunner has indeed justified his own reluctance to disintegrate by his desire to enjoy the poem as much as he can. He can sympathize, he tells us, with those persons who are "so intoxicated with the beauty of a great creation, that they do not care a whit how it arose."[1] But he forgets that the true critic is not a mere dissector, but analyzes in order to reconstruct, and that there are disintegrating critics (take for instance Dr. Walter Leaf[2]) who are in no respect hindered by their criticism from the fullest æsthetic enjoyment of the work of art which they criticize.

I may indeed venture to go further and ask, Is the Book of Job, as it now stands, really such a great work of art? I know all that can be said on the difference between Eastern and Western art, and between Eastern and Western pyschology; but the difference must not be pressed to an extreme. I am willing to admit—indeed, I did in 1887 expressly admit—that the six accretions indicated in my *Job and Solomon* (pp. 67—69) need not have come from as many different writers. The Elihu-speeches, however, which are the most obvious of the accretions, cannot have come from the writer of the Dialogues

---

[1] Davidson, *Expositor*, 1883, p. 88.
[2] See Leaf, *Companion to the Iliad*, p. 18.

(though Kamphausen once thought so). Nor, as it would seem, can the Epilogue. I grant that the author of the Dialogues prefixed to his work not only chap. iii., but also chaps. i. and ii. But I cannot believe that he meant xlii. 7—17 to be the *dénoûment* of the story;—that hypothesis at least no ingenuity can render plausible. "The only possible close of the poem, if the writer is not untrue to his deepest convictions, is that the Satan should confess before Jehovah and the court of heaven that there are 'perfect and upright' men who serve God without interested motives."[1] Such at least is still my own opinion. That we do not now find such a close, only proves either (what we knew before) that the original poem has not come down to us intact, or that the Book of Job, like that of Koheleth, was left in an unfinished state by the author.

Whether the other passages were, or were not, added by the author is to some extent an open question. It seems to me extremely hazardous to suppose that the writer went on retouching his own work, but this is the only possible course for those who hold out against the view, which for some at least of the added passages I cannot help advocating. But at any rate one thing is certain, viz. that even after removing the speeches of Elihu, the Book of Job does not form a genuine whole—that some of the original passages have been retouched and new

[1] *Critical Review*, May 1891, p. 253 (the present writer's review of Hoffmann's *Hiob*).

ones added. That eminent critic Dillmann, who in spite of himself continually makes such gratifying concessions to young scholars, is in the main point on my side,[1] and so are all the chief workers in this department. Against me, as I have good cause to know, there stands arrayed the host of English theological reviewers. But how many of these have made a serious critical study of the Book of Job? How many have even read carefully—much less worked at—any critical work in which the unity of Job is denied, and have assimilated the *positive* side of a disintegrating theory? I complain of my friend Dr. Driver because, with the best intentions, he has made it *more difficult* for ordinary students to come to the knowledge of important facts, and made it possible for a thoroughly representative, and in some respects not illiberal, writer in a leading Anglican review to use language which must, I fear, be qualified as both unseemly and misleading.[2]

And what has the author to say on the date of the poem, or rather since the poem has, by his own admission, been added to, on the date of the original work and of the Elihu-speeches? To answer that the latter were added by "a somewhat later writer" is, I think, only defensible if the original poem be made post-Exilic. For surely, if anything has grown clearer of late years, it is that the language and ideas

---

[1] See Dillmann, *Hiob* (1891), *Einl.*, p. xxviii, and cf. his emarks on the controverted passages in the course of the book.
[2] *Guardian*, Dec. 2, 1891.

of " Elihu " are those of some part of the post-Exilic period.

The new edition of Dillmann's *Hiob* may be taken as evidence of this. He still makes the original poem pre-Exilic (though nearer to B.C. 586 than formerly), but whereas in 1869 he thought that the Elihu-speeches " might have been written in the course of the sixth century " (*i.e.* possibly before the Return), in 1891 he tells us that they are probably to be assigned to the fifth century. As to the original poem, our author states (as I did myself in 1887) that " it will scarcely be earlier than the age of Jeremiah, and belongs most probably to the period of the Babylonian captivity." [1]

Both Dillmann and Dr. Briggs favour the former date; Umbreit, Knobel, Grätz, and Prof. Davidson the latter. Gesenius also prefers an Exilic date, but will not deny the possibility of a still later one. And it is a post-Exilic date which many critics (*e.g.* Kuenen, Wellhausen, Stade, Hoffmann,[2] Cornill)

---

[1] Prof. Bissell, I observe, hopes to prove a considerably earlier date *by the help of Glaser's discoveries in Arabia* (*Presbyterian and Reformed Review*, Oct. 1891). He refers to Prof. Sayce. I trust that Prof. Whitehouse will be more cautious (see *Critical Review*, Jan. 1892, p. 12).

[2] Prof. G. Hoffmann's arguments (*Hiob*, 1891) do not perhaps materially advance the discussion, though his book ought to have been referred to by our author. His linguistic proposals are too violent, and his references to Zoroastrianism do not show enough study. Nor am I sure that he has added much of value to the argument from parallel passages. On the latter I venture to add these remarks for comparison with Dr. Driver's valuable section (p. 408). On the parallels between Job and the

are in our day inclined to accept. Ought not this to have been mentioned? I feel myself that in the present position of the criticism of the Hagiographa a post-Exilic date has acquired a greater degree of plausibility.[1] If, for instance, the Book of Proverbs is in the main a composite post-Exilic work, it becomes at once in a higher degree probable that the Book of Job is so too. It is still of course a question to be argued out in detail; there is no escaping from the discipline of hard and minute investigation. But, so far as I can see, the evidence collected, when viewed in the light of general probabilities, and of the results attained and being attained elsewhere, justifies us in asserting that the whole of the Book of Job belongs most probably to the Persian period.

---

probably or certainly Exilic parts of ii. Isaiah it is difficult to speak confidently. Nor need we perhaps consider the Prologue of Job to be indebted to Zech. iii.; the modes of representation used were "in the air" in the post-Exilic period. And as to the parallel adduced by Cornill (*Einl.*, p. 234) between Job xlii. 17 and Gen. xxxv. 29, xxv. 8 (both P), this, if admitted as important, will only affect the date of the Epilogue. Then we turn to the Psalms, the Song of Hezekiah, and the Lamentations. It would be difficult indeed to say that Isa. xxxviii. 10—20, or that Pss. xxxix. and lxxxviii. were not written in the same period as Job, and these works can, I believe, be shown to be post-Exilic. If this seems doubtful to any one, yet Ps. viii. 5 "is no doubt parodied in Job vii. 17" (Driver), and there is no reason for not grouping Ps. viii. with the Priestly Code. I admit that Lam. iii. is, by the same right as Ps. lxxxviii., to be viewed as in a large sense contemporary with Job (see Delitzsch, *Hiob*, p. 24). But what is the date of the Lamentations? See farther on.

[1] Comp. *Bampton Lect.*, p. 202.

On linguistic grounds[1] I should like to put the main part of the book in the first half of this period, and the Elihu-speeches in the second, but these grounds are not by themselves decisive.

A word must here be said on a subject which will be in the mind of many readers. These critical results must have some bearing on theories of inspiration. But what bearing? I have an uneasy feeling that the remark on page 405—that "precisely the same inspiration attaches to [the Elihu-speeches] which attaches to the poem generally"—is hardly penetrating enough, and that by such a half-truth Dr. Driver has unwisely blunted the edge of his critical decision. Of course, the Elihu-speeches *are* inspired; **they are touched by the same religious influences which pervade all the genuine Church** records of the Exilic or post-Exilic period which are contained in the Hagiographa. But it can hardly be said that these speeches have the same *degree* of inspiration as the rest of the Book of Job, at least if the general impression of discriminating readers may be trusted. The creator of "Elihu" may have some deeper ideas, but he has not as capacious a vessel to receive them as the older poet.[2] And though it may be true that he had a good motive, and that the course which he took was sanctioned by the religious

---

[1] These grounds are briefly indicated by Dr. Driver on p. 404 (§ 8) and p. 406 (top); cf. my *Job and Solomon*, pp. 291—295. Besides Budde's *Beiträge*, Stickel (*Hiob*, 1842, pp. 248—262) still deserves to be consulted on the Elihu-portion.

[2] See *Job and Solomon*, pp. 42—44.

authorities of the day, yet it is certain both that he has defects from which the earlier writer is free, and that he has for modern readers greatly hindered the beneficial effect of the rest of the poem. We must not, in short, force ourselves to reverence these two poets in an equal degree.

I admit that the difficulties which theories of inspiration have to encounter in the Song of Songs, Ecclesiastes, and Esther are still greater, and I think that Dr. Driver would have facilitated the reception of his critical results on these books if he had at once taken up a strong position with reference to these difficulties. It might even have been enough to quote a luminous passage from a lecture by Prof. Robertson Smith,[1] the upshot of which is that these three books "which were still disputed among the orthodox Jews in the apostolic age, and to which the New Testament never makes reference,"[2] and, let me add, which do not seem to be touched by the special religious influences referred to above, are not for us Christians in the truest sense of the word canonical.[3] These books however are intensely interesting, and a "frank and reverent study of the texts" shows that

---

[1] *The Old Testament in the Jewish Church*, pp. 174, 175; cf. Wildeboer, *Die Entstehung des alttest. Kanons* (1891), pp. 150, 152.

[2] See however Trench, *Seven Churches of Asia*, pp. 225, 226.

[3] Of the Song of Songs, Lowth, writing to Warburton in 1756, says: "If you deny that it is an allegory, you must exclude it from the Canon of Holy Scripture; for it holds its place there by no other tenure" (Warburton's *Works*, by Hurd, xii. 458).

they "have their use and value even for us," and my only regret is that in Esther and Ecclesiastes, at any rate, Dr. Driver is slightly more "moderate" than was necessary, and that he does not make it quite as easy as it might have been for some of his readers to agree with him.

I pass to a book in which I have long had so special an interest that it will require an effort to be brief—the glorious Song of Songs. Our author rejects the old allegorical interpretation as artificial and extravagant (p. 423), but does not regard Delitzsch's modification of it as untenable, provided it be admitted that there is nothing in the poem itself to suggest it. His meaning, I presume, is this —that the Song is only allegorical in so far as all true marriage to a religious mind is allegorical,[1] but that we cannot suppose the poet to have thought of this allegory when he wrote, and that, his own meaning being so beautiful, it is almost a pity to look beyond it. Dr. Driver's treatment of the Song is marked by much reserve. He does indeed commit himself to the lyrical drama theory, without considering whether the poet may not to some extent have worked up current popular songs (just as Poliziano did in Mediæan Florence); and though he puts two forms of this theory (Delitzsch's and Ewald's) very thoroughly before the reader, he evidently prefers the latter, with some modifications from Oettli. Still one

[1] Cf. Julia Wedgewood, *The Moral Ideal* (1888), pp. 269, 270.

feels after all that he has not given us a thorough explanation of the Song. This was perhaps justifiable in the present state of exegesis. For though the poem has not been altogether neglected by recent scholars, with the exception of Grätz and Stickel none of them has seriously grappled afresh with the problem of its origin. To Grätz (in spite of his many faults as a scholar) and Stickel the student should have been expressly referred;[1] the mention of the former on p. 423 seems to me far from sufficient. Help may also be got from Prof. Robertson Smith's able article in the *Encyclopædia Britannica* (1876), and by the section relative to the Song in Reuss' French edition of the Bible.

For determining the date of the Song the linguistic argument is of more than common importance. Here I must complain that such a thorough Hebraist as Dr. Driver hesitates so much. The only fresh ground for uncertainty is the discovery of a weight on the site of Samaria, ascribed to the eighth century, with של as in Song i. 6 (viii. 12), iii. 7. Apart from this, a linguist would certainly say that this pleonastic periphrasis *proved* the late date of the poem as it stands, but now it seems permissible to Dr. Driver to doubt. That I reluctantly call an unwise compromising with tradition. In 1876 (the date of Prof. Robertson Smith's article) we did not see our way in the post-Exilic period as we do now. If there is

[1] Stickel's book appeared in 1888, and was ably reviewed by Prof. Budde (*Theol. Lit.-ztg.*, 1888, No. 6).

anything in the contents of the Song which expresses a pre-Exilic date, let it be pointed out. Meantime all the facts as yet elicited by exegesis can be explained quite as well on the assumption of a late date as of an early one. Let us then (failing any fresh exegetical evidence) hear no more of the Song of Deborah and the early north-Israelitish dialect. It is certain that the use of שׁ for אשר is specially characteristic of late writings; certain, that שֶׁלְּמָה Song i. 7 is analogous to שֶׁלְּמִי Jon. i. 7, and also to בְּשֶׁל אֲשֶׁר Eccles. viii. 17, and אֲשֶׁר לְמָה Dan. i. 10 (the fuller relative used as in Jon. i. 8[1] [contrast ver. 7], in a carefully expressed speech); certain, too, that some at least of the loan-words mentioned on pp. 422, 423 (note [3]) point definitely to the post-Exilic period (even one or two Greek words seem highly probable). Kuenen in 1865, in spite of his preconceived theory of an early date, admitted that "the language seemed, at first sight, to plead for the Persian period"; Gesenius and M. Sachs—a great Christian and a great Jewish Hebraist—have expressed themselves still more strongly on the "modern Hebrew" of the Song of Songs. It is also highly probable that a careful study of the names of plants in the Song would favour a post-Exilic date. Nor can the parallelisms between this book and that "song of loves" (or, love), the 45th Psalm, be ignored. If that psalm is post-Exilic, so also presumably is the Song

[1] I do not take the fuller phrase in ver. 8 to be a gloss (cf. the four lines added by Dr. Driver on p. 301 in 2nd edition).

of Songs.[1] But Dr. Driver's researches on the Psalms have not yet perhaps led him to see what to me is now so clear, and I am therefore content to have shown that, quite apart from this, the facts admitted by Dr. Driver point rather to a late than to an early date, and that we cannot therefore safely assume, with our author, that the poem has a basis of fact. Readers of Delitzsch's delightful essay on "Dancing, and Pentateuch-Criticism"[2] do not need to be assured that the post-Exilic period was not without the enlivenment of secular dancing and song.

And now comes another little disappointment—another little compromise with conservatism, which I should prefer to glide gently over, but for the illusion which is growing up among us that paring down the results of criticism is necessary for a truly Christian teaching. The Book of Ruth, according to our author, is a prose idyll, similar, I presume, to that which may have lain in the mind of the author of that idyllic group of quasi-dramatic *tableaux*—the Song of Songs, and based, like the Song (according to Dr. Driver), on tradition. We are told that "the basis of the narrative consists, it may reason-

---

[1] See *Bampton Lectures*, pp. 167, 179 (cf. p. 298). On p. 167 (foot), read "*can be better accounted for.*" I do not see where to find a situation for either of these poems before the Greek period. One of the early and fortunate reigns must of course be selected. But I hold myself open to correction.

[2] Delitzsch, *Iris* (E. T.), pp. 189—204. The Mishna (*Taanith*, iv. 8; see Wünsche, *Talm.*, i. 473) tells how Song iii. 11 was sung in the vineyard dances.

ably be supposed, of the family traditions respecting Ruth and her marriage with Boaz. These have been cast into a literary form by the [pre-Exilic] author, who has, no doubt, to a certain extent idealized both the characters and the scenes. Distance seems to have mellowed the rude, unsettled age of the Judges" (pp. 427, 428).

This description seems to soften the facts a little too much. It is not merely a "mellowed" picture that we have before us, but, as Mr. Cobb has remarked,[1] complete "*contrariety* of spirit, style, social life, and public affairs." Nor is anything gained by postulating an uncertain amount of traditional material; the story of Ruth is practically as imaginative as that of Tobit, and is none the less edifying on this account. But let us see how the acute and learned author endeavours to prove a pre-Exilic date. The genealogy, as he admits, "appears to suggest an Exilic or post-Exilic date," but this "forms no integral part of the book," while, in spite of many isolated expressions[2] which, taken together, seem at first sight to point to the post-Exilic period, the

---

[1] *Bibliotheca Sacra*, Oct. 1891, p. 662.

[2] לָהֵן, שָׂפַר, קָיָם are, I think, decisive. I incline to add שַׁדַּי, which before the Exile is poetical (see *Bampton Lectures*, p. 84). Dr. Driver regards Ruth iv. 7 (קִיָּם) as a gloss, cf. 1 Sam. ix. 9. But the latter passage is embedded in a *pre-Exilic* section, whereas Ruth iv. 7 occurs *ex hyp.* in a post-Exilic narrative. The narrator tries to throw himself back into early times, but *has to explain* a custom unknown to his post-Exilic readers Nor is there any special reason to regard לָהֵן as a word of the early northern dialect (p. 427).

"general beauty and purity of the style of Ruth point decidedly to the pre-Exilic period." We are not told whether the book was written before or after Deuteronomy (which is referred on p. 82 to the reign of Manasseh), but it is pointed out that the peculiar kind of marriage referred to in chapters iii. and iv. is not strictly that of levirate (Deut. xxv. 5), and that the reception of Ruth into an Israelitish family "appears to conflict with Deuteronomy xxiii. 2." In reply, it may be said (1) that in order to give the "present condition of investigation" it was important to give a much fuller statement of the grounds on which "most modern critics consider Ruth to be Exilic (Ewald) or post-Exilic (Bertheau, Wellhausen, Kuenen, &c.)"; (2) that by Dr. Driver's very candid admission "the style of the prose-parts of Job ['most probably' Exilic, p. 405] is not less pure"; (3) that the religious liberality of the writer and the family relations which he describes in the book are perfectly intelligible in the post-Exilic period (cf. on the one hand the Book of Jonah, and on the other Kuenen's remark on Leviticus xviii. and xx., *Hexateuch*, p. 268); and (4) there is clearly no *necessity* to suppose the genealogy to have been added in a later age. In fact the one excuse for giving this book an earlier date than that of Jonah is the greater flavour of antiquity which it possesses (notice the points of contact with Samuel given by Bertheau in the *Kurzgef. Handbuch*, p. 286).[1] Its real design is, not to glorify the Davidic

---

[1] See Dr. Driver, p. 302, and cf. *Bampton Lectures*, p. 306.

house, but to show the universality of God's love. Just as our Lord exhibits a Samaritan as the model of practical piety, so the unknown writer of this beautiful little book brings before us a Moabitish woman as the model of an affectionate daughter who receives the highest earthly reward.[1]

The five Lamentations deserve attention, not only for some classic beauties of expression which have endeared them to the Christian heart, but as (perhaps) the earliest monuments of the piety of regenerate Israel, and as (perhaps) supplying presumptive evidence of the cultivation of religious lyric poetry long before the Exile. Nowhere perhaps does Dr. Driver's individuality show itself more strikingly than here. What pains he takes to soften the prejudices of old-fashioned readers, and give the principal result of criticism in its most moderate form! To unprejudiced students, however, he may seem timid, and it is certainly strange to hear that "even though the poems be not the work of Jeremiah, there is no question that they are the work of a contemporary (or contemporaries)." Nägelsbach long ago saw that at any rate Lamentations ii. implies an acquaintance with the Book of Ezekiel, and, to Dr. Driver, the affinities between all the Lamentations and the prophecies of Jeremiah ought surely to suggest that the author (or authors) had made a literary study of that book. A considerable interval must therefore

---

[1] Comp. Talm. Bab., *Sanhedrin*, 96 *b* (Wünsche, iii. 188), where still bolder flights are taken.

have elapsed between B.C. 586 and the writing of the Lamentations,[1] and the language used in Lamentations v. 20 (comp. Isa. xlii. 14, lvii. 11) points rather to the *end* than to the beginning of the Exile. This period is, moreover, the earliest which will suit the parallelisms between Lamentations iii. and the Book of Job (referred in this work to the Exile), which are more easily explained on the supposition that the elegy is dependent on Job than on the opposite theory.[2] It ought however to be mentioned that there are plausible grounds for giving a still later date to the third elegy, in which Jerusalem is not once mentioned, and which it is difficult not to associate with the Jeremianic psalms. If Psalm xxxi. is post-Exilic (and any other theory seems to me extremely improbable), so also is Lamentations iii., and of course we must add, if the poem of Job (as a whole) is post-Exilic, so also is Lamentations iii. And though I do not for a moment deny that lamentations were indited during the Exile (the Books of Ezekiel and of ii. Isaiah sufficiently prove this), yet the mere fact that the authors of Lamentations i., ii., iv., and v. refer so prominently to the fall of Jerusalem, is no conclusive proof that these lamentations too were not written in Judah after the Return. The dramatic imaginativeness of the psalmists has, I believe, been proved,[3] and the peculiar rhythm called

---

[1] See Prof. W R. Smith's excellent article in *Encyclopædia Britannica*.

[2] See my *Lamentations* (*Pulpit Comm.*), Introd. p. iii.

[3] Cf. my commentary on Pss. lxxiv. and cxxxvii. The Second

"elegiac" has been traced by Budde (though not with certainty) in many productions of the post-Exilic age. It seems to me far from impossible that, just as the Church of the Second Temple composed its own psalms, so it preferred to indite fresh elegies for use on the old fast-days.[1]

The next section is one of the very best in this part of the volume—it is on Ecclesiastes. I will not occupy space with summarizing it, but urge the student to master its contents. I quite agree with Dr. Driver that the work may possibly be a work of the Greek period. The language, as I remarked in 1887, favours (though it does not absolutely require) a later date than that suggested by Ewald (close of the Persian period). The objection that if the book be of the Greek period, we have a right to expect definite traces of Greek influence, I now see to be inconclusive; the Wisdom of Jesus the Son of Sirach contains none, and yet belongs to the Greek period.[2]

Isaiah, too, describes imaginatively in "elegiac rhythm" (if Budde may be followed) the state of captured Jerusalem (Isa. li. 17—20).

[1] Discussion of this delicate question I must here renounce. Since these chapters were written Dyserinck has favoured us with some valuable remarks of Kuenen on the possibility of a post-Exilic date for these poems (*Theol. Tijdschr.* July 1892). It was his wish that the book might be studied anew from a linguistic point of view. But he admitted the difficulty caused by the alphabetic form of the poems and their similarity to certain psalms. Dyserinck himself proposes to publish an elaborate treatment of the subject.

[2] On supposed Greek influences, see, besides Menzel, *Qohelet und die nacharistotelische Philosophie*, von August Palm (1885).

Moreover, Hellenism must have influenced very many who did not definitely adopt Greek theories. Certainly the work is very un-Jewish. Very probably Kuenen is correct in dating it about 200 B.C., *i. e.* about forty years before the great Maccabæan rising (so too Mr. Tyler). Dr. Driver admits the force of his reasoning, though he still not unreasonably hesitates. He is himself strongest on the linguistic side of the argument; see especially his note on the bearings of Prof. Margoliouth's attempted restorations of Ben Sira (p. 447). I cannot equally follow him in his argument against a theory which I myself hold, viz. that the text of Ecclesiastes has been manipulated in the interests of orthodoxy. As was remarked above, the book is not in the strictest sense canonical, and we have therefore no interest in creating or magnifying difficulties in a theory which is intrinsically probable, and is supported by numerous phenomena in the later period.

The section on Esther is also in the main very satisfactory. But why are we told that this narrative (which was not canonical according to St. Athanasius, and which, fascinating as it is, we can hardly venture to call inspired) cannot reasonably be doubted to have a historical basis? Is it because of the appeal to Persian chronicles (Esth. ii. 23; x. 2; cf. ix. 32)? But it is of the essence of the art of romance not to shrink from appeals to fictitious authorities. One may however admit that a story like Esther, which professed to account for the origin of a popular festival, probably had a traditional, though not a historical, basis. On this point reference may be made to Kuenen's *Onderzoek* (ed. 2), p. 551, and Zimmern in Stade's *Zeitschrift*, 1891, p. 168. The latter thinks (and both Jensen and Lagarde agree) that the Feast of Purim may be derived ultimately from a Babylonian New Year's Feast, and that the story of the struggle between *Mordecai* and Haman was suggested by a Babylonian New Year's legend of the struggle between *Marduk* and Tiâmat. This coincides curiously with the views proposed above to explain the origin of the Jonah-narrative. Of course, the story may have been enriched with Persian elements (on which see Lagarde and Kuenen [1]) before it was Hebraized by a Jewish story-teller.

Dr. Driver's linguistic argument for placing Esther in the fourth or third century B.C. is excellent. But there is one important omission in his brief discussion. If the date is so early, how is it that the earliest independent evidence for the observance of Purim in Judæa is in 2 Maccabees (see p. 452)? Moreover, there is no mention of Mordecai and Esther [2] in Ben Sira's "praise of famous men" (Eccles. xliv.—xlix.), which would be strange if Purim and its story were well known in Judæa in B.C. 180. May not the festival have been introduced into Judæa, and the Book of

---

[1] Lagarde's treatise *Purim* (1887) is important ; Dr. Driver's reference gives no idea of this. See also his *Mittheilungen*, ii. 378—381, iv. 347. On Persian legendary elements, see also Kuenen, *Ond.*, ed. 2, ii. 551, and cf. Cornill, *Einl.*, p. 253.

[2] Cf. Ben Sira's silence as to Daniel (see *Job and Solomon*, p. 194).

Esther have been written some time after the Maccabæan War (so Reuss, Kuenen, and Cornill)? Or, though this seems less probable, the book may have been written by a Persian Jew in the third century, but not brought to Palestine till later. Dr. Driver ought perhaps to have mentioned this theory (Mr. Bevan, *Daniel*, p. 29, notes two significant words which Esther has in common with Daniel). He might also have added to his "literature" my article "Esther" in *Enc. Brit.* (1878); Cassel's *Esther* (1888); and Dieulafoy, "Le livre d'Esther et le palais d'Assuérus" in *Revue des études juives*, 1888 (Actes et Conférences).

Nor can I help giving hearty praise to the sections on Chronicles, Ezra, and Nehemiah. The details, especially on style, are worked out with great care. The only objection that I shall raise relates to the sketch of the method and spirit of the Chronicler, which I could have wished not less reverent, but bolder and more distinct in expression. We are all familiar with the attacks to which writers like Dr. Driver are exposed; some of the most vigorous passages of Bishop Ellicott's recent Charge are directed against that strangest of all theories—"an inspiration of repainting history"—to which these reverent-minded writers are supposed to have committed themselves. If Dr. Driver had only been a little clearer on the subjects of inspiration and of the growth of the Canon, how much simpler would have been his task, especially in dealing with the

Hagiographa! Of course, the Chronicles are inspired, not as the prophecies of Isaiah and Jeremiah, but as even a sermon might be called inspired, *i.e.* touched in a high degree with the best spiritual influences of the time. Dr. Driver says (preface, p. xvi)—"It was the function of inspiration to guide the individual [historian] in the choice and disposition of his material, and in his use of it for the inculcation of special lessons."

But clearly this can be true of the Chronicler only with those limitations, subject to which the same thing could be said of any conscientious and humble-minded preacher of the Christian Church. And if these limitations cannot be borne in mind, it is better to drop the word altogether, and express what we mean by some other term. That there are some passages in Chronicles which have a specially inspiring quality, and may *therefore* be called inspired, is not of course to be denied. But upon the whole, as Prof. Robertson Smith truly says,[1] the Chronicler "is not so much a historian as a Levitical preacher on the old history." The spirit of the Deuteronomistic editor of the earlier narrative books has found in him its most consistent representative. He omits some facts and colours others in perfect good faith according to a preconceived religious theory, to edify himself and his readers. He also adds some new facts, not on his own authority, but on that of earlier

---

[1] *The Old Test. in the Jewish Church*, ed. 1, p. 420.

records, but we dare not say that he had any greater skill than his neighbours in sifting the contents of these records, if indeed he had any desire to do so. Dr. Driver's language (p. 501) respecting the "traditional element" used by the Chronicler seems therefore somewhat liable to misunderstanding.[1]

The only remaining section of the book relates to the Book of Daniel, and upon this, as might be expected, Dr. Driver's individuality has left a strong impress. It is needless to say that the student can fully trust the facts which are here stored up in abundance, also that the conclusions arrived at are in the main judicious, and the mode of their presentation considerate. And yet helpful, very helpful, as this section is, it does not fully satisfy a severely critical standard. Far be it from me to blame the author for this; I sympathize too deeply with the conflict of feelings amid which he must have written. I would speak frankly, but (on the grounds already mentioned) without assumption of superiority. First of all, I think it a misfortune that the sketch of the contents of the book could not have been shortened. I know the excuse; there existed in English no commentary on Daniel sufficiently critical to be referred to. But on the other hand, there was the most urgent need for more preliminary matter,

---

[1] To the "literature" of Ezra I should add Nestle, "Zur Frage nach der ursprünglichen Einheit der Bücher Chronik, Esra, Neh.," in *Studien u. Kritiken*, 1879, pp. 517—520; van Hoonacker, "Néhémie et Esdras; nouvelle hypothèse," in *Le Muséon*, 1890.

especially on the characteristics of this book. Ordinary readers simply *cannot* understand Daniel. Modern culture supplies no key to it, as the late Mr. Gilbert's interesting paper in the *Expositor* for June 1889 conclusively shows. I do not undervalue the judicious remarks on pp. 480—482, but on "apocalyptic" literature something more was wanted than bare references to various German authors, one of whom (Smend) ought, as I think, to have been made much more prominent.[1] Secondly, I think that a freer use should have been made of the cuneiform inscriptions, especially considering the unfriendly criticisms of Prof. Sayce. In this respect I believe myself to have long ago set a good example, though my article on Daniel (*Enc. Brit.*, 1876) of course requires much modification and expansion.[2] And here let me repair an omission in chap. xi. Dr. Driver should, I think, in dealing with Hexateuch criticism, have taken some account of Assyrian and Egyptian investigations. Even if he thought it safer not to speak too positively on the bearings of these researches on the question of the dates of documents, he ought, I think, to have "indicated the way for future progress" (editor's preface), and so have prevented (so far as in him lay) the vehement but

---

[1] Dr. Wright's work on Daniel in the *Pulpit Commentary* will, I am sure, be full of learned and honest discussion. But when will it appear? Mr. Bevan's *Short Commentary on Daniel* (1892) is so good that we may even ask him for something more complete, though not more careful and critical.

[2] See also *Bampton Lect.*, pp. 105—107 (cf. 94, 296).

erroneous criticisms of Prof. Sayce.[1] But on the relation of cuneiform research to the criticism of Daniel no reserve was called for. It would have been quite right to say that the statement respecting Belteshazzar in Daniel iv. was erroneous, and that the names Ashpenaz, Shadrach, and Meshach could not have been put forward as Babylonian in Exilic times;[2] also that Hamelsar (probably) and Abednego (certainly) are ignorant deformations of Babylonian names, and that though Arioch is doubtless Eri-aku, yet this name was probably obtained from Genesis xiv. 1. And much more might, I think, have been made of the writer's slight acquaintance with Babylonian ideas and customs. Above all, while on "the Chaldæans" and on Belshazzar very just remarks are made, on "Darius the Mede" we get this unfortunate compromise between criticism and conservatism (p. 469; cf. p. 479, note[2])—"Still the

[1] I referred to this at the Church Congress in 1883 (*Job and Solomon*, p. 6), and Prof. Robertson Smith wrote an acute paper on "Archæology and the Date of the Pentateuch" in the *Contemp. Rev.* for October 1887. Against the coloured statements of Prof. Sayce's paper in the *Expository Times* for December 1881 I have already protested. The Tell-el-Amarna tablets introduce a fresh element, not of simplicity, but of complication ("development" is, alas! not such a simple matter as theorists used to suppose). But E. Meyer's critical inference from Egyptian history in Stade's *Zt.*, 1888, pp. 47—49 (cf. his *Gesch. des Alt.*, i. 202), appears to be worth a corner even of Dr. Driver's limited space.

[2] Few probably will accept Kohler's suggestions on "the Chaldean names of Daniel and his three friends," in the *Zt. für Assyriologie*, 1889, pp. 46—51.

circumstances are not perhaps such as to be absolutely inconsistent with either the existence or the office of 'Darius the Mede'; and a cautious criticism will not build too much on the silence of the inscriptions, when many certainly remain yet to be brought to light."

Now it is quite true that in the addenda to the second edition it is stated, in accordance with the contract-tablets published by Strassmaier, that neither "Darius the Mede" nor even Belshazzar bore the title of king between Nabûna'id and Cyrus. But it is not the very venial error in the original statement on which I lay stress, but the attitude of the writer. Out of excessive sympathy with old-fashioned readers, he seems to forget the claims of criticism. The words of Daniel v. 31 should be in themselves sufficient to prove the narrative in which they occur to have been written long after B.C. 536.[1]

Thirdly, against the view that chap. xi. contains true predictions, the author should, I think, have urged Nestle's *certain* explanation of the so-called "abomination of desolation" in Stade's *Zeitschrift*

---

[1] That Mr. Pinches should have come forward on the side of conservatism at the Church Congress in 1891 is, I presume, of no significance. He is far too modest to claim to have studied the Book of Daniel critically. The same remark probably applies to Mr. Flinders Petrie (see *Bampton Lect.*, pp. 9, 10). On "Darius the Mede," compare Meinhold (*Beiträge*, 1888), and Sayce, *Fresh Light*, &c. (1884), p. 181, who however unduly blunts the edge of his critical decision. See also my own article "Daniel," for an incidental evidence of the confusion between Cyrus and Darius Hystaspis from 1 Kings x. 18, Sept.

for 1883 [1] (see *Bampton Lectures*, p. 105). That an Exilic prophet should have used the phrase explained by Nestle, Bishop Ellicott himself will admit to be inconceivable. I will not blame Dr. Driver for his remark on p. 477 (line 28, &c.), but I believe that it is not **quite** critical, and that Nestle's discovery supplies the last fact that was **wanted** to *prove* to the general satisfaction that Daniel xi., xii. (and all that belongs to it) was written in the reign of Antiochus Epiphanes. I say "the last fact," because a faithful historical explanation of Daniel xi., xii., such as is given by the great Church-Father Hippolytus in the lately discovered fourth book of his Commentary,[2] *forces* on the unprejudiced mind the conclusion that this section was written during the Syrian persecution. Hippolytus, it is true, did not draw this conclusion, but who can wonder that the Neoplatonic philosopher Porphyry did? And should we **not be** ready to learn even from our foes?

Fourthly. (The reader will pardon this dry arrangement under heads with a view to brevity.) I

---

[1] Dr. Driver mentions this explanation in the addenda to ed. 2. But, like Mr. Bevan (*Daniel*, p. 193, who also refers to Nestle), he thinks the "abomination" was an altar. Surely, as Bleek saw, it was (primarily at least) a statue. The statue of Olympian Zeus bore the Divine name, and the altar was presumably erected before it.

[2] Fragments of the Syriac version of this fourth book were given by Lagarde, *Analecta Syriaca* (1838), pp. 79—91. Georgiades discovered, and Dr. E. Bratke edited the complete work in Greek in 1891. [In June 1892 Dr. Salmon gave an article on Hippolytus's commentary in *Hermathena*, No. 18.]

notice on p. 479 the same confusion which occurs elsewhere between "tradition" and history. I do not think that any critic who agrees on the main point with Dr. Driver would maintain that "Daniel, it cannot be doubted, was a historical person" except the newly-converted Delitzsch, who, as his article in the second edition of Herzog's *Encyclopædia* shows, had not worked his way to perfect clearness. Listen to the late Prof. Riehm, who is now just obtaining recognition among us. "The material of his narratives the author may partly have taken from folk-tales (*aus der Volkssage*), though at any rate in part he invented it himself. . . . And even if there was a folk-tale (*Volkssage*), according to which Daniel was a prophet living during the Exile and distinguished for his piety, yet the historical existence of an Exilic prophet Daniel is more than doubtful."[1]

One must, I fear, add that the two statements mentioned in note[2] as resting possibly or probably on a basis of fact are, the one very doubtful, the other now admitted to be without foundation.

Fifthly, as to the date of the composition of the book. Dr. Driver states this to be at earliest about B.C. 300, but more probably B.C. 168 or 167 (p. 467). Delitzsch is bolder and more critical; he says about B.C. 168. But to be true to all the facts, we ought rather to say that, while some evidence points to a date not earlier than B.C. 300, other facts point

---

[1] *Einleitung in das A.T.*, ii. 329.

to the reign of Antiochus Epiphanes, and perhaps more definitely still to the period between the end of Dec. 165 (the dedication of the temple, which is mentioned in Daniel viii. 14) and June 164 (the end of the seventieth year-week, when the writer of Daniel expected the tyrant Antiochus to "come to his end ").[1]

It was a pity that so little could be said on the composition of the book. Reuss and Lagarde both held that the book was made up of a number of separate "fly-sheets," and Dr. C. H. H. Wright maintains that it is but an abridgment of a larger work. The theories of Lenormant, Zöckler, and Strack also deserved a mention. On Meinhold's theory a somewhat too hesitating judgment is expressed (p. 483), which should be compared with Mr. Bevan's more decided view in his *Daniel*. From the form of the opening sentence of par. 3 on page 482, I conjecture that something on this subject may have been omitted. But if by so doing the author obtained more room for his *linguistic* arguments, I can but rejoice. Gladly do I call attention to the soundness of the facts on which these are based and the truly critical character of his judgments, and more particularly to what is said on the Aramaic of the Book of Daniel, and the eminently fair references to Prof. Margoliouth.[2]

---

[1] The fullest justification of this is given by Cornill, *Die siebzig Jahrwochen Daniels* (Königsberg, 1889); cf. *Einleitung*, p. 258. This little treatise deserves a fuller criticism than it has yet received.

[2] Mr. Bevan's mainly linguistic commentary on Daniel and

But the treatment of the language of Daniel is but the climax of a series of linguistic contributions. To any one who has eyes to see, the special value of the book consists in its presentation of the linguistic evidence of the date of the documents (cf. p. 106). I do not say that I am not sometimes disappointed. No wonder; did not a good scholar like Budde, in 1876, claim the Elihu-speeches for the original Book of Job on grounds of language? Often I could have wished both that more evidence were given and a more definite conclusion reached (*e. g.* on Joel); but I recognize the difficulties with which Dr. Driver had to contend, arising partly from his limited space, partly from the unfamiliarity of the reader with this style of argument. With Dr. Driver's remark in the *Journal of Philosophy*, xi. 133 (note [1]), I agree, and when Dr. Briggs suggests that in my researches on the Psalms "the argument from language is not employed with much effect,"[1] I feel that if not quite as firm as I might have been, I have been at least as bold as Dr. Driver would have been; indeed, I am indebted to my colleague for criticisms of my "Linguistic Affinities of the Psalms," which tended rather to the limiting than to the heightening of their "effect." I think that I should now be able to put

---

Mr. Brasted's study on the order of the sentences in the Hebrew portions of Daniel (*Hebraica*, July 1891, p. 244, &c.) appeared after the completion of Dr. Driver's work.

[1] In a very generous notice of *Bampton Lecture*, *North American Review*, Jan. 1892, p. 106.

forward a few somewhat more definite conclusions (positive and negative), but Dr. Driver's self-restraint on p. 361 will perhaps show Dr. Briggs that if I erred, it was in good company. Let me add that the author himself has not lost the opportunity of giving some sufficiently definite conclusions on the development of Hebrew style. It is on a paragraph which begins by stating that "the great turning-point in Hebrew style falls in the age of Nehemiah" (p. 473). The result thus indicated is based upon much careful observation. It agrees substantially with the view of H. Ewald (*Lehrbuch*, p. 24), which is a decided improvement upon Gesenius's (*Gesch. der hebr. Spr.*), but must however, as I believe, be qualified, in accordance with the great variety of Hebrew composition.

In bringing this review to an end, let me say once more how much more gladly I would have echoed the words of that generous-minded eulogist of this book—Prof. Herbert E. Ryle.[2] I have written because of the illusions which seem gathering fresh strength or assuming new forms among us, and if I have shown some eagerness, I trust that it has been a chastened eagerness. The work before us is a contribution of value to a great subject, and if the facts and theories which it so ably presents should influence the higher religious teaching, no one would rejoice more than

---

[1] Cf. *Bampton Lecture*, pp. 460—463; Geiger, *Urschrift*, pp. 40, 41. I need not say that I am by no means a disciple of this brilliant but too hasty critic.

[2] See *Critical Review*, Jan. 1892.

myself. But solid, judicious, and in one place brilliant as it is, it requires much supplementing as a sketch of the present state of criticism—not merely in the sense in which this must be true of even the best handbooks, but for reasons which have, as I hope, been courteously stated. The author appears to have thought that criticism of the Bible was one of those shy Alpine plants of which it has been well said that "we can easily give our plants the soil they require, but we cannot give them the climate and atmosphere; the climate and atmosphere are of as much importance to their well-being as carefully selected soil." I venture, however, to hope that he is unduly fearful, and that the mental climate and atmosphere of England is no longer so adverse as formerly to a free but reverent Biblical criticism. Indeed, one of my chief grounds for advocating such a criticism is that it appears to me to be becoming more and more necessary for the maintenance of true evangelical religion. It is, therefore, in the name of the Apostle of Faith that one of the weakest of his followers advocates a firmer treatment of all parts of the grave historical problem of the origin of our religion.[1]

[1] On the relation of the criticism of the Gospels to faith see some wise remarks of Herrmann in the *Zt. f. Theol. u. Kirche*, 1892, p. 258.

THE END.

www.ingramcontent.com/pod-product-compliance
Lightning Source LLC
Chambersburg PA
CBHW030408230426
43664CB00007BB/795